LEAD
VOCABULARY

LEAD VOCABULARY

초판1쇄	2021년 11월 15일
초판2쇄	2022년 11월 10일

지 은 이	DAVID CHIN
디 자 인	최주호(PETER CHOI)
펴 낸 이	박영은
펴 낸 곳	리드에듀북스
등록번호	395-91-01356
전 화	070-4512-5236
팩 스	0504-489-4844
이 메 일	leadedubooks@naver.com
홈페이지	https://leadedubooks.modoo.at
저작권자	DAVID CHIN, 리드에듀북스

ISBN   979-11-973714-4-8   13740

이 책의 저작권은 저자와 출판사에 있습니다.
저작권자와 출판사의 허락없이 책의 일부 또는 전재 및 복제, 발췌하는 것을 금합니다.

낙장 및 파본은 구매처에서 교환해 드립니다.

값 17,500 원

PREFACE

　새로운 언어를 배울 때 가장 어렵고 힘든 부분 중 하나가 어휘 입니다. 대부분의 학생들은 매일 매일 영어 단어를 외우는데 많은 시간을 보내고 있습니다.

　원어민들 역시 새로운 단어를 접하고 일상 생활에 적용하는데 적지 않은 시간을 보냅니다. 그렇기 때문에 생소한 단어를 발견하더라도 당황하거나 실망할 필요가 없습니다. 원어민들조차 학생 여러분들이 보고 있는 단어들을 이해하지 못하는 경우도 많기 때문입니다.

　저는 한국에서 십수년간 토플을 학생들에게 가르치면서 한국 학생들 사이에서 어휘 암기에 대한한가지 패턴을 발견했습니다. 학생들 대부분이 영어 단어와 한국어 뜻을 연습장에 반복해서 적는 소위 깜지 라는 형태로 단어를 암기하고 있다는 것이었습니다. 이 공부 방법은 예전부터 계속해서 전해져 왔습니다.

　안타깝게도 이러한 방법을 통해 암기한 단어들은 당일 단어 시험을 통과하거나 단기 기억에 머무를 수 밖에 없습니다.

　새로운 어휘를 온전히 자신의 것으로 만들기 위해서 학생들은 두 가지 부분을 기억하면 됩니다. 그것은 응용과 창의성 입니다. 물론 이런 식으로의 단어 암기 접근법이 처음에는 어색하게 들릴 수 있습니다, 그러나 폭넓게 확장하여 단어들을 사용하면 분명 여러분 생활에 자연스럽게 녹아들 것 입니다. 또한, 새로운 어휘들을 떠올릴 수 있는 창의적인 방법들을 생각해 봅시다. 본인이 스스로 창의적인 문장을 생각해 내거나 이미지화 시켜 연관성을 만들기 까지 힘들고 긴 시간이 필요합니다, 그러나 걱정할 필요 없습니다. 리드 어휘집이 그 시간을 훨씬 단축시켜 주고 여러분의 실력을 향상시켜줄 것입니다.

　리드 어휘 책은 TOEFL, TEPS, IELTS, SAT 등 표준화된 영어 시험에서 빈번하게 나타나고 중요하게 나오는 단어들의 구성으로 이루어져 있습니다. 어휘암기를 지루해 하고 힘들어 할 필요가 없습니다. 리드 어휘 책에 나오는 각 세트를 통해 여러분 어휘 실력의 범위는 매우 넓어질 것입니다.

DAVID CHIN

HOW TO STUDY

The vocabulary in each set are from a plethora of academic fields and everyday language. These words are common and appear frequently in standardized tests.

SOME WORDS DO NOT CONTAIN THE OBVIOUS DEFINTIONS. For example in SET 1, the word SCHOOL is not defined as a place of learning since that is the most accepted meaning. It is important to be familiar with the secondary definitions of the words.

After each set, a test is given to make sure you memorized the vocabulary. The best way of finding out if you memorized properly is using the word in a sentence. Each set test is made up of twenty fill in the blank sentences, with answers at the bottom. Sometimes, a crossword puzzle will be given just to put a little fun in the process.

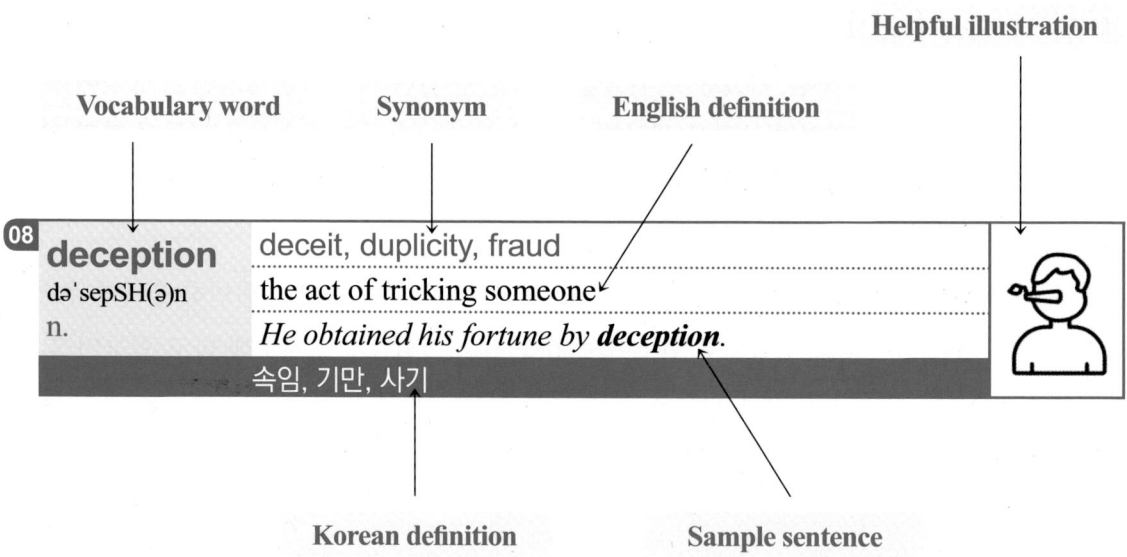

STUDY PLAN

2,000 words in 40 days

	SET 1	SET 2	SET 3	SET 4	SET 5
DAY 1	Memorize set				
DAY 2	Review	Memorize set			
DAY 3	Quick review	Review	Memorize set		
DAY 4	Quick review	Quick review	Review	Memorize set	
DAY 5	Quick review	Quick review	Quick review	Review	Memorize set

Memorize one set per day and take the set test afterwards.

A batch of 5 sets is the appropriate amount to review. Reviewing the previous set may seem too much, but constant review is a sure way to memorize for the long term.

PROGRESS CHECK

	SET 1	SET 2	SET 3	SET 4	SET 5	SET 6	SET 7	SET 8	SET 9	SET 10
VOCAB										
TEST										

	SET 11	SET 12	SET 13	SET 14	SET 15	SET 16	SET 17	SET 18	SET 19	SET 20
VOCAB										
TEST										

	SET 21	SET 22	SET 23	SET 24	SET 25	SET 26	SET 27	SET 28	SET 29	SET 30
VOCAB										
TEST										

	SET 31	SET 32	SET 33	SET 34	SET 35	SET 36	SET 37	SET 38	SET 39	SET 40
VOCAB										
TEST										

TABLE OF CONTENTS

Latin Root Words / Greek Root Words / Prefix / Suffix — 07

Set 1	17	Set 21	249
Set 2	29	Set 22	261
Set 3	41	Set 23	273
Set 4	53	Set 24	285
Set 5	65	Set 25	297
Set 6	75	Set 26	307
Set 7	87	Set 27	319
Set 8	99	Set 28	331
Set 9	111	Set 29	343
Set 10	123	Set 30	355
Set 11	133	Set 31	365
Set 12	145	Set 32	377
Set 13	157	Set 33	389
Set 14	169	Set 34	401
Set 15	181	Set 35	413
Set 16	191	Set 36	423
Set 17	203	Set 37	435
Set 18	215	Set 38	447
Set 19	227	Set 39	459
Set 20	239	Set 40	471

LEAD
Latin Root Words
Greek Root Words
Prefix
Suffix
VOCABULARY

LATIN ROOT WORDS

Root	Examples	Meaning
ab	abstain, abstract	to move away
acer (acri)	acrimony, acrid	bitter
acid	acidity, acidulous	acidic, sour
aev (ev)	longevity, medieval	age
ambi	ambidextrous, ambiguous	both
ann	anniversary, annual	yearly
aqua	aquamarine, aquarium	water
aud (audi)	auditorium, audience, audible	hear
bene	benefactor, benign, benevolent	good
bi	bicep, bicycle	two
brev	abbreviate, brevity	short
cent	century, centimeter	one hundred
circum (circ)	circulate, circle, circumvent	round
civ	civic, civil	citizen
clar	clarity, clarify	clear
contra (counter)	encounter, contradict	against
cred	credible, credit	believe
dict	edict, dictate, dictation	say
duc (duct)	produce, deduce, conduct	lead, make
fac	manufacture, factory	to do, to make
form	reform, conform	shape
fort	fortress, fortitude	strength
fund	founding, funding	bottom
fract	fraction, fracture	to break
gen	generate, gene	to give birth
hab	inhabit, habitation	to have
hal	inhale, exhale	breath
hospit	hospitality, hospice	host
ject	rejection, projection	throw
jud	prejudice, judicial	judge
jur	jury, justice	law
lax	relax, laxative	not tense
lev	leverage, elevate, levitate	to lift
liber	liberty, liberate	free
libr	library, libretto	book
log (logue)	logic, analogy	thought
luc (lum)	translucent, illuminate, lucid	light
lun	lunar, luna	moon
magn	magnificent, magnitude	great, large
mal	malefactor, malevolent, maleficent	bad
manu	manicure, manual	hand

Root	Examples	Meaning
mater	maternity, maternal	mother
miger	migrant, immigration	wander
miser	miserable, commiseration	unhappy
mit (mis)	transmit, permit	send
mort	mortician, mortal	death
multi	multiple, multimedia	many
neg	negate, negativity	no
nov	novel, innovative	new
omni	omnipotent, omnivorous	all
pac	pacifist, pacify	peace
pater	paternity, paternal	father
port	import, export, portable	carry
prim	primary, prime	first
proxim	proximity, approximate	nearness
ques	question, request	seek
quit	requiem, tranquil	silent
retro	retrogress, retrospective	backward, behind
rupt	disruption, bankrupt	to break
san	sanitary, sanitize	healthy
sci	omniscience, conscience	to know
scrib (scribe)	proscribe, script, inscription	to write
sect (sec)	section, bisect	to cut
semi	semi-final, semi-annual	half
sens	sentient, sensual	to feel
sent	resent, consent	to feel, to send
soci	social, associate, society	group
sol	solitude, isolation	alone
spect	spectator, inspection	to look
struct	restructure, destruction	to build
suav	assuage, suave	sweet
surg	resurgence, surge	rise
tempor	temporal, tempo	time
terr	territory, terrain	earth
tim	timorous, timid	to fear
tot	total, totality	whole
vac	vacate, vacuum	empty
ver	verdict, veracity	to be true
vid (vis)	vivid, video, invisible	to see
viv	revive, survive, viable	live
voc	advocate, vocalize	voice, to call

GREEK ROOT WORDS

Root	Examples	Meaning
aer	aerosol, aeronautics	air, atmosphere
amphi	amphibian, amphoteric	around, both
anthropo	anthropologist, philanthropy	man, humanity
anti	antithesis, antidote, antibacterial	against
aqu	aquatic, aquifers	water
arch	monarch, matriarch	ruler or leader
arche (archaeo)	archaeology, archaic	primitive, ancient
ast(er)	astronaut, astrology, asteroid	star
auto	automate, automatic, automobile	self
bar	barograph, barometer	weight, pressure
basi	basic, basis	at the bottom
biblio	bibliophile, bibliography	book
bio	biology, biography	life
botan	botany, botanical	plant
byss	abyss, hypabyssal	bottom
chrome	phytochrome, monochrome	color
chron (chrono)	chronicle, synchronize, chronological	time
cosm	cosmology, cosmonaut	universe
cycl	cyclone, recycle	circle or ring
cylind	cylinder, cylindroma	roll
dem	democracy, demographics	people
derma	dermatologist, hypodermic	skin
doc	doctrinal, document	teach
dyna	dynamite, dynamic, dynasty	power
dys	dyslexic, dysfunctional	bad, hard, unlucky
ethn (ethno)	ethnic, ethos	nation, race
exo	exotic, exosphere	outside
gam	monogamy, polygamy	marriage
geo	geology, geography	earth
gen	genealogy, genetic	family, race
gno	agnostic, acknowledge	to know
gram	epigram, telegram	written
graph	graphic, autograph, demographic	write
hetero	heterogeneous, heteronym	different
homo	homogenous, homonym	same
hydr	hydropower, hydrant, dehydrate	water
hypo	hypothermia, hypoglycemia	below, beneath
ideo	ideology, ideologue	idea
kinesis	photokinesis, kinetic	movement
logos	theology, biology	word, study
logy	psychology, geology, biology	study of

mech	mechanic, mechanism	machine
meter (metr)	thermometer, diameter	measure
micro	microscope, microbe	small
mis (miso)	misogyny, misanthrope	hate
mono	monotonous, monologue	one
morph	morphing, morphology	form, shape
narc	narcolepsy, narcotic	sleep
nym	synonym, antonym	name
ono (onum)	anonymous, onomatopoeia	name
opt	optical, optician	eye
path	apathy, empathy	feel
ped	pediatrics, pediatrician	child
phil	philanthropy, bibliophile	love
phobia	phobic, claustrophobia	fear
phon	telephone, microphone	sound
photo (phos)	photon, photocopy, photograph	light
pneu	pneumonia, pneumatic	air, breath
polis	metropolis, cosmopolitan	city
pseudo	pseudoscience, pseudonym	false
psycho	psychic, psychology	soul, spirit
pyr	pyromaniac, pyrogen	fire
saur	dinosaur, stegosaurs	lizard
schem	schematic, scheme	plan
scope	telescope, microscope	viewing instrument
strat	stratonic, strategy	army
syn	synchronize, synonym	together, with
techno	technological, technique	art, science, skill
tele	telescope, telephone	far
the (theo)	theology, apotheosize	god
therm	thermometer, thermal	heat
tropos	heliotrope, troposphere	turning

PREFIX

Prefix	Examples	Meaning
a- (an-)	amoral, acellular, abyss	without, lack of
ab-	absent, abstinent	away from
ante-	antecedent, anterior, antedate	before, earlier
anti-	antibacterial, antibody, anticlimax	against
auto-	autobiography, autopilot, automobile	self
bene-	benefit, benevolent, benefactor	well, good
bi-	bicycle, bilateral, binoculars	two
bio-	biology, biometrics, bioscience	life
circum-	circumvent, circumnavigate	around
co-	cooperate, coworker, copilot	with, together
com- (con-)	combination, companion, contact	together with
contra- (contro-)	contradict, contrast, controversy	against, opposite
de-	devalue, deactivate, degrade	down, off
dis-	disbar, disagreeable, disappear	not
en-	enclose, entangle, enslave	put into, cover with
ex-	exit, extract, exhale	out
extra-	extracurricular, extravagant	beyond, outside
geo-	geology, geothermal, geoscience	earth
hetero-	heterosexual, heterogeneous	different, other
homo- (homeo-)	homeostasis, homophone	same, alike
hyper-	hypertension, hypercritical, hyperactive	over
hypo-	hypodermic, hypothermia, hypothesize	under, beneath
im- (il-, ir-)	impossible, irresponsible, illegal	not
in-	incomplete, inconsiderate	not
inter-	interstate, interstellar, intervene	between
intra- (intro-)	intravenous, introvert	within, inside
macro-	macroeconomics, macrostructure	large, prominent
mal-	malevolent, malefactor, maleficent	bad, ill
micro-	microbiology, microbe, microscope	small
mid-	midway, midday, midair	middle
mis-	misunderstood, misspell, miscarriage	wrong, mistaken
mono-	monorail, monologue, monogamy	one
non-	nonsense, nonfiction, nonessential	not
omni-	omniscient, omnivorous, omnidirectional	all, every
post-	post-test, posterior, postscript	after
pre- (pro-)	pre-test, precede, prologue	before, forward
re-	repeat, rebuild, refold	do again
sub-	subway, submarine, substandard	under

sym- (syn-)	symmetry, synchronize, synapse	same time
tele-	television, telephone	over a distance
trans-	transatlantic, transmit, transaction	across
un-	unhappy, unfinished, unfriendly	not
uni-	unity, unicellular, unicycle	one
up-	upgrade, uphill, upscale	higher, better

SUFFIX

Suffix	Examples	Meaning
-able (-ible)	portable, credible	can do something
-age	drainage, salvage	action, process of
-al	fictional, musical	pertaining to
-ance (-ence)	importance, attendance	an action or state
-ant	assistant, participant	a person
-ate	collaborate, eradicate	become
-ible	edible, comprehendible	can do something
-ed	walked, loved	past tense
-ee	referee, franchisee	a person
-ence	difference, correspondence	an action or state
-er (-or)	teacher, administrator	a person who performs the action
-ery	bakery, creamery	a type or place of work
-ess	waitress, goddess	turns into a feminine form
-ful	hopeful, spoonful	full of
-fy	magnify, oversimplify	to make
-ing	walking, painting	present tense
-ion	decoration, experimentation	a process, state, or result
-ious	pious, religious	characterized by
-ish	greenish, childish	a little
-ism	Judaism, totalitarianism	a belief or condition
-ist	artist, florist	someone performing the action or a believer
-ity (-ty)	extremity, security	quality of
-ive	attentive, active	having the quality of
-ize	victimize, photosynthesize	to make
-less	hopeless, careless	not having
-like	lifelike, gentlemanlike	similar to
-ly	softly, slowly	related to
-ment	amendment, measurement	the action of
-ness	brightness, sickness	condition of
-ology	zoology, biology	the study of
-ory	laboratory, dormitory	relating to
-ose	verbose, adipose	full of
-osis	diagnosis, hypnosis	process, condition
-ous	joyous, hazardous	full of, having
-some	troublesome, cumbersome	a tendency to
-pathy	sympathy, neuropathy	feeling, diseased

Suffix	Examples	Meaning
-phone	telephone, microphone	sound
-ship	friendship, membership	position held
-sion	confusion, depression	state, quality of being
-sophy (-sophic)	philosophy, theosophy	wisdom, knowledge
-th	depth, length	state or quality
-tion (-ation)	creation, transition	action, process of
-tude	fortitude, certitude	state, quality of being
-ure	departure, erasure	action or resulting state
-ward	forward, afterwards	shows direction
-ware	hardware, kitchenware	things of the same type
-ways	sideways, crossways	shows direction
-wise	clockwise, weatherwise	in relation to
-y	funny, greedy	characterized by

notes:

LEAD
SET 1
VOCABULARY

SET 1

01 rare
rer
adj.

infrequent, scarce, sparse

a condition, event, or situation that does not occur often

*My cousin has a **rare** genetic disorder.*

(자주 있는 일이 아니어서) 드문(보기 힘든/희귀한)

02 intense
inˈtens
adj.

severe, extreme, fierce

of extreme degree, force, or strength

*The job requires **intense** concentration.*

극심한, 강렬한

03 mate
māt
n.

partner, spouse, lover

a person or an animal's sexual partner

*A male bird will sing to court his **mate**.*

배우자, 배필 (남편 또는 아내); 짝(한 쌍)의 한쪽

v.

breed, couple, copulate

animals or birds coming together to breed; copulate

*A single male lion will **mate** with several females.*

짝짓기를 하다

04 alpha
ˈalfə
n.

first, start

denotes the dominant animal or human in a group

*A wolf pack is led by the **alpha**.*

우두머리, 수컷

05 circumvent
ˌsərkəmˈvent
v.

avoid, evade, bypass

to find a way around, usually an obstacle

*If there is something blocking your path, you should **circumvent** it.*

(길을 막고 있는 것을) 피해 가다(둘러 가다)

06 ritual
ˈriCH(oo)əl
n.

ceremony, rite, service

a religious or a solemn ceremony made up of a series of actions done according to a given order

*Buddhists follow a strict **ritual** in their temple.*

(특히 종교상의) 의식 절차, (제의적) 의례

07 fertilize
ˈfərdlˌīz
v.

impregnate, inseminate, pollinate

cause an egg, female animal, or plant to create a new individual by introducing male reproductive material

*Male dogs will **fertilize** their partners and stay until the pups are born.*

수정시키다

08 deception
dəˈsepSH(ə)n
n.

deceit, duplicity, fraud

the act of tricking someone

*He obtained his fortune by **deception**.*

속임, 기만, 사기

09 comprise
kəmˈprīz
v.

contain, constitute, form

consist of; made up of

*The United States is **comprised** of fifty states.*

…으로 구성되다(이뤄지다)

10 roughly
ˈrəflē
adv.

about, around

approximately

*The hospital is **roughly** 20 miles away.*

대략, 거의

11 distinguish
dəˈstiNGgwiSH
v.

discriminate, discern, differentiate

to recognize or treat someone or something as different

*It is too dark to **distinguish** the objects.*

구별하다

12 spawn
spôn
v.

create, generate, hatch

(relating to fish, frog, etc.) be laid as eggs

*The salmon can precisely locate where they were **spawned**.*

알을 낳다

13 reproduction
ˌrēprəˈdəkSH(ə)n
n.

breeding, procreation, propagation

the production of offspring by a sexual or asexual process

*Humans and animals must go through **reproduction** to proliferate.*

생식, 번식

SET 1

14 mature
məˈCHoor
adj.

adult, grown

fully developed physically; full-grown

*He is now a **mature** man.*

성인이 된, 다 자란

15 delay
dəˈlā
v.

retard, linger, detain

make someone or something late or slow

*Due to the storm, the plane was **delayed**.*

지연, 지체

16 mass
mas
n.

pile, stack, lump

a large body of matter with no definite shape

*A **mass** of clothes were seen on the bedroom floor.*

(정확한 형체가 없는) 덩어리

17 predator
ˈpredədər
n.

carnivore, animal of prey

an organism that preys on others

*Cats are major **predators** of mice.*

포식자, 포식 동물

18 colony
ˈkälənē
n.

territory, dominion, province

a country or area under the full or partial political control of another country, typically a distant one, and occupied by settlers from that country

*Japanese forces attacked the French **colony** of China.*

식민지

n.

community, group, population

a community of animals or plants of one kind living close together or forming a physically connected structure

*A **colony** of seals were seen off the coast.*

무리

19 excavate
ˈekskəˌvāt
v.

dig, gouge, unearth

to make a hole or channel by digging

*The ground was **excavated** in order to build a canal.*

(구멍 등을) 파다

20. depression
/dəˈpreSH(ə)n/
n.

- dent, dip, pit
- the act of lowering something or pushing something down
- *The shallow **depressions** were turned into rivers.*
- (지면의) 구멍, 팬 곳, 구덩이

n.
- recession, slump, decline
- a long and severe recession in an economy
- *The country was suffering from an economic **depression**.*
- 불경기

21. emerge
/əˈmərj/
v.

- appear, become visible
- come out or move away from something and come into sight
- *The ghostly ship **emerged** from the fog.*
- (어둠 속이나 숨어 있던 곳에서) 나오다(모습을 드러내다)

22. proportion
/prəˈpôrSH(ə)n/
n.

- ratio, distribution, relationship
- the relationship of one thing to another in terms of quantity, size, or number
- *The **proportion** of free time to work time is vastly different.*
- (다른 것과 규모, 양 등을 대조한) 비(비율)

23. divert
/dīˈvərt/
v.

- reroute, redirect
- cause someone or something to change course or turn from one direction to another
- *The river was **diverted** to irrigate the farmland.*
- 방향을 바꾸게 하다(전환시키다), 우회시키다

24. secrete
/səˈkrēt/
v.

- discharge, emit, excrete
- produce and discharge a substance
- *The insect **secreted** poison to defend itself.*
- 분비하다

25. procreative
/prōˈkrē-āˈtĭv/
adj.

- fruitful
- producing new life or offspring
- *Organisms engage in reproduction as a **procreative** act.*
- 출산(생식)의, 출산(생식)력이 있는

SET 1

26 meek
mēk
adj.

- patient, submissive, gentle
- quiet, gentle, and easily imposed on
- *My mother did not talk much, so many considered her **meek**.*

온순한, 온화한

27 seek
sēk
v.

- pursue, explore
- attempt to find something
- ***Seek** and you will find.*

(…을 발견하기 위해) 찾다

28 adjacent
əˈjās(ə)nt
adj.

- adjoining, close to
- next to or adjoining something else
- *The siblings live in **adjacent** rooms.*

인접한, 가까운

29 breed
brēd
v.

- reproduce, procreate, multiply
- mate and then produce offspring
- *Some animals **breed** on a seasonal basis.*

새끼를 낳다

n.
- stock, strain, type
- animals or plants having a distinctive appearance
- *The new **breed** of monkeys were put in the zoo.*

품종

30 school
skool
n.

- group, faction, circle
- a group of people, particularly writers, artists, or philosophers, sharing the same or similar ideas, methods, or style
- *The **school** of scholars met to discuss the big bang theory.*

무리의

31 exacerbate
igˈzasərˌbāt
v.

- aggravate, inflame, worsen
- to make a situation worse
- *Lying to my father **exacerbated** the situation.*

악화시키다

32 accelerate
əkˈseləˌrāt
v.

speed, expedite, boost
to increase in amount of extent
*The police car **accelerated** to catch up with the car thief.*
속도를 높이다

33 malpractice
malˈpraktəs
n.

wrongdoing, misconduct, unprofessionalism
improper or illegal activity done by a professional
*Doctors in Asia perform medical **malpractice** to earn more money.*
(전문 직종에서의) 위법(부정/배임) 행위, (의사의) 의료 과실

34 advise
ədˈvīz
v.

counsel, guide, educate
to offer suggestions
*The old man **advised** the child to return the stolen item.*
조언하다, 충고하다, 권고하다

35 doctrine
ˈdäktrən
n.

creed, dogma, belief
a belief practiced and taught by a political, religious, or any group
*Christians believe in the **doctrine** of salvation.*
교리, 신조, 정책, 주의

36 relieve
rəˈlēv
v.

alleviate, mitigate, assuage
to cause a pain or difficulty to become less severe
*The medicinal cream helped **relieve** the pain.*
(불쾌감,고통 등을) 없애(덜어)주다, 안도하게(후련하게) 하다

37 revive
rəˈvīv
v.

resuscitate, revitalize, reanimate
to bring to life or consciousness
*Frankenstein was **revived** with a jolt of electricity.*
활기를 되찾다(되찾게 하다), 회복(소생)하다(시키다)

38 dispense
dəˈspens
v.

distribute, allocate, apportion
to distribute or provide something to many people
*The health center **dispensed** free multivitamin pills to the townspeople.*
나누어 주다, 내놓다

SET 1

39 anticipate
anˈtisəˌpāt
v.
expect, predict, foretell
to regard as likely to happen
She **anticipated** that someone would ask her to dance.
예상하다

40 thorough
ˈTHərō
adj.
exhaustive, scrupulous, meticulous
performing a task very carefully and completely, paying attention to detail
Doctors must be very **thorough** when performing surgery.
빈틈없는, 철두철미한

41 controversy
ˈkäntrəˌvərsē
n.
dissension, contention, dispute
a disagreement
The couple had a **controversy** on whether to adopt a dog or not.
논란

42 ignorant
ˈignərənt
adj.
uneducated, unsophisticated, mindless
an overall lack of knowledge or awareness
Some people are just **ignorant** and stupid.
무지한, 무식한; 무학의

43 stem
stem
v.
arise, derive, originate
to originate in
Hatred **stems** from jealousy.
비롯되다, 유래하다

44 adverse
adˈvərs
adj.
unfavorable, detrimental, antagonistic
preventing development or success
The hot weather is having an **adverse** effect on agriculture.
부정적인, 불리한

45 dispose
dəˈspōz
v.
discard, scrap, trash
to get rid of by throwing it away or giving it to someone else
Batman **disposed** his old suit when Alfred made him a new one.
…을 없애다, 처리하다

46 external
ikˈstərnl
adj.

exterior, outer, extrinsic

relating to the outer surface or structure

*The **external** armor of the spaceship absorbed the radiation from the sun.*

외부의, 밖의, 외면의

47 internal
inˈtərnl
adj.

interior, inner, inside

relating to the inside

*The victim was suffering from **internal** bleeding.*

내부의

48 viral
ˈvīrəl
adj.

flourishing, burgeoning, expanding

information that is circulated quickly and widely

*The scandalous news went **viral** in a matter of minutes.*

무성한, 급증하는

49 replicate
ˈrepləˌkāt
v.

duplicate, copy, clone

to make a copy

*China tends to **replicate** products that are already made, but inferior in quality.*

모사(복제)하다

50 exceptional
ˌikˈsepSH(ə)n(ə)l
adj.

outstanding, remarkable, special

unusually good

*The hamburger was **exceptional** when compared to McDonalds.*

이례적일 정도로 우수한, 특출한

SET 1 TEST

1. The news that North and South Korea reunified went _____ and every news channel delivered the major event.

2. The lab rat decided to _____ the obstruction in its path by finding a new path in the maze.

3. Watching too much television has proven to show _____ effect in the development of a child.

4. His _____ was clearly evident, so people walked away from his offer.

5. Every year, Santa Claus _____ gifts to children who have been good and leaves behind coal to those who misbehaved.

6. The runners were _____ from their path due to a car accident.

7. There are still some _____ people who believe that their ethnicity should dominate others.

8. Students who are _____ tend to be the ones who are bullied in school.

9. Brian _____ the situation when he arrived late for a meeting that was already delayed.

10. Accountants in major corporations conduct _____ when they try to evade paying taxes to the government.

---

1. viral   2. circumvent   3. adverse   4. deception   5. dispense
6. divert   7. ignorant   8. meek   9. exacerbate   10. malpractice

11. It was _____ that Michelle forgot to pick up the clothes because she usually never forgets what she needs to do.

12. My son showed _____ skills playing chess, considering he is only six-years-old.

13. The butterfly _____ from its cocoon and took flight for the first time.

14. Koreans _____ their trash by separating the items, even at fast food restaurants.

15. It is difficult to _____ a lost item if one's room is unorganized.

16. In order to _____ the pain, she decided to take some medication.

17. The two males fought in order to fulfill the position of being the _____ in the group.

18. M&M chocolate is _____ of different colors with the chocolate logo on each piece.

19. Picasso and Duchamp were in the same _____ of art.

20. Doctors must be very _____ during surgery or the patient will suffer afterwards.

---

11. rare	12. exceptional	13. emerge	14. dispose	15. seek
16. relieve	17. alpha	18. comprise	19. school	20. thorough

SET 1

notes:

LEAD SET 2
VOCABULARY

SET 2

01 tilt
tilt
v.

lean, slant, incline
move or cause to move into a sloping position
*The ground was **tilted** slightly so it had to be leveled.*

기울다, (뒤로) 젖혀지다, 갸우뚱하다

02 resident
ˈrez(ə)dənt
n.

inhabitant, local, citizen
a person or an animal of a species that lives somewhere permanently or on a long-term basis
*The small town was a peaceful place with just 50 **residents**.*

거주자

03 diminutive
dəˈminyədiv
adj.

petite, minute, minuscule
unusually small
*The **diminutive** woman arrived to the party dressed in a child's dress.*

아주 작은

04 tactic
ˈtaktik
n.

scheme, stratagem, maneuver
an action or strategy carefully planned to obtain a specific goal
*The military academy taught basic **tactics** in warfare.*

(어떤 일을 달성하기 위한) 전략(작전)

05 agility
əˈjilədē
n.

dexterity, swiftness, quickness
ability to move easily and quickly
*Although she received no training, her **agility** was notable in sports.*

민첩, 명민함

06 fortunate
ˈfôrCH(ə)nət
adj.

advantageous, providential, welcome
auspicious or favorable
*It was a **fortunate** match for the disabled player.*

다행스럽다

07 significant
sigˈnifikənt
adj.

notable, remarkable, outstanding
important enough to give attention; noteworthy
*The team was given a medal to award them in their **significant** win.*

특별한 의미가 있는, 중요한

08 stalk
stôk
v.

trail, follow, shadow

pursue or approach with unwanted and obsessive attention

*The cheetah **stalked** the antelope, ready to attack any minute.*

몰래 접근하다

09 halt
hôlt
v.

cease, curb, suspend

bring or come to a sudden stop

*The two warring countries made truce to **halt** the bloodshed.*

멈추다, 서다

10 mimicry
ˈmiməkrē
n.

imitation, copying, impersonation

the action or art of imitating someone or something

*Certain insects use **mimicry** to intimidate predators.*

흉내

11 disguise
disˈgīz
n.

camouflage, concealment, costume

a method of changing one's appearance or hiding one's identity

*He told everyone that he was a detective in **disguise**.*

위장하다, 숨기다

12 fashion
ˈfaSHən
n.

method, approach, way

a way of doing something

*The office work is done in a casual **fashion**.*

방식

13 markings
ˈmärkiNG
n.

patterns

a mark or pattern of marks on an organism's fur, feather, or skin

*The **markings** on the frog indicate that it is poisonous.*

무늬

14 establish
əˈstabliSH
v.

institute, inaugurate, install

set up (a group, system, or rules) on a permanent basis

*The British **established** a trade system with India.*

설립(설정)하다

SET 2

SET 2

15 maneuver
məˈnoovər
n.

- operation, action, exercise
- movement or series of moves requiring skill and care
- *The stuntman carried out spectacular **maneuvers** throughout the film.*
- 조심해서 기술적으로 하는 동작

16 eject
ēˈjekt
v.

- emit, discharge, expel
- force or throw something out, usually in a violent or sudden way
- *Igneous rocks are **ejected** from an exploding volcano.*
- 배출(분비) 하다, 뿜어내다

17 accomplish
əˈkämpliSH
v.

- fulfill, realize, attain
- achieve or complete successfully
- *The military successfully **accomplished** their mission.*
- 완수하다, 성취하다, 해내다

18 jeopardy
ˈjepərdē
n.

- peril, endangerment, insecurity
- danger of failure, harm, or loss
- *The company was in **jeopardy** due to the stock market crash.*
- 위험

19 acquiesce
ˌakwēˈes
v.

- consent to, assent to, comply with
- to accept something reluctantly without protesting
- *Michelle **acquiesced** in the decision after losing the game.*
- …의 의견에 순순히 따르다

20 velocity
vəˈläsədē
n.

- pace, rate, tempo
- speed
- *The rocket flew up at an incredible **velocity**.*
- 속도

21 trick
trik
n.

- ploy, ruse, scheme
- a cunning or skillful act or plan to deceive or outwit the other
- *He is a two-face conman capable of performing any **trick**.*
- 속임수

22 shield
SHēld
v.

protect, cover, shade

protect someone or something from a danger, risk, or anything unpleasant

*He put on his sunglasses to **shield** his eyes from the sun.*

보호하다, 가리다

23 arrange
ə'rānj
v.

fix, schedule, plan

organize or make plans for an upcoming event

*The two families **arranged** to have a wedding.*

마련하다, (일을) 처리(주선)하다

24 lure
lŏor
v.

entice, attract, persuade

tempt to do something or to go someplace, by offering a reward

*The child was **lured** by the dentist, who offered a piece of candy.*

꾀다, 유혹하다

25 fitness
'fitnəs
n.

strength, robustness, vigor

the state of being physically fit and healthy

*Lack of **fitness** will lead to sickness.*

신체 단련, (신체적인) 건강

26 sneak
snēk
v.

creep, slink, slip

to move in a furtive or stealthy way

*She **snuck** in to the house through the garage.*

살금살금(몰래) 가다

27 effective
ə'fektiv
adj.

productive, constructive, fruitful

successful in creating a wanted or intended result

*The World Health Organization came up with **effective** solutions to fight the pandemic.*

효과적인

28 entice
en'tīs
v.

allure, lure, tempt

attract or tempt by providing pleasure or benefit

*The new toy should **entice** children to want it as a Christmas gift.*

유도(유인)하다

SET 2 · 33

SET 2

29. nimble
ˈnimbəl
adj.
- agile, acrobatic, light-footed
- quick and light in action or movement
- *The ballerina danced with **nimble** feet.*
- 빠른, 날렵한

30. multiplicity
ˌməltəˈplisədē
n.
- array, variety, myriad
- a large variety
- *The Amazon Rainforest is home to a **multiplicity** of species.*
- 다수, 다양성

31. espouse
iˈspouz
v.
- embrace, champion, adopt
- to adopt or support a cause or belief
- *Many Koreans **espoused** the abandonment of Japanese products.*
- (주의, 정책 등을) 옹호(지지)하다

32. proper
ˈpräpər
adj.
- orthodox, conventional, established
- appropriate
- *It is **proper** to applaud after someone gives a speech.*
- 적절한, 제대로 된

33. delve
delv
v.
- probe, rummage, inquire
- to reach inside and search for something
- *She **delved** into her purse to look for her keys.*
- (무엇을 찾으려고 가방 등을) 뒤지다

34. splinter
ˈsplin(t)ər
v.
- shatter, split, fracture
- to break into small sharp fragments
- *The glass sculpture **splintered** when it fell from its podium.*
- 쪼개지다, 깨지다

35. contrast
ˈkänˌtrast
n.
- disparity, distinction, polarity
- the state of being different from something else
- *The two paintings were observed for **contrast** and comparison.*
- 차이; 대조, 대비

36. forefront
ˈfôrˌfrənt
n.

vanguard, spearhead, lead

at the front, the most important position

NASA is at the **forefront** of space exploration.

맨 앞, 선두

37. avenue
ˈavəˌn(y)oō
n.

method, approach, way

a way of handling a problem

A practical **avenue** was proposed by the teacher to solve the problem.

방안/방법/접근수단

38. wizen
ˈwizən
adj.

wrinkled, lined, creased

wrinkled with age

The **wizened** old man played chess in the park.

시들다

39. tout
tout
v.

commend, endorse, recommend

to persuade someone the advantages of someone or something

The mayor **touted** that his city was the best place to relax.

(사람들을 설득하기 위해) 장점을 내세우다

40. berate
bəˈrāt
v.

rebuke, reprimand, admonish

to scold or criticize someone

The boss **berated** his employees for making a mistake.

질책하다

41. fraction
ˈfrakSH(ə)n
n.

fragment, hint, tad

a small part, amount, or proportion of a whole

I only want a small **fraction** of that cake.

부분, 일부

42. robust
rōˈbəst
adj.

vigorous, sturdy, tough

strong and healthy

Arnold Schwarzenegger is **robust** even after retirement.

원기 왕성한, 팔팔한

SET 2

43. placebo
plə'sēbō
n.

a harmless pill or medicine that is given to the patient for positive psychological effect

The sugar pill acted as a **placebo** and helped my uncle cope with the sickness.

플라세보, 속임약, 위약

44. placate
'plākāt
v.

pacify, appease, mollify

to make someone less angry or hostile

The rioters were **placated** when their demands were answered.

(화를) 달래다

45. willing
'wiliNG
adj.

prepared, inclined, disposed

ready or eager to do something

He was **willing** to take out the trash.

기꺼이 하는, 자발적인, 열렬한, 적극적인

46. prescribe
prə'skrīb
v.

advise, authorize, direct

to recommend a medicine or action for someone

The doctor **prescribed** cold medicine to the patient.

처방을 내리다, 처방하다; 처방전을 쓰다

47. couple
'kəpəl
n.

pair, duo, match

two people of the same kind

A **couple** of tennis players were already on the court.

두 사람

v.

attach, join, link

to connect

The two railroad tracks were **coupled** midway.

연결(결합)하다

48. ailment
'ālmənt
n.

disorder, affliction, malady

a minor sickness

The child was suffering from an **ailment** and needed to rest at home.

질병

49 vouch
affirm, verify, confirm

vouCH
v.

to assert or confirm an experience as something true or accurately portrayed

*I can **vouch** that my brother is an honest man.*

보증(보장)하다

50 dummy
imitation, substitute, representation

ˈdəmē
n.

something that resembles and serves as a replacement for the real thing

*Car crashes were tested by using **dummies**.*

모조품

SET 2 TEST

1. Everyone was shocked at the _____ size of the puppy.

2. I can _____ that he will be a resourceful worker at your company.

3. _____ of someone should be done with the smallest attention to detail if they wish to impersonate the person.

4. Even the most vicious animals can be _____ by playing a song or melody.

5. The _____ that she approached the problem was ingenious.

6. Professional wrestlers must be _____ in order to defeat their opponents on the ring.

7. The team was in _____ because their main players were all injured and the coach had given up.

8. Even if your boss _____ you, you should work harder so that next time you can receive a compliment.

9. The children _____ to sleeping early when they were allowed to watch television the next morning.

10. The little boy _____ his hand into the cookie jar to find the biggest cookie.

---

1. diminutive 2. vouch 3. mimicry 4. placate 5. fashion 6. robust 7. jeopardy 8. berate 9. acquiesce 10. delve

11. The hunter tried to _____ the deer by smearing the tree with the scent of its mate.

12. Ballerinas must be _____ in order to receive high marks.

13. What sort of _____ are you suffering from?

14. The cheetah ran with such _____ that it was able to catch up with its prey.

15. The pilot gracefully _____ his plane so that it looked like the aircraft was dancing in the sky.

16. I love going to the buffet, even though I cannot eat much, because of the _____ of menus.

17. He was able to solve only a _____ of the puzzle.

18. Electric cars stand in the _____ of car engineering.

19. This is a _____ of the actual satellite that will be launched into space next month.

20. The military general carefully planned a _____ to surprise the enemy.

---

11. lure   12. nimble   13. ailment   14. agility   15. maneuver
16. multiplicity   17. fraction   18. forefront   19. dummy   20. tactic

SET 2

notes:

LEAD
SET 3
VOCABULARY

SET 3

01 pursue
pərˈsoō
v.

- chase, hunt, stalk
- follow someone or something in order to attack or catch them
- *The police officer **pursued** the thief.*

(붙잡기 위해) 뒤쫓다

v.
- seek, strive for
- seek to attain or accomplish something over an extended time
- *Individuals **pursue** their own happiness.*

추구하다, (어떤 일을 어느 정도의 기간을 두고) 밀고 나가다

02 succumb
səˈkəm
v.

- yield, surrender, cave in
- fail to resist pressure, temptation, or anything negative
- *The hard worker finally **succumbed** to the pressures of office work.*

굴복하다, 무릎을 꿇다

03 allure
əˈloor
n.

- attraction, appeal, glamour
- the trait of being attractive or fascinating in a powerful and mysterious way
- *Some people find no **allure** for gold or diamonds.*

매력

04 alter
ˈôltər
v.

- change, adjust
- change in character or composition
- *The author was persuaded to **alter** the plot of the story.*

바꾸다, 고치다

05 prominent
ˈprämənənt
adj.

- distinguished, eminent, leading
- important; famous
- *The politician is a **prominent** member of the city.*

중요한, 유명한

06 rear
rir
n.

- back, hind, stern
- the back part of something
- *The garage is at the **rear** of the house.*

뒤쪽

v.
- nurture, parent, look after
- care for until the animal or child is fully grown
- *I was born and **reared** in Seoul.*

키우다

42 · LEAD VOCABULARY

07 dorsal
'dôrsəl
adj.

back, hind, behind

relating to the top or back of an animal, plant, or organ

*The dolphin has a tracker on its **dorsal** fin.*

(물고기나 동물의) 등에 있는

08 medium
'mēdēəm
n.

form, vehicle, tool

the material or form used by an artist or writer

*During the Renaissance, oil paint was the most popular **medium** for art.*

예술가의 표현수단(중개물)

09 ample
'ampəl
adj.

sufficient, abundant, plentiful

enough or more than adequate

*There is **ample** time to tour the entire museum.*

충분한

10 symbolic
sim'bälik
adj.

figurative, representative, illustrative

serving as a symbol

*The number eight on its side is **symbolic** of continuity.*

상징적인, 상징하는

11 enhance
en'hans
v.

magnify, amplify, strengthen

increase the quality, value, or extent of

*The president carried out many reforms to **enhance** his reputation.*

(좋은 점, 가치, 지위를) 높이다(향상시키다)

12 endure
en'd(y)oor
v.

last, persist, continue

remain in existence

*The ancient cities have **endured** the passing of time.*

오래가다(지속되다)

13 primarily
ˌprī'merəlē
adv.

essentially, fundamentally, firstly

for the most part

*Around 60 percent of computers are used **primarily** for online games.*

주로

SET 3

14 deceased
də'sēst
adj.

dead, expired, departed
no longer living
*The **deceased** relative was buried in the family cemetery.*

고인

15 pragmatic
prag'madik
adj.

practical, realistic, sensible
dealing with things in a sensible and realistic way
*The scientist proposed a **pragmatic** method to solve global warming.*

실용적인

16 scarce
skers
adj.

scant, meager, sparse
insufficient for demand
*Fossil fuel has become **scarce**, so renewable energy should be developed.*

부족한, 드문

17 adept
ə'dept
adj.

expert, proficient, skillful
skilled or proficient at something
*She is **adept** at repairing damaged artwork.*

능숙한

18 import
im'pôrt
v.

bring goods or services into a country from outside
*America is known to **import** many foreign cars.*

수입하다

19 artisan
'ärdəzən
n.

craftsperson, mechanic
someone in a skilled trade, usually something made by hands
*Street markets are famous for local **artisans** displaying their handmade goods.*

장인, 기능 보유자

20 native
'nādiv
n.

resident, local, aborigine
a local inhabitant
*Summers in South Korea are too hot even for the **natives**.*

… 태생(출신)인 사람

21. gnarled
närld
adj.

knotted, lumpy, rough

rough and twisted, especially with age

*The **gnarled** oak tree has been standing in our backyard for decades.*

울퉁불퉁하고 비틀린, 옹이가 많은

22. irregular
əˈregyələr
adj.

crooked, asymmetrical, nonuniform

not even or balanced in shape or order

*The **irregular** features in the painting attracted many viewers.*

고르지(가지런하지) 못한

23. counterpart
ˈkoun(t)ər‚pärt
n.

equivalent, parallel, complement

a person or thing in a position or carrying out a function that corresponds to another person or thing

*The president held a meeting with his French **counterpart**.*

…의 대응(인)물

24. associate
əˈsōsēˌāt
v.

link, relate, couple

connect someone or something with something else

*The teenager **associated** freedom with the idea of moving out.*

연상하다, 결부(연관)짓다

n.

colleague, coworker, workmate

a partner in business or at work

*My **associate** will help you get used to working at our company.*

같이 일하는 동료

25. composition
‚kämpəˈziSH(ə)n
n.

constitution, configuration, makeup

the ingredients or constituents of something

*The social **composition** of the village is divided into three tiers.*

구성 요소들, 구성

26. alternative
ôlˈtərnədiv
adj.

other, substitute, possible

something to be available as another possibility

*There are other **alternative** methods to solve the problem.*

대체 가능한, 대안이 되는

SET 3

27 employ
əmˈploi
v.

hire, recruit
give work to someone and compensate them
*The company **employs** over 100 people.*

고용하다

28 pigment
ˈpigmənt
n.

coloring, tint, hue
the natural coloring matter of an animal or plant
*The **pigment** of an octopus changes according to its environment.*

(동물,식물 등에 자연 상태로 존재하는) 색소

29 sporadic
spəˈradik
adj.

infrequent, periodical, scattered
occurring at irregular times or only in a few places
***Sporadic** fighting broke out during the civil war.*

산발적인, 이따금 발생하는

30 resurrect
ˌrezəˈrekt
v.

revive, regenerate, revitalize
restore something or someone that has died back to life
*He was dead, but he has **resurrected**.*

부활시키다

31 prior
ˈprī(ə)r
adj.

preceding, antecedent, previous
coming before in regards to time, order, or importance
*Strangely, he brushed his teeth **prior** to eating his meal.*

사전의

32 violate
ˈvīəˌlāt
v.

breach, infringe, break
to disregard or fail to follow the rules
*They **violated** the terms of the contract.*

(법,합의 등을) 위반하다(어기다)

33 ethic
ˈeTHik
n.

integrity, moral, virtue
moral principles
*The **ethic** of not telling a lie is broken when the truth actually hurts someone.*

(개인 행동 규범으로서의) 윤리

34 legitimate
ləˈjidəmət
adj.

authorized, legalized, permitted

following laws and regulations

*The son had a **legitimate** claim to the family fortune.*

정당한, 타당한, 적당한

35 tempt
tem(p)t
v.

entice, convince, induce

to attract someone to do something they know is wrong

*Jim was **tempted** to steal the candy when no one was looking.*

유혹하다(부추기다)

36 optimistic
ˌäptəˈmistik
adj.

positive, hopeful, cheerful

hopeful and confident regarding the future

*Our group leader is **optimistic** and always encourages and pushes the group.*

낙관적인, 낙관하는

37 pessimistic
ˌpesəˈmistik
adj.

negative, cynical, gloomy

inclined to believe the worst for everything

*Our teammates are **pessimistic** and never try hard nor arrive on time.*

비관적인, 비관주의적인

38 retrospect
ˈretrəˌspekt
n.

hindsight, recollection, reminiscence

a review of past events or course of time

*A full **retrospect** of the game was required for the player to improve.*

회상, 회고, 추억, 회구

39 breach
brēCH
v.

violate, infringe, contravene

to break or not follow a law or an agreement

*The country **breached** the Paris Agreement when it produced too much carbon emission.*

(합의나 약속을) 위반하다(어기다)

40 nocebo
nəˈsēbō
n.

a harmful effect on health made from psychological factors, such as negative expectations

*The **nocebo** effect caused the patient to pass away much faster than anticipated.*

노세보(치료가 유해할 것이라고 믿는 부정적 생각)

SET 3

41. numerous
'n(y)oom(ə)rəs
adj.

countless, innumerable, copious

great in number

*The popular celebrity attended **numerous** social events.*

많은

42. foreign
'fôrən
adj.

unknown, exotic, alien

to be strange and unfamiliar

*It must be **foreign** for you to eat with chopsticks.*

이질적인, …과 맞지 않는

43. infect
in'fekt
v.

contaminate, affect, poison

to affect with a disease-causing organism

*Eating spoiled food **infected** him with food poisoning.*

감염시키다

44. differentiate
ˌdifə'ren(t)SHē ˌāt
v.

distinguish, discriminate, discern

to recognize what makes the subject different

*Sometimes the parents are unable to **differentiate** the twins.*

구별하다

45. engulf
in'gəlf
v.

flood, immerse, envelop

to surround or cover something completely

*The house was **engulfed** in flames.*

완전히 에워싸다, 휩싸다

46. neutralize
'n(y)ootrə ˌlīz
v.

counteract, offset, counterbalance

to make something ineffective or harmless by inputting an opposite force or effect

*The poison was **neutralized** when the antidote was administered.*

무효화(상쇄)시키다

47. attain
ə'tān
v.

accomplish, achieve, obtain

to succeed in obtaining

*The student was able to **attain** his goals by organizing his plans.*

이루다(획득하다)

48	**excrete**	expel, discharge, eject
	ikˈskrēt	to release as a waste
	v.	We **excrete** carbon dioxide every time we breathe.
	배설(분비)하다	

49	**liberate**	release, emancipate, free
	ˈlibəˌrāt	to set free from a situation
	v.	Slaves were **liberated** when the North won the Civil War.
	자유롭게(벗어나게) 해주다	

50		ban, oust, dismiss
	expel	to remove the membership or involvement of someone in a school or organization
	ikˈspel	
	v.	The student was **expelled** from school when he vandalized the founder's statue.
	퇴학시키다, 축출(제명)하다	

SET 3 TEST

1. The revolutionists decided to _____ their fellow comrades from prison.

2. The spy finally _____ to torture and spilled top secret information to the enemy.

3. The forest fire _____ the cabin, trapping its inhabitants inside the house.

4. The children in the costume grabbed _____ amounts of candy from the jar.

5. The citizen _____ the law when he decided to rob the bank.

6. Engineers think of _____ ways to harness renewable sources of energy.

7. In _____, I used to lie to my parents all the time.

8. The painter was very _____ at using the paintbrush to color his work.

9. The _____ terrorist acts were committed in different parts of the country.

10. He was _____ from the group for cheating.

---

1. liberate   2. succumb   3. engulf   4. ample   5. breach   6. pragmatic   7. retrospect   8. adept   9. sporadic   10. expel

11. King Midus was able to _____ anything he touched into gold.

12. Parents are somehow able to _____ identical twins.

13. The _____ celebrity made a sizeable donation to charity.

14. Because he was the _____ son, he was given his father's fortunes.

15. In recent years, fossil fuels have become _____ so humanity has turned to other energy sources.

16. The _____ of coffee in America is tea in China.

17. The _____ only produces a handful of items every year, so they are sought after.

18. People _____ happiness their entire lives.

19. The vaccine was able to _____ the virus when it entered the body.

20. The _____ wheel was unable to move on the ground.

---

11. alter   12. differentiate   13. prominent   14. legitimate   15. scarce
16. counterpart   17. artisan   18. pursue   19. neutralize   20. irregular

SET 3

notes:

LEAD SET 4 VOCABULARY

SET 4

01 sensible
ˈsensəb(ə)l
adj.

practical, realistic, reasonable

(concerning a statement or action) chosen according to wisdom or prudence

*I cannot believe that people find it **sensible** to spend so much on clothes.*

분별(양식) 있는, 합리적인

02 uniform
ˈyoonəˌfôrm
adj.

constant, steady, invariable

stay the same in all situations; not changing in character or form

*The laborer made bricks all **uniform** in size.*

획일적인, 균일한, 한결같은

03 elegant
ˈeləgənt
adj.

refined, sophisticated, tasteful

graceful and stylish in looks and manner

*She looked **elegant** in that white dress.*

품격 있는, 우아한

04 somber
ˈsämbər
adj.

solemn, grave, sober

serious or sober in mood

*He said goodbye to her with a **somber** expression.*

침울한, 우울한

05 perceptive
pərˈseptiv
adj.

insightful, observant, discerning

having or showing insight

*The psychiatrist had an excellent **perceptive** in understanding her situation.*

통찰력(직관력) 있는

06 incompetent
inˈkämpədənt
adj.

inept, amateurish, unskilled

unable to do or show the skills to perform a task successfully

*He was an **incompetent** assistant and will be replaced soon.*

(업무·과제 등에 대해) 무능한(기술이 부족한)

07 resilient
rəˈzilyənt
adj.

strong, tough, hardy

able to recover quickly or withstand a difficult situation

*Baby kangaroos are not so **resilient**, so they stay inside their mother's pouch.*

(충격·부상 등에 대해) 회복력 있는

08 proficient
prə'fiSHənt
adj.

skilled, expert, experienced

capable or skilled in performing or using something

*With many years of experience, he was very **proficient** at his job.*

능숙한, 능한

09 luster
'ləstər
n.

shine, brightness, radiance

a gentle reflection of light or soft glow

*The **luster** of the diamond captured my wife's eyes.*

광택, 윤; 광채, 빛남

10 routine
roo͞'tēn
n.

pattern, drill, regime

a sequence of actions that are carried out regularly

*The war veteran was still used to the **routine** of waking up early and exercising.*

규칙적으로 하는 일의 통상적인 순서와 방법

11 utilize
'yoo͞dl,īz
v.

use, employ, exploit

to make practical and effective use of

*A good leader will **utilize** his resources carefully.*

활용(이용)하다

12 monetary
'mänə,terē
adj.

financial, economic, fiscal

relating to money or some form of currency

*That relic has no **monetary** value.*

통화(화폐)의

13 depict
də'pikt
v.

portray, represent, picture

show or symbolize by a drawing or other form

*The ceiling **depicts** a scene from the Bible.*

(말이나 그림으로) 묘사하다(그리다)

14 deity
'dēədē
n.

god, goddess, divinity

a god or goddess

*Zeus is a **deity** of ancient Greece.*

신

SET 4

15 elite
əˈlēt
n.

best, aristocracy, nobility

an individual or a group that is superior in regards to ability or qualities compared to the rest

The school's **elite** published neverbeforeseen works and ideas.

엘리트 (계층)

16 craft
kraft
n.

profession, work, activity

the use of making things by hand

My mother is in the **craft** of pottery.

(특정 활동에 필요한 모든) 기술(기교)

v.

manufacture, produce, generate

to create something

My mother **crafted** a beautiful piece of pottery.

(특히 손으로) 공예품을 만들다, 공들여 만들다

17 drastic
ˈdrastik
adj.

extreme, serious, dire

likely to have a strong or far-reaching effect

There was a **drastic** need to improve the working conditions.

과감한, 극단적인; 급격한

18 indigenous
inˈdijənəs
adj.

native, aboriginal, local

to be from or occur naturally in a specific place

The **indigenous** tribe did not welcome the Europeans.

(어떤 지역) 원산의(토착의)

19 civilization
ˌsivələˈzāSH(ə)n
n.

advancement, development, progress

an advanced stage of human development and organization

The **civilization** perished when the invaders attacked with better weapons.

문명

20 vanish
ˈvaniSH
v.

dissipate, disappear, fade

disappear completely

The boyfriend **vanished** into the night when the girl's father came home.

(갑자기, 불가사의하게) 사라지다

21. inhabitant
in'habədnt
n.

resident, occupant, dweller

an animal or a person that lives or occupies a space

The **inhabitant** of the cave was heard grunting as it came close to its home.

(특정 지역의) 주민(서식 동물)

22. attempt
ə'tem(p)t
v.

strive, aim, endeavor

to make an effort to achieve or accomplish something

The runner **attempted** to win the race.

(특히 힘든 일을) 시도하다, 애써 해보다

23. ruins
'roōin
n.

debris, remnants, rubble

the remains of a building or structure from decay or collapse

The city of Pompeii was left in **ruins** after the volcano erupted.

붕괴, 몰락

24. withstand
wiTH'stand
v.

resist, defy, brave

to remain undamaged or unaffected

The rebel forces were able to **withstand** the might of the empire.

견뎌(이겨) 내다

25. integrate
'in(t)ə‚grāt
v.

amalgamate, merge, fuse

combine with another so that they can become one

The dead animal will decay and eventually **integrate** with the environment.

통합시키다(되다)

26. enable
en'āb(ə)l
v.

authorize, sanction, permit

to give someone or something the power or means to do something

The extra energy will **enable** the machine to stay on for a few more days.

(무엇을) 가능하게 하다

27. seamless
'sēmləs
adj.

coherent, consistent, smooth

smooth and continuous

His logic was **seamless** as he persuaded the audience to his side.

(중간에 끊어짐이 없이) 아주 매끄러운, 천의무봉의

SET 4 · 57

SET 4

28 haphazard
ˌhapˈhazərd
adj.

random, disorganized, unplanned

unplanned and showing no form of organization

*The clothes were inside the closet in a **haphazard** manner.*

무계획적, 닥치는 대로 하는

29 lack
lak
n.

absence, deficiency, shortage

the condition of being without or not having adequate amount

*There was a **lack** of food in the homeless shelter.*

부족, 결핍

30 extensive
ikˈstensiv
adj.

substantial, considerable, ample

covering or influencing a large area

*An **extensive** garden stretched in front of the mansion.*

아주 넓은(많은), 대규모의

31 intimidate
inˈtiməˌdāt
v.

menace, overawe, harass

to frighten someone in order to have them do what one wants

*The monarch butterfly **intimidates** its enemies by spreading out its wings.*

겁을 주다(위협하다)

32 wholly
ˈhōl(l)ē
adv.

completely, totally, fully

entirely

*The ill mannered child displayed **wholly** inappropriate behavior.*

완전히, 전적으로

33 excess
ikˈses
n.

surplus, superfluity, plethora

an amount that is more than needed or allowed

*The student felt that he was overburdened by an **excess** of workload.*

지나침, 과도, 과잉

34 endanger
inˈdānjər
v.

imperil, jeopardize, threaten

to put someone or something in danger or at risk

*The smog coming out of the factory is **endangering** the environment.*

위험에 빠뜨리다, 위태롭게 만들다

35 utmost
'ət‚mōst
adj.

greatest, maximum, most
the most extreme
*It is of **utmost** importance we clean the house before mom comes home.*

최고의, 극도의

36 terrain
tə'rān
n.

topography, landscape, land
an area of land, including its physical features
*The antelopes are able to run even in the toughest **terrains**.*

지형, 지역

37 aggregate
'agrigət
n.

total, sum, gross
a whole made by combining different elements
*The team was an **aggregate** of the fastest and the slowest runners.*

합계, 총액

38 compress
kəm'pres
v.

contract, condense, compact
to squeeze or press to be made smaller
*The clothes were **compressed** to fit into the luggage bag.*

압축하다(되다), 꾹 누르다(눌러지다)

39 lubricate
'loōbrə‚kāt
v.

facilitate, ease, polish
to make a process run smoothly
*The mechanic **lubricated** the gears by adding oil.*

윤활유를 바르다, 기름을 치다

40 pristine
'pris‚tēn
adj.

immaculate, untarnished, unblemished
clean and unspoiled
*After the wash, the car was in **pristine** condition.*

완전 새 것 같은, 아주 깨끗한

41 contention
kən'ten(t)SH(ə)n
n.

dispute, argument, discord
a heated disagreement
*Two speakers are in **contention** to win the debate championship title.*

논쟁, 언쟁

SET 4

42. fallacy
'faləsē
n.
- misconception, delusion, misbelief
- a mistaken belief
- *The idea that parents never lie is a **fallacy**.*
- 틀린 생각

43. unspoiled
ˌənˈspoild
adj.
- preserved, intact, unimpaired
- regarding a place where it has not been marred by development
- *Certain parts of the forest are **unspoiled** from human settlement.*
- 훼손되지 않은 아름다움을 지닌

44. blemish
'blemiSH
v.
- mar, deface, impair
- to damage the appearance of something
- *His reputation as a kind man was **blemished** when he was seen hitting his children.*
- 흠집을 내다

45. stale
stāl
adj.
- hardened, old, dry
- no longer fresh and appetizing
- *The loaf of bread became **stale** after a few days.*
- 신선하지 않은, (만든 지) 오래된

46. diffract
dəˈfrakt
v.
- to bend sound or light waves
- *The light was **diffracted** by the mirror.*
- (빛을) 회절시키다

47. inclusion
inˈklooZHən
n.
- involvement, incorporation, encompassing
- the state of being included in a group or structure
- *The art exhibition features such **inclusions** as post-modern art.*
- 포함

48. embed
əmˈbed
v.
- implant, lodge, set
- to fix something firmly and deeply onto something else
- *The crystals were **embedded** into the gauntlet.*
- (단단히) 박다(끼워 넣다)

49 **magnify**
'magnəˌfī
v.

augment, enlarge, enhance
to make something larger than it really is
*The camera's zoom can **magnify** the image.*

확대하다

50 **modest**
'mädəst
adj.

moderate, fair, adequate
concerning a small or limited amount, rate, or level
*Drink **modest** amounts of alcohol at the party.*

그다지 대단하지는 않은, 보통의

adj.

humble, unassuming, unpretentious
moderate in the evaluation of one's talents and success
*She was a **modest** woman and refused to accept the prize.*

겸손한

SET 4 TEST

1. He remained _____ during the funeral.

2. Even after winning the lottery, she remained _____ and worked hard everyday.

3. Cockroaches are _____ creatures and can survive most disasters.

4. My baby newphew _____ my art collection by smearing chocolate on the canvas.

5. Computer programmers are _____ in programming and coding various applications.

6. The people were misled by the _____ told by the newly elected leader.

7. The _____ of our society are the ones that truly lead our country to prosperity.

8. The project was an _____ of different members contributing their talents.

9. The newly constructed road was _____ as it stretched for miles and miles.

10. The intern was proven to be _____ when she did not know how to send an email.

---

1. somber 2. modest 3. resilient 4. blemish 5. proficient
6. fallacy 7. elite 8. aggregate 9. seamless 10. incompetent

11. Children tend to _____ their pain, even if it is just a scratch.

12. It was _____ for him to bring an umbrella since the sky was full of dark clouds.

13. Drill sergeants will _____ new cadets so they can adjust to army life.

14. My father wanted to build a log cabin in a forest that was _____ by civilization.

15. My roommate was having _____ problems because she was a shopaholic.

16. Almost every ancient civilization worshipped a _____ .

17. Edison wished to _____ his motion picture device with a music player.

18. The comic book fan had an _____ knowledge about superheroes and villians.

19. The _____ food was given to the pigs.

20. The car was in a _____ condition, even after driving it for a year.

---

11. magnify 12. sensible 13. intimidate 14. unspoiled 15. monetary 16. deity 17. integrate 18. extensive 19. excess 20. pristine

SET 4

notes:

LEAD SET 5 VOCABULARY

SET 5

01 organic
ôr'ganik
adj.

biological, natural, living
associated with or made from living matter
*The farmer used **organic** gardening, so he used no pesticides.*
유기체(생물)에서 나온(만들어진), 유기의

02 complement
'kämpləmənt
n.

supplement, accessory, accompaniment
something that completes or leads to perfection
*Milk is a perfect **complement** to chocolate chip cookies.*
보완물, 금상첨화격 요소

03 loose
loos
adj.

insecure, unattached, unsecured
not firmly fixed in place
*My son's **loose** tooth dangled in his mouth.*
묶여(매여) 있지 않은, 풀린

04 confederation
kən,fedə'rāSH(ə)n
n.

league, federation, coalition
an organization made up of different parties or groups that come together in alliance
*A **confederation** of labor unions emerged in the early 1900's.*
연합

05 supreme
soo'prēm
adj.

chief, foremost, leading
strongest, most important, or most powerful
*He was the **supreme** leader of the empire.*
최고의

06 hereditary
hə'redə,terē
adj.

genetic, inherited, inborn
determined by genes and thus passed on from parents to their offspring
*The disease is **hereditary** since most men in the family have it.*
유전적인

07 focal
'fōk(ə)l
adj.

central, nucleus, principal
relating to the main point of interest
*The man in the corner was the **focal** interest of the artwork.*
중심의, 초점의

08 descendant
dəˈsendənt
n.

heir, offspring, progeny

an animal, plant, or person that is descended from a specific ancestor

He is the last direct **descendant** of the king.

자손, 후손, 후예

09 absolute
ˈabsəˌlo͞ot
adj.

definite, certain, complete

free from imperfection

The spy swore to **absolute** secrecy for his mission.

완전한, 완벽한

10 oversee
ˌōvərˈsē
v.

supervise, direct, manage

to monitor a person or work

My father was selected to **oversee** the group project since he was the oldest.

감독하다

11 unique
yo͞oˈnēk
adj.

special, distinctive, individual

one of a kind

The design was **unique**, something that was never seen before.

유일무이한, 독특한

12 exert
igˈzərt
v.

strive, endeavor, strain

to make a mental or physical effort

The lion needs to **exert** itself to catch its prey.

있는 힘껏 노력하다, 분투하다

13 immeasurable
i(m)ˈmeZH(ə)rəb(ə)l
adj.

incalculable, unfathomable, innumerable

too extensive or extreme to measure

The prisoner of war endured **immeasurable** suffering while being tortured.

헤아릴(측정할) 수 없는

14 phonetic
fəˈnedik
adj.

oral, spoken, vocal

relating to sounds made in speech

The king made the alphabet using **phonetic** information.

음성(발음)을 나타내는

SET 5

15 transmit
tranz'mit
v.

transfer, impart, channel
to pass from one place or person to another
*The information was **transmitted** from the boss to the employee.*

전송(송신/방송)하다

16 formal
'fôrməl
adj.

official, legal, certified
officially approved or recognized
*The tenet received a **formal** complaint from his neighbor.*

정규적인

17 interpret
in'tərprət
v.

clarify, elucidate, explain
to explain the meaning of words, actions, or information
*The boyfriend's actions were difficult to **interpret**.*

(의미를) 설명(해석)하다

18 inscribe
in'skrīb
v.

engrave, etch, chisel
to write or carve words or pictures on something
*The winning team's name was **inscribed** on the trophy.*

(이름 등을) 쓰다(새기다)

19 primitive
'primədiv
adj.

ancient, antique, prehistoric
relating to a character of an early stage in time or history
***Primitive** human beings hunted with bow and arrows.*

초기의, 원시적인 단계의

20 convey
'kən'vā
v.

relay, transmit, communicate
communicate a message or information
*The baby tried hard to **convey** his thoughts with gurgles and screams.*

(생각,감정 등을) 전달하다

21 relay
'rē,lā
v.

transfer, retail, impart
receive and pass on information or a message
*The messenger **relayed** the information to the general.*

(정보뉴스 등을 받아서) 전달하다

22. overlap
ˌōvərˈlap
v.

imbricate, overhang

to cover the same area of interest, time, responsibility, etc.

*The sibling's duties in the house sometimes **overlapped**.*

겹치다; 겹쳐지다, 포개지다

23. spectacular
spekˈtakyələr
adj.

breathtaking, striking, picturesque

beautiful in an eye-catching way

*The Rocky Mountains is a **spectacular** scenery in America.*

장관을 이루는, 극적인

24. relic
ˈrelik
n.

antique, heirloom, artifact

an object that has survived from an earlier time and has historical or sentimental interest

*This object is a **relic** from China's long history.*

유물, 유적

25. forge
fôrj
v.

mold, cast, form

make or shape by heating it with fire and hammering it

*The one ring was **forged** from the fires of Mt. Doom.*

구축하다

26. appraise
əˈprāz
v.

evaluate, gauge, assess

to determine the value or quality of

*The curator **appraised** the lost artwork to be worth several million dollars.*

평가하다

27. durable
ˈd(y)oorəb(ə)l
adj.

resistant, strong, tough

ability to withstand wear or damage

*The backpack is **durable** so it can even withstand rain and snow.*

내구성이 있는, 오래가는

28. intimate
ˈin(t)əmət
adj.

close, familiar, friendly

having very close connection

*The mayor has an **intimate** involvement in the community.*

친(밀)한

SET 5

29 compatible
kəmˈpadəb(ə)l
adj.

congruous, suited, fitting

two things or people able to exist or occur without causing conflict

The two lovers are **compatible** with one another.

호환이 되는

30 reign
rān
v.

rule, prevail, preside

to prevail or dominate an area or domain

The notorious dictator **reigns** over the country.

다스리다

31 homestead
ˈhōmˌsted
n.

cabin, cottage, farm

a house, usually a farmhouse

The farmers returned to their **homestead** after plowing the field.

주택(농가)

32 transpire
tran(t)ˈspī(ə)r
v.

occur, ensue, befall

to happen

The events that **transpire** will determine the future.

일어나다, 발생하다

33 communal
kəˈmyo͞on(ə)l
adj.

common, public, shared

shared by all members of a community

The dormitory has a **communal** bathroom and kitchen.

공동의(공용의)

34 oasis
ōˈāsis
n.

refuge, haven, retreat

a pleasant or peaceful place or time in the midst of a difficult or troubling situation

The small park is an **oasis** in the middle of the urban district.

오아시스 (같은 곳), 위안(휴식)을 주는 곳

35 hygiene
ˈhīˌjēn
n.

sanitation, cleanliness, wholesomeness

a condition or practice useful to the maintenance of health

Personal **hygiene** is important in order to prevent sickness.

위생

36 sanitize
ˈsanəˌtīz
v.

sterilize, disinfect, purify
to make clean
*Doctors **sanitize** their tools before a surgery.*

위생 처리하다, 살균하다

37 relent
rəˈlent
v.

yield, accede, acquiesce
to give up or decrease a harsh intention or treatment
*Jason was going to refuse her request, but **relented** when Jane started to cry.*

(거부하다가 마침내) 동의하다

38 meager
ˈmēgər
adj.

scanty, paltry, modest
lacking in quality or quantity
*His **meager** wage was not enough to support his family.*

메마른

39 unrest
ˌənˈrest
n.

upset, turmoil, tumult
a state of agitation or dissatisfaction
*The leader sensed **unrest** in the group when he announced his retirement.*

불안(불만)

40 apex
ˈāpeks
n.

summit, pinnacle, peak
the highest point of something
*The athlete reached the **apex** of his career when he broke the record.*

꼭대기, 정점

41 formidable
ˈfôrmədəb(ə)l
adj.

intimidating, daunting, threatening
to instill fear or respect by being impressively large or powerful
*No one dared to fight against the **formidable** warrior.*

가공할, 어마어마한

42 implicate
ˈimpləˌkāt
v.

imply, suggest, insinuate
to convey a meaning indirectly
*Her response **implicates** that she did not want to be bothered.*

원인임을 보여주다(시사하다)

SET 5 · 71

SET 5

43 aggression
əˈgreSHən
n.

hostility, antagonism, offense

hostile or violent behavior

The enemy showed **aggression** when they fired the first shot.

공격성

---

44 plunder
ˈpləndər
n.

looting, robbery, marauding

the acquirement of property through violence and dishonesty

The pirates hid their **plunder** inside a cave.

약탈, 강탈

---

45 asylum
əˈsīləm
n.

refuge, sanctuary, sanctum

a place of protection from danger

Criminals find **asylum** inside a jail after they betray their boss.

망명

---

46 dire
ˈdī(ə)r
adj.

dreadful, terrible, frightful

very serious or urgent

The military found themselves in a **dire** situation when they ran out of ammunition.

대단히 심각한, 엄청난, 지독한

---

47 correspond
ˌkôrəˈspänd
v.

parallel, comparable, analogous

to match or agree closely

His essay **corresponds** to the one found on the Internet.

일치하다, 부합하다

v.

communicate, write

to communicate by writing letters

The pen pals **correspond** with each other on a monthly basis.

(~와) 서신을 주고받다

---

48 plummet
ˈpləmət
v.

plunge, dive, drop

to fall down at high speed

The asteroid **plummeted** through Earth's atmosphere.

곤두박질치다, 급락하다

49 outbreak
ˈoutˌbrāk
n.

epidemic, breakout, eruption

the sudden or violent beginning of an unwanted event, such as war or disease

*The **outbreak** of the zombie virus forced humanity into the brink of extinction.*

(전쟁,사고,질병 등의) 발생

50 reverse
rəˈvərs
v.

back, backtrack, inverse

to move backward

*The driver **reversed** his car into the parking garage.*

후진 하다

v.

undo, alter, overturn

to make something the opposite of what it was

*The damage done to the economy can be **reversed**.*

(정반대로) 뒤바꾸다, 반전(역전)시키다

SET 5 CROSSWORD PUZZLE

Across

1. to convey a meaning indirectly
3. ability to withstand wear or damage
9. lacking in quality or quantity
11. to happen
13. officially approved or recognized
14. too extensive or extreme to measure
15. communicate a message or information

Down

2. to match or agree closely
4. shared by all members of a community
5. associated with or made from living matter
6. a state of agitation or dissatisfaction
7. having very close connection
8. to make a mental or physical effort
10. to determine the value or quality of
12. relating to the main point of interest

1. implicate   2. correspond
3. durable   4. communal
5. organic   6. unrest
7. intimate   8. exert
9. meager   10. appraise
11. transpire 12. focal
13. formal   14. immeasurable
15. convey

LEAD
SET
6
VOCABULARY

SET 6

01 traverse
trəˈvərs
v.
- cross, roam, span
- to travel across
- *Columbus **traversed** the Atlantic Ocean to reach the New World.*
- 가로지르다, 횡단하다

02 realm
relm
n.
- domain, sphere, area
- a field or domain of interest or activity
- *The study of cells lie in the **realm** of biology.*
- 영역(범위)

03 pathetic
pəˈThedik
adj.
- pitiful, poignant, poor
- showing pity, especially because of vulnerability or sadness
- *The dog looked so **pathetic**, I took him home and gave him a bath.*
- 불쌍한, 애처로운

04 apprehensive
ˌaprəˈhensiv
adj.
- worried, uneasy, concerned
- anxious that something horrible or unpleasant will occur
- *He felt **apprehensive** about going back to his house after running away.*
- 걱정되는, 불안한

05 timid
ˈtimid
adj.
- fearful, apprehensive, afraid
- showing lack of confidence or courage
- *The child was **timid** to ask for more food.*
- 소심한, 용기(자신감)가 없는

06 pulverize
ˈpəlvəˌrīz
v.
- annihilate, crush, pound
- destroy completely
- *Our basketball team completely **pulverized** the rival team.*
- 완전히 쳐부수다, 분쇄하다

07 cultivate
ˈkəltəˌvāt
v.
- till, plow, fertilize
- to prepare and use the land for farming or gardening
- *The farmers who **cultivated** the land became rich.*
- (땅을) 경작하다, 일구다

08	**frugal** ˈfroogəl adj.	thrifty, economical, prudent
		sparing or cheap with money or food
		*My grandfather lived a **frugal** lifestyle with very few personal belongings.*
	소박한, 간소한	

09	**merit** ˈmerət n.	value, profit, advantage
		a characteristic or fact that deserves reward or praise
		*The **merits** of living alone far outweigh having roommates.*
	가치 있는(훌륭한) 요소, 장점	

10	**mandate** ˈmanˌdāt n.	directive, decree, command
		an official order to carry out a task
		*The president issued a **mandate** to cease the riot.*
	명령	

11	**insurrection** ˌinsəˈrekSH(ə)n n.	rebellion, revolt, mutiny
		a violent uprising against a government or authority
		*The **insurrection** was quickly dissolved by the army.*
	반란(내란) 사태	

12	**arid** ˈerəd adj.	dry, parched, dehydrated
		having little or no rain
		*The Sahara Desert is an **arid** environment.*
	매우 건조한	

13	**precipitation** prəˌsipəˈtāSH(ə)n n.	rain, snow, drizzle
		rain, snow, or hail that falls to the ground
		*The clouds that are forming in the distance will produce **precipitation**.*
	강수, 강수량	

14	**artificial** ˌärdəˈfiSHəl adj.	synthetic, simulated, faux
		made by human beings and not occurring naturally
		*The **artificial** light gave warmth to the cold-blooded reptile.*
	인공(인조)의	

SET 6

15 sedentary
ˈsednˌterē
adj.

stationary, inactive, still

somewhat inactive or showing minimal physical movement

*A couch potato is someone who has a **sedentary** lifestyle.*

주로 앉아서 지내는, 몸을 많이 움직이지 않는

16 scrutiny
ˈskro͞otnē
n.

inspection, survey, scan

critical examination or observation

*Upon close **scrutiny**, one can find a scar under the chin.*

정밀 조사, 철저한 검토

17 rational
ˈraSH(ə)n(ə)l
adj.

logical, reasonable, sensible

based on reason or logic

*There is a **rational** explanation for his silly behavior.*

이성(합리)적인

18 eschew
əsˈCHo͞o
v.

shun, forgo, refrain

deliberately avoiding the use of

*He did not bring his wallet so that he could **eschew** from buying dinner.*

피하다, 삼가다

19 fiscal
ˈfisk(ə)l
adj.

tax, revenue, budgetary

relating to taxes and government revenue

*The Economic Department is in change of **fiscal** matters.*

국가 재정(세제)의

20 vast
vast
adj.

extensive, broad, boundless

of great extent or quantity

*The Great Plains of America is a **vast** plain of grass.*

(범위,크기·양 등이) 어마어마한

21 restrict
rəˈstrikt
v.

limit, impede, confine

limiting the movement of someone or something

*The mother **restricted** her son from using the mobile phone.*

(크기,양,범위 등을) 제한(한정)하다

22	**curtail** kərˈtāl v.	reduce, diminish, cut
		shorten the extent or quantity of
		*Basic freedom was **curtailed** from slaves during the colonial era.*
		축소(삭감/단축)시키다

23	**obscene** əbˈsēn adj.	scandalous, atrocious, heinous
		offensive to moral standards
		*Animal rights activists view fur coats as **obscene**.*
		터무니없는, 가당찮은

24	**appeal** əˈpēl v.	beseech, implore, entreat
		to apply to a judicial court for a change in decision
		*The court was given 24 hours to **appeal** the decision.*
		심판에게 항의하다
	v.	attract, interest, please
		to be attractive or interesting
		*The Fall collection of dresses will **appeal** to young women.*
		흥미를 일으키다

25	**adamant** ˈadəmənt adj.	unwavering, unshakeable, inflexible
		refusing to change one's mind
		*She was **adamant** that she would be crowned homecoming queen.*
		요지부동의, 단호한

26	**strict** strikt adj.	stern, harsh, severe
		demanding complete obedience to rules
		*He is a **strict** vegetarian and will not eat anything made from animals.*
		(규칙 등이) 엄격한

27	**taboo** təˈboo adj.	forbidden, banned, proscribed
		prohibited by social custom
		*Religion and politics are **taboo** subjects to be spoken amongst friends.*
		금기 (사항), 터부

SET 6

28 integrity
in'tegrədē
n.
- uprightness, honor, honesty
- the state of being honest and having moral principles
- *My mother is a person of **integrity**.*
- 진실성

29 amiable
'āmēəb(ə)l
adj.
- amicable, cordial, warmhearted
- having or showing a friendly behavior
- *My grandmother is an **amiable** old lady, who will not hurt a fly.*
- 쾌활한, 정감 있는

30 invariably
ˌin'verēəblē
adv.
- always, every time
- on every occasion or in every case
- *The portions at this restaurant are **invariably** big and delicious.*
- 변함(예외)없이, 언제나

31 impure
im'pyoor
adj.
- mixed, blended, combined
- mixed with outside substance
- *The gold necklace was actually made of **impure** metals.*
- 순수하지(깨끗하지) 못한, 불순물이 섞인

adj.
- immoral, corrupt, dishonorable
- morally wrong
- *His **impure** thoughts clouded his judgement.*
- 불결한, 부도덕한, 음란한

32 quest
kwest
n.
- expedition, undertaking, mission
- a long or difficult search for something
- *The knight set on his **quest** to save the princess.*
- 탐구, 탐색

33 impervious
im'pərvēəs
adj.
- immune, resistant, unaffected
- not affected by
- *After taking the vaccine, she was **impervious** to the virus.*
- …에 영향받지(휘둘리지) 않는

34. definitive
/dəˈfinədiv/
adj.

final, decisive, absolute

to have reached a conclusion or agreement decisively and with authority

*The jury gave a **definitive** verdict regarding the case.*

최종적인, 확정적인

35. classify
/ˈklasəˌfī/
v.

categorize, group, sort

to arrange someone or something in classes or categories

*The list of things she had to do were **classified** according to urgency.*

분류(구분)하다

36. pinpoint
/ˈpinˌpoint/
v.

locate, detect, find

to find or locate precisely

*The doctor was able to **pinpoint** the source of his pain.*

정확히 찾아내다(보여주다)

37. resist
/rəˈzist/
v.

withstand, counter, repel

to withstand the action or influence of someone or something

*The building was able to **resist** the shaking of the earthquake.*

저항(반대)하다

38. upheaval
/ˌəpˈhēvəl/
n.

disturbance, disorder, turbulence

a violent or sudden disruption

*The rats that came out of the kitchen caused an **upheaval** in the restaurant.*

격변, 대변동

39. civil
/ˈsiv(ə)l/
adj.

nonmilitary, civilian

in regards to ordinary citizens and their well being

*Men and women fought for **civil** rights in the early 1900's.*

시민(들)의

adj.

polite, courteous, refined

well mannered

*As men of intellect, they should be **civil**.*

예의 바른, 공손한, 정중한

SET 6

40 heritage
ˈherədij
n.

tradition, culture, customs

cultural and historic objects and qualities that have been passed down for generations

The museum displays the **heritage** of the Native Americans.

유산

41 procure
prəˈkyoor
v.

secure, acquire, obtain

to obtain with care and effort

The mother bird was able to **procure** food for her chicks.

구하다(입수하다)

42 contiguous
kənˈtigyooəs
adj.

neighboring, bordering, adjacent

sharing a common boundary

The European continent is made up of several **contiguous** nations.

인접한, 근접한

43 brittle
ˈbridl
adj.

fragile, frail, delicate

likely to break or shatter with ease

Osteoporosis is a disease where the bone is **brittle**.

잘 부러지는

44 coincide
ˌkōənˈsīd
v.

concur, coexist, parallel

to occur at the same time

The two parties **coincided** so I had to choose which one to attend.

동시에 일어나다

45 mutual
ˈmyoōCH(oō)əl
adj.

reciprocal, common, shared

concerning an emotion or action which is experienced by each of two or more groups

The two champions shared a **mutual** respect for one another.

상호간의, 서로의

46 eradicate
əˈradəˌkāt
v.

eliminate, exterminate, obliterate

to put an end to

The pesticide **eradicated** most of the insects in the field.

근절하다, 뿌리뽑다

47 foremost
'fôr‚mōst
adj.

principal, premier, prime

most important in rank or position

*Edison was one of the **foremost** intellectuals of the century.*

가장 중요한(유명한), 맨 앞에 위치한

48 predominant
prə'dämənənt
adj.

chief, primary, central

to be the strongest or main part

*The **predominant** color of the room was black.*

두드러진, 뚜렷한

adj.

dominant, controlling, superior

having or exercising control or power

*The **predominant** species in the ecosystem stood at the top of the food chain.*

우세한, 지배적인

49 variant
'verēənt
n.

variation, alternative, mutant

a version of something that is different from the norm

*A **variant** form of the virus began to appear.*

변종, 이형

50 afflict
ə'flikt
v.

oppress, exasperate, plague

to cause pain or suffering

*The child was **afflicted** with a mild skin disease.*

괴롭히다, 피해를 입히다

SET 6 TEST

1. Superman was _____ to the bullets shot by the henchmen.

2. My wife handles the _____ matters since I am not good with money.

3. The number four is considered _____ in Korea because it represents death.

4. In a parasitic relationship, the parasite will often _____ its host to gain benefits.

5. It was difficult to _____ this item since it is very rare.

6. Lewis and Clark _____ the Frontier of the United States.

7. The diner was very _____ so he left a very small tip for the waitress.

8. People tend to _____ from electronic devices they have never used.

9. The movie had to be _____ because it was already five hours long.

10. The admission office described the _____ of the university so that I would enroll.

---

1. impervious   2. fiscal   3. taboo   4. afflict   5. procure   6. traverse   7. frugal   8. eschew   9. curtail   10. merit

11. The movie was rated R because some of the scenes were too _____.

12. My grandfather was _____ about his opinion regarding the current president.

13. It is normal for people to be _____ about starting a new job since everything will be new.

14. The dictator _____ that the citizens pay a monetary tribute each month.

15. Edward Snowden lost his _____ when he gave classified information to a foreign country.

16. Satellites help _____ enemy bases in the midst of battle.

17. The Black Death _____ millions of Europeans in the fourteenth century.

18. The rain helped _____ the land for farming.

19. A sloth is a _____ animal and rarely moves from its spot.

20. School counselors are _____ so students have no trouble talking to them.

11. obscene 12. adamant 13. apprehensive 14. mandate 15. integrity 16. pinpoint 17. eradicate 18. cultivate 19. sedentary 20. amiable

SET 6

notes:

LEAD
SET 7
VOCABULARY

SET 7

01 curb
kərb
v.

restrain, repress, suppress
to hold back or keep in check
The father promised he would **curb** his temper.
억제(제한)하다

02 regulate
ˈregyəˌlāt
v.

supervise, oversee, police
control or monitor something though rules and regulations
The police **regulates** the rallies that take place in the capital.
규제(통제/단속)하다

03 evoke
əˈvōk
v.

arouse, elicit, invoke
to bring forth a response
His actions **evoked** a response from the community.
불러내다, 끌어내다

04 purge
pərj
v.

cleanse, exclude, remove
remove an unwanted quality or a group of people from an organization
The king **purged** the corrupt members from his group of counselors.
제거하다

05 downfall
ˈdounˌfôl
n.

undoing, ruin, defeat
a loss of power, prosperity, or status
The dictator's indifference toward his people will be his **downfall**.
몰락, 몰락의 원인

06 elevate
ˈeləˌvāt
v.

hoist, promote, raise
to rise or lift up to a higher position
The congressman was **elevated** to a higher seat when he beat his opponent.
(높은 곳이나, 위치로) 올리다

07 shift
SHift
v.

transfer, carry, move
move from one place to another
The penguin **shifted** to its other leg to avoid being cold.
(장소를) 옮기다; 자세를 바꾸다

08 indulgent
in'dəljənt
adj.

easygoing, tolerant, forgiving

having a tendency to be too generous

*He is known to be **indulgent**, since he forgives anyone that wrongs him.*

너그러운(관대한)

09 intricate
'intrəkət
adj.

complex, convoluted, entangled

complicated or detailed

*An **intricate** network of rivers run through the Amazon Rainforest.*

복잡한

10 equitable
'ekwədəb(ə)l
adj.

impartial, fair, just

fair and unbiased

*The president must show an **equitable** decision while in office.*

공정한, 공평한

11 manifestation
ˌmanəfə'stāSH(ə)n,
n.

demonstration, expression, indication

the action or fact of displaying something abstract

*The student showed a **manifestation** of anxiety over the final exams.*

징후(표명)

12 spectate
spek'tāt
v.

attend, view, observe

to watch an event

*The soccer fans decided not to **spectate** the match due to the thunderstorm.*

지켜보다(구경하다)

13 ensue
in'sōō
v.

follow, spring, stem

to come after; result

*She had to face the consequences that **ensued** after her lies.*

(어떤 일, 결과가) 뒤따르다

14 craze
krāz
n.

fad, vogue, trend

an enthusiasm for an activity or object that appears suddenly and achieves a short-lived popularity

*Baggy pants were a **craze** in the 90's.*

(특히 일시적인) 대유행(열풍)

SET 7

15 satiate
ˈsāSHēˌāt
v.

quench, stuff, gorge
to satisfy to the fullest
*I will **satiate** my hunger at the buffet.*

(식욕, 성욕 등을) 실컷 만족시키다

16 frenetic
frəˈnedik
adj.

frantic, hectic, feverish
quick and energetic in a wild, uncontrolled way
*The wedding planner carried out her duties at a **frenetic** pace.*

정신없이 바쁘게 돌아가는, 부산한

17 intervention
ˌin(t)ərˈven(t)SH(ə)n
n.

intercession, interposing, involvement
action carried out to improve a situation
*Due to his obsessive drinking, we decided to hold an **intervention** to help.*

개입, (내정) 간섭

18 akin
əˈkin
adj.

similar, corresponding, comparable
of similar character
*Something **akin** to sorrow overwhelmed him at the funeral.*

~와 유사한

19 entrepreneur
ˌäntrəprəˈnər
n.

businessman, businesswoman
a person who operates a business
*Many new **entrepreneurs** seek fortune in their business.*

사업가(기업가)

20 hitherto
ˌhiTHərˈtoō
adv.

previously, formerly, earlier
until now
*There is no need to discuss about what has **hitherto** been a troublesome talk.*

지금까지, 그때까지

21 expeditious
ˌekspəˈdiSHəs
adj.

swift, prompt, punctual
performed with speed and efficiency
*The detectives carried out an **expeditious** investigation.*

신속한, 효율적인

22. ingenious
in'jēnyəs
adj.

creative, imaginative, original
clever and inventive
*Einstein had several **ingenious** ideas.*

기발한

23. contraption
kən'trapSH(ə)n
n.

device, gadget, apparatus
a device or machine that appears difficult to operate
*My father loved making **contraptions** out of old electronics.*

(기묘한) 기계(장치)

24. generate
'jenə,rāt
v.

cause, produce, spawn
to cause something to arise or appear
*Their argument is likely to **generate** a rift in their relationship.*

발생시키다, 만들어 내다

25. boast
bōst
v.

brag, swagger, gloat
talk with pride and satisfaction over one's achievements, possessions, or talents
*Napoleon **boasted** about his many victories.*

뽐내다, 자랑하다

26. initial
i'niSHəl
adj.

commencing, inceptive, opening
existing or happening at the beginning
*Our **initial** impression of the movie was good, until it reached the climax.*

처음의, 초기의

27. propensity
prə'pensədē
n.

inclination, predisposition, tendency
a natural tendency to act in a certain way
*Carnivores display a **propensity** for violence at a young age.*

경향(성향)

28. affix
ə'fiks
v.

bind, post, secure
attach or fasten something to something else
*The mailman **affixed** the stamp on the envelope.*

부착하다, 붙이다

SET 7

29. apparatus
ˌapəˈradəs
n.

gear, equipment, rig

the equipment or machine required for a particular activity or purpose

*The laboratory **apparatus** was set up to conduct the experiment.*

기구, 장치

30. impede
imˈpēd
v.

hinder, obstruct, hamper

to delay or prevent something by blocking them

*The car accident will definitely **impede** traffic.*

(진행을) 지연시키다(방해하다)

31. reciprocal
rəˈsiprək(ə)l
adj.

joint, corresponding, correlative

to affect two groups equally

*The peace treaty included a **reciprocal** share in the natural resources.*

상호간의

32. canny
ˈkanē
adj.

shrewd, astute, discerning

having or showing insight and good judgement, particularly in money or business affairs

*The **canny** shopper made her purchase at night to receive additional discounts.*

(특히 재계, 정계에서) 약삭빠른(영리한)

33. asymmetric
ˌāsəˈmetrək
adj.

uneven, misaligned, malformed

having parts that do not match to one another in shape, size, or order

*The **asymmetric** building was constructed on purpose as an architectural novelty.*

비대칭의

34. empower
əmˈpou(ə)r
v.

authorize, license, sanction

to give authority or power

*The police are **empowered** by the state to arrest suspicious individuals.*

권한을 주다

35. efface
əˈfās
v.

expunge, cancel, eliminate

to erase from a surface

*The pencil marks were **effaced** with erasers.*

지우다, 없애다

36 buttress
'bətrəs
v.

strengthen, fortify, reinforce

to increase the strength of or support

*The professor's qualifications were **buttressed** by his many degrees and achievements.*

지지하다, 힘을 실어 주다

37 liable
'lī(ə)b(ə)l
adj.

accountable, responsible, chargeable

responsible by law

*The company is **liable** for mistreating its employees.*

법적 책임이 있는

adj.

inclined, disposed, prone

likely to do something

*Students are **liable** to relax after their final exams.*

~하기 쉬운, ~할 것 같은

38 interval
'in(t)ərvəl
n.

interlude, interim, meantime

a passing of time

*There was an **interval** of several years before the two were able to talk again.*

(두 사건 사이의) 간격

n.

intermission, break, recess

a pause or rest

*There should be a 5 minute **interval** between each exercise.*

중간 휴식 시간

39 clarify
'klerə,fī
v.

elucidate, illuminate, simplify

to make something less confusing

*My tutor **clarified** the difficult lesson I learned in school today.*

명확하게 하다, 분명히 말하다

40 ordinance
'ôrd(ə)nəns
n.

decree, law, command

an authoritative order

*A city **ordinance** prohibited smoking in public facilities.*

법령, 조례

SET 7

41 homogenous
həˈmäjənəs
adj.

analogous, identical, uniform
similar in structure
*A coat and a jacket are **homogenous** in function.*
균질의, 동질의

42 sentiment
ˈsen(t)əmənt
n.

attitude, view, thought
an opinion toward a situation
*She did not agree with my **sentiments** regarding finance.*
정서

n.

feeling, emotion
an emotion
*The Korean drama stirred a strong **sentiment** of sadness.*
감정

43 embody
əmˈbädē
v.

incorporate, manifest, personify
to give a concrete form to an idea, quality, or feeling
*The trophy **embodies** victory and hard work.*
상징(구현)하다

44 mend
mend
v.

repair, fix, restore
to repair something that is damaged
*The construction workers were **mending** the damaged buildings.*
수리하다, 고치다

45 retard
riˈtärd
v.

delay, postpone, inhibit
to slow down or hold back
*The construction of the bridge was **retarded** by the snowstorm.*
지연(지체)시키다

46 divulge
dəˈvəlj
v.

disclose, reveal, expose
to make private information known
*Coworkers usually do not **divulge** their weekend plans to one another.*
(비밀을) 알려주다(누설하다)

47 mingle
'miNGgəl
v.

socialize, circulate, fraternize
associating with people
*Employees find it awkward to **mingle** with their bosses.*

돌아다니다, (사람들과) 어울리다

48 supplant
sə'plant
v.

replace, supersede, displace
to replace with something else
*The old bike chain was **supplanted** with a new and improved part.*

대신(대체)하다

49 blight
blīt
v.

ruin, wreck, spoil
to have a detrimental effect
*The scandal **blighted** the celebrity's career.*

망치다, 엉망으로 만들다

n.

plague, affliction, contamination
something that spoils or damages
*The tomatoes were suffering from **blight** and could not be consumed.*

(곡식의) 병충해

50 edible
'edəb(ə)l
adj.

succulent, digestible, wholesome
fit or appropriate to be eaten
*The **edible** roots were gathered by the farmers.*

먹을 수 있는

SET 7 TEST

1. It is difficult to _____ one's desires if they have no money.

2. Children have the _____ to lie when they are in trouble.

3. The hotel manager _____ our room when we found bugs on the floor.

4. Our flight was _____ because of the snowstorm.

5. The alcohol swab helped _____ the pen marks on the table.

6. Korean pottery shows _____ designs that can only be made by experienced craftsman.

7. A cast helps to _____ broken bones.

8. Children with _____ parents tend to be spoiled since they get whatever they want.

9. An _____ was needed in order to help the friend overcome his shopping spree.

10. The security gaurd was able to _____ the thief from getting away with the money.

---

1. satiate 2. propensity 3. supplant 4. impede 5. efface 6. intricate 7. mend 8. indulgent 9. intervention 10. curb

11. The delivery company was able to carry out an _____ service by delivering the next day.

12. Servants used to eat the food before the king to make sure the food was _____.

13. The computer hacker was able to _____ the coded message.

14. Exterminators may spray the house with insecticides to _____ unwanted pests.

15. The jury must deliever an _____ verdict based on facts.

16. Da Vinci made various _____ that were way ahead of his time.

17. The ring _____ the halfling and gave him supernatural abilities.

18. The president issued an _____ which required citizens to wear masks in public.

19. The driver was _____ to pay for the damages he created from smashing his car.

20. The mother _____ a cup holder onto the stroller's handle.

---

11. expeditious 12. edible 13. divulge 14. purge 15. equitable
16. contraption 17. empower 18. ordinance 19. liable 20. affix

SET 7

notes:

LEAD
SET 8
VOCABULARY

SET 8

01 attribute
əˈtriˌbyo͞ot
v.
- ascribe, credit, assign
- to regard as resulting from something specific
- He **attributed** his success to the efforts of his wife.
- (~을 …의) 결과로(덕분으로) 보다

02 affirm
əˈfərm
v.
- declare, assert, proclaim
- to state strongly and publicly
- The religious leader **affirmed** the religion's purpose to the public.
- 단언하다

03 commit
kəˈmit
v.
- perform, enact, execute
- to carry out an action
- The thief **committed** a horrible crime.
- 일을 저지르다

v.
- pledge, devote, dedicate
- to pledge to a certain course, organization, or policy
- The thief **committed** never to steal again.
- (엄숙히) 약속하다

04 apparel
əˈperəl
n.
- clothes, garments, attire
- clothing
- The models were dressed in dark **apparel**.
- 의류

05 erect
əˈrekt
v.
- build, assemble, construct
- to construct a building or an upright structure
- The castle was **erected** in the seventeenth century.
- 건립하다

06 commence
kəˈmens
v.
- start, begin
- to begin
- The allied forces **commenced** the military operation.
- 시작되다(하다)

07 intermittent
ˌin(t)ərˈmitnt
adj.

sporadic, irregular, spasmodic

happening at irregular intervals

*Hawaii has **intermittent** rain falling throughout the day.*

간헐적인, 간간이 일어나는

08 frenzy
ˈfrenzē
n.

hysteria, madness, insanity

a state of uncontrolled excitement or behavior

*The immense workload drove him into a **frenzy**.*

광분, 광란

09 rite
rīt
n.

ritual, ceremony, service

a solemn ceremony or act, usually of religious nature

*The Spartans had a **rite** of manhood for their children.*

(특히 종교상의) 의식(의례)

10 inspire
inˈspī(ə)r
v.

arouse, ignite, trigger

create a positive feeling in a person

*The music **inspired** the athletes to try harder.*

영감을 주다

11 cohesion
kōˈhēZHən
n.

unity, bond, continuity

the act of forming a whole

*The team lacks **cohesion** since everyone works on their own.*

화합, 결합

12 ensure
inˈSHoor
v.

secure, guarantee, warrant

make sure that something occurs or be the case

*The lawyer must **ensure** the safety of the victim.*

반드시 …하게(이게) 하다, 보장하다

13 divine
dəˈvīn
adj.

saintly, religious, holy

being sacred, devoted to God

*He walked amongst us like a **divine** figure sent from heaven.*

신(하느님)의, 신성한

SET 8

14 pledge /plej/ n.
- vow, word, commitment
- a solemn promise
- The conference ended with the countries' **pledge** to end global warming.
- (굳은) 약속, 맹세, 서약

15 deem /dēm/ v.
- consider, judge, regard as
- to consider in a specified way
- The birthday party was **deemed** successful since everyone went home happy.
- (…로) 여기다[생각하다]

16 harmony /ˈhärmənē/ n.
- euphony, consonance, tunefulness
- the combination of musical notes having a pleasant effect
- The **harmony** produced by the orchestra satisfied everyone's ears.
- 화음, 화성(법)

17 exclude /ikˈsklo͞od/ v.
- eliminate, bar
- remove from consideration
- Women were **excluded** from political activities early on in the century.
- 제외(배제)하다

18 remarkable /rəˈmärkəb(ə)l/ adj.
- extraordinary, exceptional, astounding
- worthy of attention
- It was a **remarkable** coincidence that the two sat next to each other in the bus.
- 놀랄 만한, 놀라운, 주목할 만한

19 novel /ˈnävəl/ n.
- new, original, unconventional
- something new and unusual
- The scientists approached the problem with a **novel** method.
- (이전에 볼 수 없던) 새로운, 신기한

20 extinct /ikˈstiNG(k)t/ adj.
- vanished, lost, dead
- no longer in existence
- Dinosaurs became **extinct** millions of years ago.
- 더 이상 존재하지 않는, 사라진

21 intertwine
ˌin(t)ərˈtwīn
v.

entwine, interweave, interlace

twist together

*The fishing net was made with ropes that had to be **intertwined**.*

뒤얽히다, 뒤얽다, 엮다, 엮이다

22 influx
ˈinˌfləks
n.

rush, flood, incursion

the entry of a large number of people or things

*There was a massive **influx** of diners during dinner time.*

(많은 사람, 자금, 물건이) 밀어닥침(밀려듦)

23 amend
əˈmend
v.

revise, alter, modify

to make changes in order to make it more fair, accurate, or better

*The law was **amended** to satisfy the needs of the foreigners.*

(법 등을) 개정(수정)하다

24 motto
ˈmädō
n.

maxim, proverb, axiom

a short sentence or phrase that portrays a belief or an idea

*I live by the **motto**, "No pain, no gain."*

좌우명

25 wane
wān
v.

diminish, decline, dwindle

become weaker

*Superman's power **waned** as the kryptonite moved closer.*

약해지다, 줄어들다, 시들해지다

26 asset
ˈaset
n.

strength, blessing, advantage

a useful or valuable object, person, or characteristic

*The ability to think quick was his strongest **asset**.*

자산(이 되는 사람, 물건)

27 advocate
ˈadvəkət
n.

champion, supporter, proponent

a person who supports a particular cause or policy

*He was an **advocate** of women's rights.*

옹호자, 지지자

SET 8

28 render
ˈrendər
v.

supply, furnish, offer

to provide or give

*Honor serves as a reward for services **rendered** to the military.*

제시(제출)하다

29 correspondence
ˌkôrəˈspändəns
n.

correlation, resemblance, compatibility

a similarity or connection

*There is a **correspondence** between the hours of television viewing and intelligence.*

관련성(유사함)

30 navigate
ˈnavəˌgāt
v.

maneuver, sail, steer

plan and direct the route of a transport

*Salmons **navigate** back to freshwaters using their sense of smell.*

길을 찾다(방향을 읽다)

31 liken
ˈlīkən
v.

compare, correlate, associate

to point out the similarity

*Egyptian pharaohs were **likened** to a god.*

비유하다, 비기다

32 provocative
prəˈväkədiv
adj.

irritating, provoking, exasperating

causing anger, annoyance, or other strong reaction

*The **provocative** review angered the movie director.*

도발적인, 화(부아)를 돋우려는

33 pictorial
pikˈtôrēəl
adj.

illustrated, graphic, drawn

expressed in pictures

*Children's books are often **pictorial** so kids can understand easily.*

그림을 이용한, 그림이 포함된

34 crude
kro͞od
adj.

raw, unprepared, natural

not yet processed or refined

*The wooden chair was **crude** and required improvement.*

원자재의, 가공되지 않은

adj.

vulgar, rude, offensive

a manner which is offensive

*His **crude** joke made everyone uncomfortable.*

무례한, 예의 없는, 버릇없는

35 puncture
'pəNGk(t)SHər
v.

pierce, penetrate, rupture

to make a hole in something

*The magician **punctured** a hole in the balloon.*

펑크(구멍)를 내다

36 industrious
in'dəstrēəs
adj.

diligent, assiduous, productive

hard working

*The **industrious** immigrants worked hard in their new home.*

근면한, 부지런한

37 bicker
'bikər
v.

squabble, quarrel, dispute

to argue about small matters

*The children **bickered** about who will go down the slide first.*

(사소한 일로) 다투다

38 eminent
'emənənt
adj.

distinguished, renowned, esteemed

famous and respected in a particular field

*Stephen Hawking is an **eminent** scholar in astrophysics.*

저명한

39 cloister
'kloistər
n.

arcade, walkway, corridor

a courtyard in a religious establishment

*The **cloister** in the cathedral is the perfect place to meditate.*

(지붕이 덮인) 회랑

40 sober
'sōbər
adj.

clearheaded, abstinent, temperate

not drunk with alcohol

*He has been clean and **sober** for almost a year now.*

술 취하지 않은

adj.

solemn, grave, somber

serious and sensible

*Mr. Scrooge has a **sober** view of life.*

냉철한, 진지한

SET 8

41 womb
wo͞om
n.
an organ in the female body where the offspring is conceived and developed
*A human child develops in the **womb** for 10 months.*
자궁

42 accord
əˈkôrd
n.
settlement, deal, pact
an official agreement
*After many days arguing, the two sides came to an **accord**.*
합의

v.
grant, present, give
to give someone authority, status, or recognition
*The soldier was **accorded** with the highest honor in the military.*
부여하다

43 envision
ənˈviZHən
v.
visualize, picture, imagine
to imagine as a possibility
*The boy **envisioned** himself as an architect as he stacked the blocks.*
마음속에 그리다(상상하다)

44 ramify
ˈraməˌfī
v.
diversify, divide, fork
to form branches or divisions
*The government group was **ramified** into smaller departments.*
가지를 내다(내게 하다), 분기(분파)하다(시키다)

45 perpetuate
pərˈpeCHəˌwāt
v.
preserve, sustain, maintain
to make something continue without stopping
*Matters in motion will continue to **perpetuate** in an unperturbed system.*
영구화하다, 영속시키다

46 dispel
dəˈspel
v.
banish, dismiss, eliminate
to make a feeling or belief disappear
*There was nothing that could **dispel** the sadness he felt.*
떨쳐 버리다(없애다)

47 prerequisite
prē'rekwəzət
n.

precondition, requirement, essential
something that is required before something else to occur or exist
Concentration is a **prerequisite** before one attempts to study.

전제 조건

48 judicious
jōō'diSHəs
adj.

sensible, prudent, wise
having good judgement or sense
The **judicious** decision made by the judge prevented an innocent man from going to jail.

신중한, 판단력 있는

49 hilarity
hə'lerədē
n.

merriment, laughter, mirth
extreme amusement
There was much **hilarity** in the audience from the comedian's performance.

아주 우스움

50 affinity
ə'finədē
n.

empathy, rapport, connection
a natural liking or sympathy for someone or something
Thanos had an **affinity** for the infinity stones.

친밀감

SET 8 TEST

1. The fire from the cigarette _____ in the forest, causing devastation.

2. The _____ comment angered my friend and he refused to talk to me.

3. Squirrels have an _____ for nuts.

4. The district attorney _____ his commitment to rid the city of crime.

5. The United Nations is a _____ of countries to make the world a better place.

6. There was a large _____ of shoppers during the annual sale.

7. Martin Luther King Jr. was an _____ of free speech.

8. The king's authority over the people began to _____ as he aged.

9. My son mumbles in his sleep at _____ times throughout the night.

10. The Bible is a _____ book for Christians.

1. perpetuate 2. provocative 3. affinity 4. affirm 5. cohesion 6. influx 7. advocate 8. wane 9. intermittent 10. divine

11. In order to _____ their relationship, the father bought his son a car.

12. Oompa Loompas are _____ workers who work at the chocolate factory.

13. The _____ sketch of the house was immediately liked by the family.

14. The girls were in a _____ when they met their favorite boy band.

15. The boyfriend made a _____ to his girlfriend that he would never cheat on her.

16. A swiss army knife is small, but it is an important _____ when one is out in the wild.

17. The large company was _____ into several small parts due to mismanagement.

18. The _____ of the situation made everyone laugh and forget their troubles.

19. Learning how to add and subtract is a _____ before learning how to multiply and divide.

20. The businessman _____ his success to his lucky tie.

11. amend 12. industrious 13. crude 14. frenzy 15. pledge 16. asset 17. ramify 18. hilarity 19. prerequisite 20. attribute

SET 8

notes:

LEAD
SET
9
VOCABULARY

SET 9

01 resemble
rəˈzembəl
v.

mirror, mimic, parallel

to have similar qualities or features as someone or something else

*Children often **resemble** their parents in appearance.*

닮다, 비슷(유사)하다

02 align
əˈlīn
v.

situate, position, orient

to organize or place in a straight line

*The orchestra conductor makes sure that the seats are perfectly **aligned**.*

나란히(가지런히) 만들다, 일직선으로 하다

03 discharge
disˈCHärj
v.

dismiss, remove, expel

to dismiss or release someone from a place, position, or situation

*The student was **discharged** from school for his misconduct.*

(어떤 장소나 직무에서) 떠나는 것을 허락하다, 해고하다

v.

release, liberate, free

allow a liquid or gas to be released from where it was confined

*The insect is known to **discharge** a poisonous chemical when threatened.*

배출하다

04 simultaneous
ˌsīməlˈtānēəs
adj.

concurrent, coincident, synchronized

happening or done at the same time

*Thunder and lightening occur at a **simultaneous** time, but we see lightening first.*

동시의

05 modulate
ˈmäjəˌlāt
v.

regulate, adjust, set

to exercise influence

*The government attempts to **modulate** the businesses to help run the economy.*

조절하다

06 exude
igˈzo͞od
v.

discharge, release, emit

to discharge a chemical slowly and steadily

*The insect **exudes** a pheromone during its mating season.*

(액체나 냄새를(가)) 흘리다(흐르다/풍기다)

v.

radiate, emanate, ooze

to display an emotion or quality strongly and outwardly

*The student counselor **exuded** generosity and friendliness.*

(특정한 느낌 등을(이)) 물씬 풍기다(줄줄 흐르다)

07 perpetual
pərˈpeCH(oō)əl
adj.

everlasting, eternal, permanent

never coming to a stop or changing

*Space is a **perpetual** darkness with the occasional light from the stars.*

끊임없이 계속되는

08 in tandem
ˈtandəm
adj.

lineup, organization, unit

having two things aligned with one another

*The two tennis players play **in tandem** during a tennis match.*

(~와) 동시에(나란히)

09 perturb
pərˈtərb
v.

worry, concern, upset

to make someone nervous or unsettled

*The family was **perturbed** by their teenage daughter's behavior.*

(심리적으로) 동요하게 하다

10 coordinate
kōˈôrdəˌnāt
v.

harmonize, correlate, interrelate

to bring the different parts of an activity or organization into a relationship, which will produce efficiency or harmony

*She has to **coordinate** this year's office party.*

조직화(편성)하다

11 capable
ˈkāpəb(ə)l
adj.

competent, proficient, accomplished

having the ability or quality necessary to perform or obtain something

*He is a **capable** worker, with years of experience.*

유능한

12 amalgamate
əˈmalgəˌmāt
v.

merge, fuse, mingle

to combine to form one structure

*Facebook **amalgamated** with Instagram to form a bigger company.*

합치다

13 potential
pəˈten(t)SHəl
adj.

prospective, probable, likely

having or displaying the capacity to become something in the future

*Free gifts will attract **potential** customers to the store.*

(…이 될) 가능성이 있는, 잠재적인

SET 9 · 113

SET 9

14 miniature
ˈmin(ē)əCHər
adj.

minute, tiny, mini

something that is much smaller than normal

*The babies are dressed as **miniature** office workers.*

아주 작은(소형의), 축소된

---

15 conduction
kənˈdəkSH(ə)n
n.

the process by which electricity or heat is transmitted through a substance

*The scientists tested the **conduction** of the material by turning the heat on and off.*

(전기나 열의) 전도

---

16 deflect
dəˈflekt
v.

divert, distract, avert

to cause something to change direction after coming across a hindrance

*Captain America's shield **deflected** the bullet.*

방향을 바꾸다(바꾸게 하다)

---

17 route
rōōt
v.

send, direct, dispatch

to send or direct along a specific course

*Due to the accident, all cars were **routed** to a local road.*

(특정한 루트를 따라 무엇을) 보내다(전송하다)

---

18 resistance
rəˈzistəns
n.

opposition, struggle, confrontation

the refusal to accept or follow something

*Superman showed no **resistance** when he was taken captive by the people.*

(공격에 대한) 저항(항거)

---

19 detect
dəˈtekt
v.

perceive, discern, notice

to find or identify the existence or presence of something

*The father was able to **detect** the lie from his son's excuse.*

발견하다(알아내다/감지하다)

---

20 encode
inˈkōd
v.

cipher, conceal

to change into a coded form

*The message was **encoded** in the musical notes.*

암호로 바꾸다

21. deliberate
dəˈlib(ə)rət
adj.

intentional, calculated, conscious

performed consciously and intentionally

*The country's action was a **deliberate** attempt to start a war.*

고의의, 의도(계획)적인

22. prowess
ˈprouəs
n.

expertise, mastery, skill

talent or expertise in a specific activity or field

*Sir Lancelot displayed **prowess** in swordsmanship.*

(절묘한) 기량(솜씨)

n.

courage, valor, gallantry

bravery in a fight

*King Arthur showed **prowess** when he fought the Vikings.*

용감함

23. eligibility
ˌeləjəˈbilədē
n.

qualification, fit

the condition of having the right to do or get something

*The woman's **eligibility** for benefits will depend on her income.*

적임, 적격

24. impulse
ˈimˌpəls
n.

instinct, drive, compulsion

a sudden urge or desire to act

*I had an **impulse** to help the child who fell off his bike.*

충동

25. erupt
əˈrəpt
v.

burst, explode, detonate

break out suddenly and dramatically

*An argument **erupted** between the two friends.*

터뜨리다(폭발하다)

26. jam
jam
v.

stuff, shove, wedge

to squeeze tightly into a particular space

*Ten clowns **jammed** themselves into a small sports car.*

밀다(밀어 넣다)

n.

predicament, plight, dilemma

an awkward situation

*I'm in a **jam** so I need some help.*

곤경에 처하다(난처한 입장이다)

SET 9

27 engage
inˈgāj
v.
- immerse, involve, preoccupy
- to participate or get involved in
- *The mother **engaged** in helping her daughter learn how to cook.*
- 관여하다

28 cease
sēs
v.
- end, halt, stop
- to bring or come to an end
- *The middleman **ceased** the fight between two strangers.*
- 중단되다, 그치다; 중단시키다

29 emit
əˈmit
v.
- release, discharge, secrete
- to produce and discharge something
- *The lizard **emitted** poison from its skin as a defense mechanism.*
- (빛, 열, 가스, 소리 등을) 내다(내뿜다)

30 aggressive
əˈgresiv
adj.
- hostile, belligerent, antagonistic
- likely to confront or attack
- *A dog shows that it is **aggressive** when the hair on its neck are standing.*
- 공격적인

31 impinge
imˈpinj
v.
- affect, influence, touch
- to have a negative effect or impact
- *Watching too much television will **impinge** his academic scores.*
- (특히 나쁜) 영향(지장)을 주다

32 converge
kənˈvərj
v.
- assemble, concentrate, mingle
- to come from different areas and meet at a single point
- *Bees tend to **converge** towards the queen.*
- 모여들다, 집중되다

33 diverge
dəˈvərj
v.
- split, ramify, fork
- to separate from a single point and spread out in different directions
- *Bees will **diverge** from their hive to look for honey.*
- (다른 방향으로) 갈라지다

34	**dilute**	reduce, attenuate, mitigate
	dīˈlo͞ot	to make something weaker in strength, content, or value
	v.	The coffee was **diluted** by adding water.
		(효과 등을) 희석시키다(약화시키다)

35	**assortment**	mixture, array, variety
	əˈsôrtmənt	a collection of items or people
	n.	There was an **assortment** of candies at the convenience store.
		모음, 종합

36	**empathy**	compassion, sympathy, rapport
	ˈempəTHē	the ability to understand and share the emotions of someone else
	n.	The Tin Woodman did not have **empathy** so the wizard gave him a heart.
		감정이입, 공감

37	**contextual**	circumstantial, dependent, contingent
	kənˈteksCHo͞oəl	relating to the circumstances
	adj.	Based on **contextual** clues, Sherlock was able to guess who the culprit was.
		맥락(전후 사정)과 관련된

38	**subtle**	shrewd, perceptive, insidious
	ˈsədl	hard to perceive or understand
	adj.	The **subtle** message of the movie was barely understood by the audience.
		미묘한, 감지하기 힘든

39	**benchmark**	basis, standard, gauge
	ˈben(t)SHmärk	a point of reference or standard
	n.	The first gift becomes the **benchmark** of future gifts.
		기준(점)

40	**era**	period, age, generation
	ˈirə	a distinct time period in history
	n.	The discovery of electricity started a new **era**.
		시대

SET 9

41. sneer
snir
v.

belittle, deride, scoff
to smile or speak in a mocking way
The pro gamer **sneered** at the amateur's performance.

비웃다, 조롱하다

42. infuriate
inˈfyo͝orēˌāt
v.

enrage, madden, inflame
to make someone very angry
The angry bird was **infuriated** by the pigs.

극도로 화나게 만들다

43. vanquish
ˈvaNGkwiSH
v.

conquer, annihilate, crush
to defeat completely
Roman legions **vanquished** every foe that stood in their way.

완파하다

44. undermine
ˌəndərˈmīn
v.

weaken, compromise, diminish
to weaken the power or ability
His work in the company was **undermined** when the new boss changed the system.

약화시키다

45. cram
kram
v.

review
to study intensively just before an examination
University students **cram** during final examination week.

벼락치기 공부를 하다

v.

stuff, jam, overfill
to completely fill a space until it overflows
She **crammed** her clothes into the closet

(좁은 공간 속으로) 잔뜩 들어가다

46. annihilate
əˈnīəˌlāt
v.

destroy, obliterate, exterminate
to destroy utterly
European settlers **annihilated** the dodo birds to extinction.

전멸시키다

47. artifact
ˈärdəfakt
n.

antique, memento, remnant
an item of cultural or historical relevance
The **artifact** was placed in the museum.

인공 유물

48 plausible
ˈplôzəb(ə)l
adj.

feasible, tenable, reasonable

to be reasonable or probable

*The thief gave a **plausible** explanation for his crime.*

타당한 것 같은, 이치에 맞는, 그럴듯한

49 ponder
ˈpändər
v.

consider, contemplate, review

to think carefully before making a decision

*The student **pondered** long before writing down the answer.*

숙고하다, 곰곰이 생각하다

50 detour
ˈdētoor
n.

deviation, diversion, bypass

a route that is taken to avoid an obstacle, or to stop by someplace along the way

*She made a **detour** to a café before going to work.*

둘러 가는 길, 우회로

SET 9 TEST

1. She acted on _____ and decided to buy the dog.

2. The eye wink was _____ that only the person across the table noticed it.

3. Batman _____ his enemies and Gotham City was free of crime.

4. The family decided to take a _____ from their trip and stopped to eat the world famous ice cream.

5. The professor _____ his authority by kicking the student out of his class.

6. A solar eclipse occurs when the sun and the moon are in _____ with one another.

7. The little girl _____ the red and blue clay to form a purple clay.

8. Individuals should end relationships when their friends _____ their personality.

9. My son gave a _____ explanation for why the flower vase broke.

10. The newly wed bride _____ happiness and joy.

---

1. impulse 2. subtle 3. vanquish 4. detour 5. modulate 6. tandem 7. amalgamate 8. impinge 9. plausible 10. exude

11. Joan of Ark showed _____ on the battlefield, despite the fact that she was the only female soldier.

12. Riding the bicycle for the first time _____ the boy's parents.

13. The little girl broke her dollhouse with _____ force so that she could get a new one.

14. The two roads _____ into one.

15. My grandmother showed _____ to her neighbor who had also lost her dog.

16. Koreans are _____ when Japan claims that Dokdo is their land.

17. The basketball game and soccer match occurred at a _____ time.

18. His authority over his troops were _____ when his badge was taken away.

19. The _____ signs showed that he was in trouble.

20. Deep space seems to be a _____ stretch of vastness.

---

11. prowess 12. perturb 13. deliberate 14. converge 15. empathy
16. infuriate 17. simultaneous 18. undermine 19. contextual 20. perpetual

SET 9

notes:

LEAD

SET 10

VOCABULARY

SET 10

01 **intent**
in'tent
n.

aim, objective, goal
intention or purpose
*What is your **intent** of attacking the city?*

의도

02 **reflexive**
rə'fleksiv
adj.

compulsory, spontaneous, unintentional
performed unconsciously
*Covering the mouth while coughing is a **reflexive** behavior.*

반사 행동

03 **conflict**
'kän͵flikt
n.

dispute, quarrel, squabble
a disagreement or argument
*My parents are always in **conflict** when deciding where to eat.*

갈등(충돌)

04 **subsequent**
'səbsəkwənt
adj.

ensuing, succeeding, successive
following after something in time
*The fire drills were annually practiced **subsequent** to the great fire of 2004.*

다음의, 차후의

05 **marginal**
'märjənl
adj.

insignificant, minor, negligible
of minor importance
*What to serve as appetizers is **marginal** compared to the main dish.*

미미한, 중요하지 않은

06 **immediate**
i'mēdēət
adj.

instant, prompt, swift
happening or done at once
*The police took no **immediate** action when the store was robbed.*

즉각적인

adj.

close, adjacent, near
nearest in space
*Roads in the **immediate** range of the hospital were closed due to construction.*

아주 가까이에(바로 옆에) 있는

07 substitute
'səbstəˌt(y)o͞ot
n.

- replacement, proxy, surrogate
- a person or thing which serves or acts in place of the other
- Soy milk is often used as a **substitute** for dairy milk in coffee.
- 대신하는 사람(것), 대리자; 대용물

08 analogous
əˈnaləgəs
adj.

- comparable, parallel, corresponding
- similar in certain aspects
- The pectoral fins of a fish are **analogous** to that of human arms.
- 유사한

09 contract
ˈkäntrakt
n.

- commitment, settlement, agreement
- a written or verbal agreement
- He signed a **contract** to live in the house for two years.
- 계약(약정)

v.

- shrink, decrease, diminish
- to decrease in number, range, or size
- The puffer fish **contracts** when it does not feel threatened.
- 줄어들다, 수축하다

10 invade
inˈvād
v.

- seize, conquer, pervade
- to enter with the intent of controlling or occupying
- Demonstrators **invaded** the White House.
- 난입하다, 침범하다

11 capacity
kəˈpasədē
n.

- volume, dimensions, measurements
- the maximum number that something can hold
- The **capacity** of the movie theatre is 200 people.
- 용량, 수용력

n.

- potential, competence, ability
- the ability to do or understand something
- The CEO was impressed with the worker's **capacity** for hard work.
- 능력

12 array
əˈrā
n.

- arrangement, lineup, formation
- an incredible display or range of something
- An **array** of artwork were displayed at the gallery.
- 집합체(모음/무리)

SET 10

13 multitude
ˈməltəˌt(y)o͞od
n.

host, horde, mass

a large number

A **multitude** of diseases plagued the early American colonies.

주 많은 수, 다수

14 adopt
əˈdäpt
v.

embrace, acquire, assume

to choose to take up, follow, or use

This method has been **adopted** by many companies.

(특정한 방식이나 자세를) 쓰다(취하다)

15 limited
ˈlimədəd
adj.

finite, narrow, lean

restricted in amount, extent, or size

A **limited** number of restaurants are open at this late hour.

제한된, 아주 많지는 않은

16 settle
ˈsedl
v.

resolve, rectify, reconcile

to resolve or reach an agreement

The judge **settled** the court case once and for all.

(논쟁 등을) 해결하다(끝내다)

v.

perch, descend, flump

to come to rest in a comfortable position

The children **settled** down on their favorite couch.

편안히 앉다(눕다)

17 immigrate
ˈiməˌgrāt
v.

migrate, relocate, resettle

to go live in a foreign country permanently

My family **immigrated** to America when I was very young.

(다른 나라로) 이주해(이민을) 오다

18 nomad
ˈnōˌmad
n.

migrant, wanderer, rover

someone who does not stay in the same place for a long time

He was a **nomad** who never stayed in one place longer than a year.

방랑자

19 itinerant
īˈtinərənt
adj.

wandering, wayfaring, roaming

moving from place to place

The **itinerant** traders travelled across Asia, looking for trade routes.

떠돌아다니는(순회하는)

20. sophisticated
/sə'fistə,kādəd/ adj.

experienced, enlightened, cosmopolitan

having a great deal of experience and knowledge in cultural areas

*After living in different cities, he is now a **sophisticated** man.*

세련된, 교양 있는

21. contemporary
/kən'tempə,rerē/ adj.

concurrent, synchronic, coexistent

living or occurring at the same time

*This style of drawing is **contemporary** with other drawings of that time.*

동시대의

22. irrigation
/,irə'gāSHən/ n.

watering, flooding, soaking

the supply of water to land for farming

*The stream supplies water for **irrigation** to the farms nearby.*

관개, 물을 끌어들임

23. distinguishable
/də'stiNGgwiSHəb(ə)l/ adj.

discernible, detectable, separable

clear enough to be identified as different

*He is **distinguishable** from his twin brother.*

구별할 수 있는, 분간할 수 있는

24. belief
/bə'lēf/ n.

faith, confidence, credence

confidence in someone or something

*I have **belief** in you that you will do the right thing.*

신념, 확신

25. offshoot
/'ôf,SHoot/ n.

branch, derivative, appendage

something that develops from something else

*Evolutionists believe that humans are an **offshoot** of monkeys.*

파생물, 분파

26. disparate
/'dispərət/ adj.

contrasting, differing, unlike

different in kind

*He comes from a **disparate** country, so he cannot understand her actions.*

서로 전혀 다른, 이질적인

SET 10

27 adapt
əˈdapt
v.

adjust, accommodate, habituate

to become adjusted to new conditions

*The animal must **adapt** to its new environment in order to survive.*

(상황에) 적응하다

28 niche
niCH
n.

vocation, place, job

a suitable position in life or employment

*After becoming a politician, he felt that he had found his **niche** in the community.*

아주 편한(꼭 맞는) 자리(역할/일 등)

29 remnant
ˈremnənt
n.

remains, residue, leftovers

a remaining quantity of something

*The **remnants** of the uprising were quickly disposed of by the military.*

남은 부분, 나머지

30 scatter
ˈskadər
v.

disperse, dissipate, disband

to separate and move in different directions

*The deer **scattered** when the mountain lion attacked them.*

황급히 흩어지다

31 theory
ˈThirē
n.

hypothesis, thesis, conjecture

a supposition or a collection of ideas with the purpose of explaining something

*Charles Darwin came up with the **theory** of evolution.*

이론

32 precept
ˈprēˌsept
n.

principle, code, guideline

a general rule to control behavior or thought

*A person is innocent until proven guilty, which is a legal **precept** in the court of law.*

(행동) 수칙, 계율

33 winsome
ˈwinsəm
adj.

engaging, charming, captivating

attractive or appealing

*His **winsome** smile attracted all the girls.*

마음을 끄는, 매력적인

34. dexterous
ˈdekst(ə)rəs
adj.

adept, adroit, handy

showing or possessing skill using hands

*The guitarist showed **dexterous** playing while handling his instrument.*

손재주가 비상한, 솜씨 좋은

35. trigger
ˈtrigər
v.

prompt, cause, provoke

to cause something to happen

*The pollen in the air **triggered** him to sneeze.*

촉발시키다

36. stagger
ˈstagər
v.

sway, totter, stumble

to walk or move unsteadily

*The alcoholic **staggered** home after drinking.*

비틀(휘청)거리다

37. oversight
ˈōvərˌsīt
n.

mistake, error, omission

a failure to notice or take action

*The employee was fired because of his continuous **oversight**.*

실수, 간과

n.

supervision, inspection, management

the act of monitoring

*An effective **oversight** is required for a company to succeed.*

관리, 감독

38. publicize
ˈpəbləˌsīz
v.

announce, report, impart

to make something known to the public

*Newspapers **publicize** events from around the world.*

광고(홍보)하다

39. disclose
disˈklōz
v.

reveal, divulge, communicate

to reveal a secret or make new information known

*An anonymous informant **disclosed** the corrupt company's name to the press.*

(특히 비밀을) 밝히다(폭로하다)

SET 10

40 premium
ˈprēmēəm
n.

subcharge, fee

an amount added on top of the normal price

*Luxury bags are sold with a **premium** by private sellers if the bags are hard to obtain.*

할증료

41 reimburse
ˌrēimˈbərs
v.

compensate, refund, replace

to repay a person for spending or losing money

*The company will **reimburse** you for your flight and hotel.*

배상(변제)하다

42 insolvent
inˈsälvənt
adj.

bankrupt, ruined, liquidated

unable to pay back

*Video rental stores became **insolvent** because of internet streaming services.*

파산한

43 negotiate
nəˈgōSHēˌāt
v.

arrange, settle, bargain

to attempt to agree or compromise by discussion

*He tried to **negotiate** a good price for the used car.*

협상(교섭)하다

44 hesitant
ˈhezədənt
adj.

uncertain, undecided, tentative

unsure or slow in action or speech

*Consumers are usually **hesitant** when purchasing expensive items.*

주저하는, 망설이는, 머뭇거리는

45 bargain
ˈbärgən
n.

deal, discount, value

an item that is purchased or offered for sale at a cheaper price

*The home theatre system was a real **bargain**.*

싸게 사는 물건

n.

arrangement, understanding, pact

an understanding between two or more groups as to what each group will do for the other

*The labor union and the managers reached a **bargain** on the working conditions.*

합의, 흥정

46. mitigate
ˈmidəˌgāt
v.

alleviate, diminish, lighten

to make less severe or painful

*The medicine helped **mitigate** the headache.*

완화(경감)시키다

47. celestial
səˈlesCHəl
adj.

heavenly, astronomical, stellar

relating to the sky or outer space

*A new **celestial** body was discovered by the Hubble Telescope.*

하늘의, 천체의, 천상의

48. allude
əˈlo͞od
v.

imply, suggest, insinuate

to indirectly suggest or hint at

*The boss had a way of **alluding** the problems without hurting the employees' feelings.*

(암시적으로) 언급(논급)하다

49. parched
pärCHt
adj.

dry, arid, dehydrated

dried out

*The farmland was **parched** from the drought.*

몹시 건조한(바싹 말라 버린)

50. filter
ˈfiltər
v.

strain, sift, refine

to pass through something to remove unwanted parts

*The lake water was **filtered** to make it drinkable.*

여과하다, 거르다

SET 10 CROSSWORD PUZZLE

Across

2. a remaining quantity of something
4. a failure to notice or take action
7. to make less severe or painful
9. a large number
10. unable to pay back
13. different in kind
14. living or occurring at the same time
15. following after something in time

Down

1. relating to the sky or outer space
3. of minor importance
5. performed unconsciously
6. something that develops from something else
8. moving from place to place
11. similar in certain aspects
12. attractive or appealing

1. celestial
3. marginal
5. reflexive
6. offshoot
8. itinerant
11. analogous
12. winsome

2. remnant
4. oversight
7. mitigate
9. multitude
10. insolvent
13. disparate
14. contemporary
15. subsequent

LEAD
SET 11
VOCABULARY

SET 11

01 scheme
skēm
n.
- plan, strategy, plot
- a systematic plan or arrangement
- The police uncovered a **scheme** to steal the diamond.
- (운영) 계획, 제도

02 distinct
də'stiNG(k)t
adj.
- definite, marked, clear
- different in nature compared to something else that is similar
- The way he talks is **distinct** from the way he writes.
- 뚜렷이 다른(구별되는), 별개의

03 tie
tī
v.
- bind, tether, strap
- to attach or fasten with a string or cord
- They **tied** the prisoner to the chair.
- (끈 등으로) 묶다, 묶어 두다(놓다)

v.
- connect, relate, join
- to link
- His fate is now **tied** with the rest of the prisoners.
- 이어지다, 연결되다

04 precursor
prē'kərsər
n.
- forerunner, predecessor, antecedent
- someone or something that comes before another
- Board games are the **precursors** of video games.
- 선도자(격인 사람·사물)

05 traction
'trakSH(ə)n
n.
- grip, friction, adhesion
- the grip of a tire on a road
- The car lost its **traction** and skidded on the ice.
- (차량 바퀴 등의) 정지 마찰력

06 preserve
prə'zərv
v.
- conserve, maintain, protect
- to maintain something in its original state
- Any historical record should be **preserved** for study.
- 보존(관리)하다

07 discriminate
də'skrimə,nāt
v.
- distinguish, differentiate, separate
- to recognize the difference
- Dogs are able to **discriminate** different kinds of scents.
- 식별(구별)하다

08 fragile
'frajəl
adj.

brittle, weak, delicate

easily damaged or destroyed

*Glass and pottery are **fragile**, so make sure to wrap them carefully when not in use.*

부서지기(손상되기) 쉬운

09 regardless
rə'gärdləs
adv.

nevertheless, nonetheless, anyway

without being attentive to the present situation

*The soldiers were determined to fight **regardless** of how many of them were left.*

개의치(상관하지) 않고

10 inexplicable
ˌinek'splikəb(ə)l
adj.

incomprehensible, unfathomable

unable to be explained or imagined

*It was **inexplicable** for her not to get a perfect grade.*

불가해한, 설명할 수 없는

11 scant
skant
adj.

minimal, limited, negligible

barely enough or adequate

*The children were given **scant** meals in the orphanage.*

거의(별로) 없는, 부족한

12 abrupt
ə'brəpt
adj.

hasty, instantaneous, immediate

sudden and unexpected

*The mother was suspicious by the **abrupt** change of subject.*

돌연한, 갑작스러운

13 depart
də'pärt
v.

deviate, digress, drift

to leave or deviate from a course of action

*The manager **departed** from his original plans to incorporate the new system.*

(정도, 일상 등으로부터) 벗어남(일탈)

14 cite
sīt
v.

quote, mention, adduce

to quote someone or something as evidence for an argument or statement

*Famous people are often **cited** in the works of others.*

인용하다

SET 11

15 displace
dis'plās
v.
replace, move, shift
to cause someone or something to move from its place, position, or role
The fallen leader was quickly **displaced** by his opponent.
대신(대체)하다

16 paucity
'pôsədē
n.
scarcity, shortage, rarity
the availability of something in small or insufficient amounts
A **paucity** of evidence failed to prove the theory.
소량; 부족, 결핍

17 demise
də'mīz
n.
end, fall, ruin
the end of a person or institution
The dictator's **demise** became a celebration for the people.
종말

18 resourceful
rə'sôrsfəl
adj.
ingenious, inventive, creative
having the ability to quickly find ways to solve difficulties
He is a **resourceful** worker and is necessary for this company.
지략(기략) 있는

19 gradual
'graj(oo)əl
adj.
moderate, cautious, slow
taking place or advancing slowly
The new leader made **gradual** changes so that the people could adjust.
점진적인, 서서히 일어나는

20 secure
sə'kyoor
v.
fix, attach, fasten
to fix or fasten so that it is not loose
Secure the cargo so that it does not fall when we sail.
(움직이지 않게) 고정시키다

v.
protect, fortify, guard
to make safe and unharmed
Secure the president in his private bunker.
안전하게 보호하다

21. wander
ˈwändər
v.

stroll, ramble, dawdle
to move in a casual or aimless way
He **wandered** aimlessly through the maze.

거닐다, 돌아다니다, 헤매다

22. agrarian
əˈgrerēən
adj.

agricultural, farming, pastoral
relating to farmed land or the farming of land
China is mostly an **agrarian** society.

농업의

23. verify
ˈverəˌfī
v.

authenticate, certify, corroborate
to make sure that something is true or accurate
Let me **verify** your identification before I let you enter.

확인하다

24. obstacle
ˈäbstək(ə)l
n.

barrier, hurdle, impediment
something that blocks one's way
The fallen tree became an **obstacle** for the firetruck.

장애물

25. perish
ˈperiSH
v.

fall, disappear, vanish
to suffer complete destruction
The Roman Empire **perished** due to poor leadership.

죽다, 비명횡사하다

26. dismiss
disˈmis
v.

release, free, dissolve
to order or permit to leave
After years of service, he was **dismissed** from the army.

사직시키다

v.

banish, abandon, disregard
to treat as something not worth consideration
His ideas were immediately **dismissed** because it was so outrageous.

(고려할 가치가 없다고) 묵살(일축)하다

SET 11 · 137

SET 11

27 portray
pôr'trā
v.

represent, depict, present
to describe someone or something in a specific way
The movie **portrayed** the villain as a hero.

나타내다(보여주다)

28 obscure
əb'skyoor
adj.

unclear, uncertain, dubious
not discovered or known
The superhero's origin is **obscure** because he suddenly appeared in the story.

잘 알려져 있지 않은, 무명의

29 overtone
'ōvər,tōn
n.

connotation, implication, suggestion
a subtle quality or implication
The president's recent announcement may have social **overtones**.

함축

30 affiliate
ə'filē,āt
v.

associate, incorporate, join
to relate officially with an organization
The international program is **affiliated** with my university.

(더 큰 회사기관 등과) 제휴(연계)하다

31 premature
,prēmə'CHoor
adj.

hasty, rash, untimely
happening or finished before the usual or proper time
Spending too much time out in the sun can cause **premature** aging of the skin.

정상(예상)보다 이른

32 variance
'verēəns
n.

discrepancy, variation, incongruity
the quality of being different or inconsistent
There was a **variance** in his skills compared to what he wrote in his resume.

변화(변동)(량)

33 rebut
rə'bət
v.

refute, deny, invalidate
to show or prove that the information is wrong
The man had to **rebut** the claim that he was cheating on his girlfriend.

논박(반박)하다

34 compulsory
kəmˈpəlsərē
adj.

obligatory, mandatory, required

required by law or rule

*Korean men serve a **compulsory** military service for 2 years.*

강제적인, 의무적인, 필수의

35 perception
pərˈsepSH(ə)n
n.

discernment, recognition, cognizance

the state of being aware of something through the senses

*He did not have a **perception** of pain because his nervous system was damaged.*

지각, 자각

n.

insight, keenness, intuition

an intuitive understanding

*My mother had keen **perception** and always managed to avoid trouble.*

통찰력

36 debunk
dēˈbəNGk
v.

expose, negate, discredit

to expose the falseness of a myth, idea, or belief

*Myth busters are men who **debunk** false information.*

틀렸음을 드러내다(밝히다)

37 vicinity
vəˈsinədē
n.

locale, region, domain

the area surrounding a specific place

*The number of people living in the **vicinity** of the power plant was small.*

(…의) 부근(인근)

38 parlor
ˈpärlər
n.

lounge, salon

a sitting room inside a house

*The family spent their leisure time in the **parlor**.*

응접실, 객실; 거실

39 constitute
ˈkänstəˌt(y)o͞ot
v.

form, compose, represent

to make up a whole

*A father, mother, and children **constitute** a conventional family.*

…을 구성하다(이루다)

SET 11

40 novice
ˈnävəs
n.

beginner, fledgling, rookie
someone who is new or inexperienced in a topic or situation
*Even a professional starts as a **novice** at one time.*

초보자

41 milestone
ˈmīlˌstōn
n.

breakthrough, landmark, occasion
an action or event which signifies an important change or development
*The baby taking his first steps was a **milestone** in his development.*

중요한(획기적인) 단계(사건)

42 parsimonious
ˌpärsəˈmōnēəs
adj.

stingy, frugal, miserly
not willing to spend money or use resources
*Even the **parsimonious** Scrooge presented gifts during Christmas.*

(돈에 지독히) 인색한

43 utilitarian
yo͞oˌtiləˈterēən
adj.

functional, effective, useful
made to be useful or practical
*The **utilitarian** furniture failed to decorate the house.*

실용적인

44 delicate
ˈdelikət
adj.

frail, fragile, eggshell
easily damaged or broken
*Lego is a **delicate** toy, so it should not be played with.*

연약한, 여린, 다치기(부서지기) 쉬운

adj.

exquisite, intricate, elegant
of complex workmanship or quality
*The **delicate** dress could only be hand washed.*

섬세한, 우아한

45 versatile
ˈvərsədl
adj.

flexible, adaptable, multifaceted
able to adapt to different functions or activities
*A **versatile** employee is useful in the office.*

다재다능한

46 recipient
rəˈsipēənt
n.

beneficiary, receiver

someone or something that receives

*The **recipient** of the award will be rewarded with a cash prize.*

(어떤 것을) 받는 사람, 수령(수취)인

47 assimilate
əˈsiməˌlāt
v.

comprehend, grasp, incorporate

to take in and understand completely

*Students must **assimilate** the information to pass the class.*

완전히 이해하다(소화하다)

48 coin
koin
v.

invent, devise, conceive

to invent a new word or phrase

*Koreans **coin** new expressions which eventually fade quickly.*

(새로운 낱말・어구를) 만들다

49 exotic
igˈzädik
adj.

foreign, alien, imported

of foreign origin or character

*The annual car show also includes **exotic** cars from around the world.*

외국의, 이국적인

50 abstract
abˈstrakt
adj.

conceptual, notional, metaphysical

existing in thought or as an idea

***Abstract** ideas such as love is difficult to explain with words.*

추상적인

SET 11 TEST

1. The earliest civilizations transitioned from a hunter gatherer society to that of an _____ culture.

2. Who or what built stonehenge is still _____.

3. _____ cars lined up in his massive garage.

4. An appetizer is a _____ that comes before the main dish.

5. A rabbit was only a _____ portion of a meal for the lion.

6. From a young age, Einstein was able to _____ the knowledge that was given to him.

7. The millenia year old pottery from China was very _____ and priceless.

8. Sometimes, relationships can be an _____ in one's path to success.

9. The development of the steam engine was a _____ in human engineering.

10. It was _____ for the convict to do community service for his crimes.

1. agrarian 2. obscure 3. exotic 4. precursor 5. scant 6. assimilate 7. fragile 8. obstacle 9. milestone 10. compulsory

11. A _____ employee is able to work in any circumstance.

12. String theory is an _____ concept even for the brightest minds.

13. The Mayans and the Aztecs met their _____ when the Europeans landed on their shores.

14. The receipt _____ that the purchase was complete.

15. The FBI is _____ with the groups that monitor the safety of the United States.

16. The jetski is a _____ of a boat, but is much smaller and faster.

17. Scientists have yet _____ the existence of the Loch Ness Monster.

18. The project leader devised a _____ for everyone to participate in the project.

19. I lost my ring in the _____ of the school bench.

20. Uncle Scrooge was known to be _____, so everyone was surprised when he gave us gifts.

| 11. versatile | 12. inexplicable | 13. demise | 14. verify | 15. affiliate |
| 16. variance | 17. debunk | 18. scheme | 19. vicinity | 20. parsimonious |

SET 11

notes:

LEAD SET 12 VOCABULARY

SET 12

01 bevy
'bevē
n.

- group, gang, troupe
- a large group of people or objects
- A **bevy** of popular brands will appear in the film.
- (같은 종류의) 무리

02 exhaust
ig'zôst
v.

- overtire, fatigue, weary
- to tire someone of their physical or mental health
- Babysitting the child **exhausted** him.
- 기진맥진하게 만들다

v.
- deplete, finish, expend
- to use up resources completely
- Humanity will **exhaust** fossil fuels within a century.
- 다 쓰다

03 accurate
'akyərət
adj.

- precise, exact, correct
- correct in all information
- **Accurate** information is essential in order to win the dispute.
- 정확한

04 impetus
'impədəs
n.

- momentum, propulsion, drive
- the energy or force that moves a body
- His **impetus** to work hard was his family.
- 자극(제)(추동력)

05 renew
rə'n(y)oō
v.

- extend, prolong
- to extend the validity of something
- I had to **renew** my driver's license since it was expired.
- 갱신(연장)하다

v.
- restore, refurbish, revamp
- to replace something that is broken or used up
- The engine of the car was replaced and the batteries were **renewed**.
- 복원(복구)하다

06 feasible
'fēzəb(ə)l
adj.

- probable, possible, likely
- likely to occur
- The most **feasible** solution is to find a renewable source of energy.
- 실현 가능한

07 conventional
kənˈven(t)SH(ə)n(ə)l
adj.

normal, standard, ordinary
based on what is generally done or believed
*The **conventional** behavior at a funeral is to stay quiet.*

전통적인, 종래의

08 abundant
əˈbəndənt
adj.

copious, ample, profuse
available in large numbers
*There was **abundant** evidence to prove that he was guilty.*

풍부한

09 promise
ˈpräməs
n.

potential, aptitude, capacity
the possibility of being excellent
*He showed great **promise** to be the next star athlete.*

가능성

v.

swear, pledge, vow
to assure to another that one will do, give, or arrange something
*I **promise** to never lie again.*

약속하다

10 staple
ˈstāpəl
adj.

principal, chief, major
main or important
*Fish happens to be the **staple** food for these islanders.*

주된, 주요한

11 fallout
ˈfôlˌout
n.

aftermath, effect, reaction
the negative side effects of a situation
*The **fallout** of an economical depression is the poor quality of life.*

좋지 못한 결과

12 tantalize
ˈtan(t)lˌīz
v.

tease, tempt, entice
to excite the senses or desires of another
*Even after years of marriage, she still **tantalizes** him.*

감질나게 하다

13 conscious
ˈkän(t)SHəs
adj.

aware, alert, responsive
aware of and responding to the surroundings
*He made a **conscious** effort to get away from the problem.*

의식하는, 자각하는

SET 12

14 aspire
əˈspī(ə)r
v.
- pursue, strive, yearn
- to hope to achieve something
- Spiderman **aspired** to be a friendly neighborhood hero.
- 열망(염원)하다

15 modify
ˈmädəˌfī
v.
- alter, adjust, adapt
- to make changes to something
- He **modified** the car to go faster.
- 수정(변경)하다, 바꾸다

16 accumulate
əˈkyoom(y)əˌlāt
v.
- collect, amass, stockpile
- to gather together and increase the number of
- Old Mr. Scrooge **accumulated** his wealth and never spared a penny.
- 모으다, 축적하다

17 reservoir
ˈrezərˌvwär
n.
- stock, supply, bank
- a supply or source of something
- The internet is a **reservoir** of information.
- (많은 양의) 비축(저장/보유)

18 channel
ˈChanl
n.
- strait, neck, passage
- a length of water which connects two larger bodies of water
- The **channel** connects the two seas.
- 물의 경로

n.
- medium, instrument, mechanism
- a way of communication
- Social networking sites are a **channel** of informing social issues.
- (대중 전달용) 매체(수단)

19 extract
ikˈstrakt
v.
- remove, withdraw, extricate
- to remove or take out
- The broken tooth will have to be **extracted**.
- 뽑다(얻다), 추출하다

20 prudent
ˈproodnt
adj.
- wise, judicious, sagacious
- acting while considering for the future
- My father is a **prudent** man as he plans everything carefully.
- 신중한

148 · LEAD VOCABULARY

21. prevalent
'prev(ə)lənt
adj.

widespread, common, general

spread throughout a specific area or time

*Social injustice is **prevalent** in today's society.*

(특정 시기·장소에) 일반적인(널리 퍼져 있는)

22. harness
'härnəs
n.

yoke, gear, tack

a set of straps fit for a horse or other animal to be controlled by the rider

*The horse's **harness** was loose so she could not control him well.*

마구

v.

exploit, utilize, use

to control and use a resource

*Scientists have tried to **harness** the energy of the sun for decades.*

이용하다

23. innovation
ˌinəˈvāSH(ə)n
n.

contraption, alteration, modernization

a new method, product, or idea

*Engineers are trying to come up with new **innovations** to save energy.*

획기적인 것(사상, 방법 등)

24. eliminate
əˈliməˌnāt
v.

abolish, eradicate, obliterate

to remove or get rid of something

*Abraham Lincoln worked tirelessly to **eliminate** slavery.*

없애다, 제거(삭제)하다

25. speculate
'spekyəˌlāt
v.

conjecture, hypothesize, theorize

to guess or form a theory about something without evidence

*My friends continue to **speculate** about the professor's personal life.*

추측(짐작)하다

26. yield
yēld
v.

produce, provide, supply

to produce or provide something

*The farmland **yields** potato, corn, and grain.*

(수익결과농작물 등을) 내다(산출/생산하다)

v.

submit, relent, surrender

to surrender to arguments, pressure, or demand

*I tend to **yield** whenever my younger brother wants the same thing.*

항복(굴복)하다

SET 12

27 oscillate
ˈäsəˌlāt
v.

swing, sway, vibrate
to move or swing at a regular speed
A pendulum **oscillates** the same distance back and forth.
(두 지점 사이를) 왔다 갔다 하다

28 pivot
ˈpivət
n.

axis, hub, fulcrum
the central point of something that allows it to turn
The shoulder is the **pivot**, attaching human arms to the torso.
(회전하는 물체의 균형을 잡아 주는) 중심점

v.

revolve, swivel, twirl
to turn or rotate
The dancer swung around, **pivoting** his ankle.
회전하다(돌다)

29 latter
ˈladər
adj.

later, hindmost, final
placed or happening nearer to the end of something
The hippy era began in the **latter** half of the twentieth century.
(기간, 시기의) 후반의

30 vacuum
ˈvakˌyoo(ə)m
n.

void, emptiness, nothingness
a space completely empty of matter
Space is a dark **vacuum** with nothing but the occasional stars and planets.
진공

31 phenomenon
fəˈnäməˌnän
n.

event, circumstance, occurrence
an occurrence or circumstance which is observed or observable
A solar eclipse is a spectacular natural **phenomena**.
현상

32 contend
kənˈtend
v.

affirm, claim, assert
to assert a statement in an argument
The culprit **contended** that he did nothing wrong.
주장하다

v.

compete, contest, struggle
to engage in competition or argument
Rocky Balboa had to **contend** with the reigning champion in boxing.
다투다(겨루다)

33. eminence
ˈemənəns
n.

renown, prestige, caliber

fame or superiority

*Steven Spielberg's **eminence** in cinematography is well known.*

명성

34. impoverish
imˈpäv(ə)riSH
v.

ruin, cripple, pauperize

to make a person or an area poor

*The never ending war **impoverished** the nation.*

빈곤(가난)하게 하다

35. antecedent
ˌan(t)əˈsēdnt
n.

precursor, forerunner, predecessor

an event or something that comes before another

*The **antecedent** of the lightbulb is the candle.*

선행 사건

36. sizeable
ˈsīzəb(ə)l
adj.

substantial, considerable, significant

fairly large

*Bill Gates offered a **sizeable** donation to charity.*

꽤 큰(많은), 상당한

37. milieu
milˈyoō
n.

setting, context, atmosphere

one's social environment

*Dick Grayson grew up in a circus **milieu**.*

(사회적) 환경

38. barter
ˈbärdər
v.

trade, swap, exchange

to exchange items or services for other items or services without the use of money

*Before the invention of currency, people **bartered** for items they desired.*

물물교환하다, 물건을 교환하다

39. arduous
ˈärjoōəs
adj.

taxing, laborious, burdensome

involving or requiring great effort

*Moving to a new home can be an **arduous** task.*

몹시 힘든, 고된

SET 12

40 incentive
in'sen(t)iv
n.

stimulus, inducement, impetus
something that motivates one to do something
*The company offered a monetary **incentive** to the top salesperson.*
장려(우대)책

41 prestigious
pre'stējəs
adj.

reputable, distinguished, esteemed
having high status
*Harvard University is one of the most **prestigious** schools in the world.*
명망 있는(높은), 일류의

42 skirmish
'skərmiSH
n.

fight, battle, confrontation
a fight between small groups of soldiers, especially between armies or fleets
*Soldiers from South Korea and America participate in a **skirmish** once a year.*
(군대의, 특히 계획에 없던) 소규모 접전(충돌)

43 despot
'despət
n.

tyrant, dictator, authoritarian
one who holds absolute power and authority
*History's infamous **despots** include Hitler, Mussolini, and Stalin.*
폭군

44 hegemony
hə'jemənē
n.

dominion, supremacy, ascendancy
a country or social group's leadership or dominance over others
*The United States and China seem to have **hegemony** in global affairs.*
헤게모니, 패권

45 forfeit
'fôrfət
v.

surrender, relinquish, yield
to lose or give up something as a consequence of something else
*The girls had to **forfeit** their room to the boys when they lost the game.*
몰수(박탈)당하다

46 vaunt
vônt
v.

acclaim, extol, celebrate
to brag or praise something
*The mother **vaunted** her son's success to the neighbors.*
자랑하다, 허풍떨다

47 collaborate
kəˈlabəˌrāt
v.

cooperate, associate, unite

to work together on an activity

*Musicians and singers **collaborate** to produce excellent music.*

협력하다, 공동으로 작업하다

48 habitual
həˈbiCH(oo)əl
adj.

persistent, continuous, perpetual

doing something constantly or out of habit

*Biting her fingernails has become a **habitual** response to anxiety.*

특유의, 늘 하는

49 ascendant
əˈsendənt
adj.

predominant, superior, prevailing

rising in power or influence

*The president looked for a way to prevent the **ascendant** politician rising to power.*

상승하는, 떠오르는

n.

antecedent, predecessor, ancestor

ancestor

*Asian cultures often have ceremonies that worship their **ascendants**.*

선조, 조상

50 exile
ˈegˌzīl
v.

expel, banish, expatriate

to chase out someone from their native country, usually because of political reasons

*Edward Snowden was **exiled** from America for leaking confidential information.*

망명을 가게 만들다, 추방(유배)하다

SET 12 TEST

1. The energy drink was the _____ he needed to finish the work.

2. The _____ buisnessman had a backup plan in case his endeavor failed.

3. General Lee's _____ in his victory against the Japanese forces is legendary.

4. Children will _____ their success in order to stand out amongst their peers.

5. Boutique shops carry a _____ of popular clothing brands.

6. The likelihood that she will get the promotion is _____.

7. Kimchi is a _____ export of South Korea.

8. Mankind has _____ using water as an energy source for a very long time.

9. The trade ban _____ the nation since trade was their main economic strength.

10. Construction work is an _____ task.

1. impetus 2. prudent 3. eminence 4. vaunt 5. bevy 6. feasible 7. staple 8. harness 9. impoverish 10. arduous

11. Mussolini was an infamous _____ who ruled the people with an iron fist.

12. The _____ behavior when someone wins an award is to shake their hand and congratulate them.

13. The sweet candy _____ my taste buds.

14. The news that the country had won the gold medal was _____ within mere seconds.

15. Scientists continuously _____ the origin of the universe with different theories.

16. The gathering of clouds is an _____ before a big storm.

17. The Stevenson Award is a _____ award given to the smartest students in the country.

18. The military had _____ its food source so they had to surrender.

19. The _____ of a military victory is that there will always be casualties.

20. Leonardo da Vinci was famous for his _____ that were ahead of his time.

11. despot   12. conventional   13. tantalize   14. prevalent   15. speculate
16. antecedent   17. prestigious   18. exhaust   19. fallout   20. innovation

SET 12

notes:

LEAD
SET
13
VOCABULARY

SET 13

01 activate
ˈaktəˌvāt
v.

operate, start, trigger

to make something operate

The smoke will **activate** the fire alarm.

작동시키다, 활성화시키다

02 prototype
ˈprōdəˌtīp
n.

mock-up, precursor, model

the first preliminary model of something, from which other models are developed

Here is the **prototype** of the spaceship that will be sent to Mars.

원형

03 corrode
kəˈrōd
v.

rust, tarnish, deteriorate

to destroy or damage gradually by chemical reaction

The chains on the bicycle have been **corroded**.

녹슬게 하거나 부식시키다

04 proponent
prəˈpōnənt
n.

advocate, promoter, supporter

someone who supports an idea, proposal, or project

My father is a **proponent** of Dokdo being Korea's land.

(어떤 사상, 행동 방침의) 지지자

05 stunt
stənt
v.

inhibit, impede, restrict

to prevent from developing normally

The plant's growth will be **stunted** if no sunlight or water is provided.

성장(발달)을 방해(저해)하다

n.

feat, trick, coup

an action showing spectacular skill and risk

The **stunt** involved jumping off a cliff and diving into the water.

스턴트(고난이도 연기)

06 benevolent
bəˈnevələnt
adj.

tenderhearted, kind, gracious

well meaning and kind

The **benevolent** king handed out food to the people.

자애로운

07 undertaking
ˈəndərˌtākiNG
n.

venture, campaign, enterprise

work that is accepted

*The volunteers participated in a grand **undertaking** to clean the streets.*

(중요한, 힘든) 일(프로젝트)

08 invest
inˈvest
v.

expend, devote, contribute

to put in one's time, money, or effort for something and expecting a positive result

*My grandparents **invested** their retirement money in my business.*

(시간, 노력 등을) 투자하다(쏟다)

09 portend
pôrˈtend
v.

foreshadow, presage, foretell

to show a sign or warning that something is likely to occur

*The psychic is famous for **portending** accurate events.*

(특히 불길한) 전조(징후)이다

10 vague
vāg
adj.

indistinct, hazy, fuzzy

uncertain or unclear in meaning or description

*He was only able to remember **vague** details from last night.*

(기억 등이) 희미한(어렴풋한)

11 stimulus
ˈstimyələs
n.

stimulant, impetus, encouragement

a thing or event that evokes action or energy in someone or something

*The monthly bonus is a **stimulus** for the employees to work hard.*

자극제, 자극(고무/격려)(이 되는 것)

12 verge
vərj
n.

margin, side, brink

the edge or border

*The masculine man is on the **verge** of tears.*

맨 끝, 변두리

13 diverse
dəˈvərs
adj.

various, manifold, multiple

showing a great variety

*There are **diverse** sports to participate in college.*

다양한

SET 13

14 rely
rəˈlī
v.

trust, depend, count

to depend on with trust and confidence

Batman **relies** on Robin on their adventures.

의지하다; 신뢰하다, 믿다

15 industrial
inˈdəstrēəl
adj.

manufacturing, factory, commercial

relating to industry

The sea port had become an **industrial** area.

산업(공업)의

16 ecology
ēˈkäləjē
n.

the branch of biology that studies the relationship between organisms and their physical environment

My sister choose to study **ecology** to understand global warming.

생태(계), 생태학

17 hamper
ˈhampər
v.

obstruct, thwart, foil

to block or hinder the movement or progress of something

Thanos' plan was **hampered** by the Avengers.

방해하다

18 vital
ˈvīdl
adj.

crucial, key, indispensable

necessary or important

The heart is a **vital** organ in our body.

필수적인

adj.

lively, energetic, active

full of energy

After eating candy, he turned into a **vital** boy.

활력이 넘치는

19 reduce
rəˈd(y)o͞os
v.

condense, truncate, abridge

to make smaller in amount or size

The player's defeat in the game **reduced** his pride.

(규모,크기,양 등을) 줄이다(축소하다)

20. ramification
ˌraməfəˈkāSH(ə)n
n.

consequence, aftermath, outcome
the result of an action or event
*His actions are bound to have unexpected **ramifications**.*

파문, 영향

21. retain
rəˈtān
v.

maintain, preserve, remember
absorb and continue to hold
*Animal rights should be **retained** even during animal experimentation.*

유지(보유)하다

22. improvident
ˌimˈprävəd(ə)nt
adj.

wasteful, spendthrift, prodigal
not thinking ahead
*The **improvident** son returned home after spending all his money.*

앞날을 생각하지 않는, 돈을 되는 대로 쓰는

23. vigor
ˈvigər
n.

robustness, hardiness, stamina
physical strength and health
*He was full of **vigor** even after running the marathon.*

정력, 힘, 활력

24. synchronous
ˈsiNGkrənəs
adj.

coincident, contemporaneous
existing or happening at the same time
*The terrorist attacks were **synchronous** all over the world.*

동시 발생(존재)하는

25. wholesale
ˈhōlˌsāl
adj.

extensive, widespread, comprehensive
done on a wide scale
*The forest fire had a **wholesale** effect on the ecosystem.*

대량의, 다수의, 대규모의

26. worldly
ˈwərldlē
adj.

earthly, temporal, mortal
concerned with material values and life instead of the spiritual
*Christians should not seek **worldly** treasures, but instead those in heaven.*

세속적인, 속세의

SET 13

27 voluble
ˈvälyəbəl
adj.
- talkative, verbose, wordy
- talking fluently, or readily
- He is a **voluble** game-show host and keeps the crowd talkative.

입담이 좋다

28 barrage
bəˈrä(d)ZH
n.
- abundance, plethora, profusion
- a concentrated outpouring, such as questions or blows
- He received a **barrage** of punches from the boxer.

연속, 집중, 비처럼 쏟음

29 contaminate
kənˈtaməˌnāt
v.
- defile, debase, corrupt
- to make something impure by exposing it to a poisonous or polluting substance
- The air was **contaminated** by the factory's smoke.

오염시키다

30 proliferate
prəˈlifəˌrāt
v.
- multiply, burgeon, increase
- to increase quickly in numbers
- Science fiction movies **proliferated** during the twentieth century.

급증하다, (빠르게) 확산되다

31 persecute
ˈpərsəˌkyo͞ot
v.
- oppress, abuse, mistreat
- to treat someone with hostility because of their race, political, or religious beliefs
- Koreans were **persecuted** when Japan ruled over the country.

(인종,종교,정치적 이유로) 박해하다

32 bizarre
bəˈzär
adj.
- peculiar, outlandish, eccentric
- very strange or unusual
- Circus attractions include **bizarre** looking creatures from around the world.

기이한, 특이한

33 serendipity
ˌserənˈdipədē
n.
- fluke, luck, fortuity
- events that occur by chance in a happy or positive way
- My father winning the lottery was a stroke of **serendipity**.

뜻밖의 재미(기쁨)

34
amateur
ˈaməCHər
n.

| incompetent, beginner, novice |
| someone who is not skilled at a particular activity |
| *The **amateur** had trouble typing the commands for the online game.* |

비전문가, 아마추어

35
dissent
dəˈsent
n.

| disagreement, opposition, objection |
| an opinion that is different from the previous, common, or official one |
| *The Republicans expressed **dissent** while the Democrats favored the new law.* |

반대

36
critical
ˈkridək(ə)l
adj.

| censorious, condemning, disparaging |
| expressing negative comments |
| *Bloggers are usually **critical** when reviewing a restaurant.* |

비판적인, 비난하는

adj.

| crucial, vital, essential |
| having a crucial importance |
| *Temperature is **critical** when handling food.* |

대단히 중요한(중대한)

adj.

| grave, perilous, hazardous |
| having the possibility to become a disaster |
| *Since the fire is not out, the situation is still **critical**.* |

위태로운

37
immune
iˈmyoon
adj.

| resistant, unsusceptible, except |
| protected or excused from the effects of something or a responsibility |
| *After receiving the vaccine, the citizens are now **immune** to the virus.* |

…의 영향을 받지 않는, …에 면역이 된

38
deride
dəˈrīd
v.

| ridicule, mock, taunt |
| to make fun of |
| *Siblings will **deride** each other for no apparent reason.* |

조롱(조소)하다

SET 13

39 allege
əˈlej
v.

proclaim, assert, insinuate

to claim that someone has done something wrong without proof

*The woman **alleged** that the boy had stolen her money.*

(증거 없이) 혐의를 제기하다(주장하다)

40 mainstream
ˈmānˌstrēm
n.

dominant, general, normal

the popular trend in opinion, arts, or fashion

*Jazz was a style of music that had departed from the **mainstream**.*

(사상·견해 등의) 주류(대세)

41 offend
əˈfend
v.

affront, displease, exasperate

to make someone feel upset or annoyed

*I am sorry if what I said **offended** you.*

기분 상하게(불쾌하게) 하다

42 cherish
ˈCHeriSH
v.

treasure, adore, esteem

to protect and care for

*People will **cherish** their friends and family more than anything else.*

소중히 여기다, 아끼다

43 absurd
əbˈsərd
adj.

preposterous, ludicrous, ridiculous

incredibly unreasonable or inappropriate

*It is **absurd** that he wants a new car when he just purchased one last week.*

우스꽝스러운, 터무니없는

44 anarchy
ˈanərkē
n.

lawlessness, chaos, pandemonium

a state of disorder due to lack of authority

*There was continuous **anarchy** during the French Revolution.*

무정부 상태, 난장판

45 convulsive
kənˈvəlsiv
adj.

uncontrollable, shaking, twitching

producing or consisting of spasms

*Someone afflicted with the Parkinson's disease displays **convulsive** movement.*

경련성인, 발작적인

46. partake
pär'tāk
v.

engage, participate
to join in an activity
*Children wish to **partake** in games even if they do not understand the rules.*

참가하다

47. spontaneous
spän'tānēəs
adj.

unprompted, impulsive, impromptu
occurring from a sudden impulse without planning
*Our family decided to go on a **spontaneous** road trip.*

자발적인, 마음에서 우러난

48. burgeon
'bərjən
v.

proliferate, flourish, thrive
to grow or increase quickly
*The number of rabbits **burgeoned** when the pack of wolves moved elsewhere.*

급성장(급증)하다

49. stimulate
'stimyə,lāt
v.

motivate, rouse, kindle
to encourage interest or activity in a person or an animal
*The smell of food **stimulated** my roommate to get out of his room.*

자극(격려)하다, 활발하게 하다

50. elementary
,elə'ment(ə)rē
adj.

rudimentary, fundamental, primary
relating to the basic characteristics of a subject
*The number 101 in a university course signifies an **elementary** level lesson.*

기본적인, 근본적인

SET 13 TEST

1. The statue began to _____ after being exposed to the acid rain.

2. The turtle was _____ by his shell while he was racing the rabbit.

3. The president nominee was unable to comprehend the _____ of his loss.

4. The man was _____ with words after being stranded on an island alone for days.

5. Rats _____ within a short time and can infest a small village in just a few weeks.

6. The man was lying on the floor and exhibiting _____ motions which he could not control.

7. The _____ king awarded the peasant with an enormous plot of land.

8. Pinnochio was _____ when he sold his books to watch the play.

9. The council showed _____ by ignoring the man completely.

10. His classmates _____ him when he accidently farted in class.

---

1. corrode 2. hamper 3. ramification 4. voluble 5. proliferate 6. convulsive 7. benevolent 8. improvident 9. dissent 10. deride

11. It is _____ to think that she would go out with him after he did all those horrible things.

12. Adding and subtracting is an _____ math skill.

13. The fortune teller will _____ what will happen to her this year.

14. It is _____ to study before an exam.

15. The plastic bag was unable to _____ the garbage.

16. He was full of _____ after a good night's rest.

17. The boxing champion threw a _____ of punches at his opponent.

18. The boys went on a _____ trip to Las Vegas.

19. The new student wished to _____ on the group activity.

20. The girl was _____ with stealing the money from the car.

---

11. absurd 12. elementary 13. portend 14. vital 15. retain 16. vigor 17. barrage 18. spontaneous 19. partake 20. allege

SET 13

notes:

LEAD
SET 14
VOCABULARY

SET 14

01 suitable
ˈso͞odəb(ə)l
adj.

- acceptable, fit, appropriate
- appropriate for a particular situation, person, or purpose
- Those toys are not **suitable** for children under four.

적합한, 적절한, 알맞은

02 buoyant
ˈboiənt
adj.

- light, floating
- able to stay afloat
- The boat was **buoyant** and sailed across the sea.

(물에) 떠 있는(뜰 수 있는)

adj.

- cheery, lighthearted, carefree
- cheerful and optimistic
- Everyone left the party in a **buoyant** mood.

발랄한, 쾌활한

03 fluctuate
ˈfləkCHəˌwāt
v.

- vary, swing, waver
- to rise and fall irregularly in amount
- The exchange rate **fluctuated** during the economic depression.

변동(등락)을 거듭하다

04 incite
inˈsīt
v.

- encourage, kindle, instigate
- to encourage or stir up
- The crowd began to **incite** the fighter to finish off his opponent.

선동(조장)하다

05 jostle
ˈjäsəl
v.

- hustle, shove, thrust
- to struggle or compete
- The children **jostled** down the crowded stairs to get to the playground.

(많은 사람들 사이에서) 거칠게 밀치다(떠밀다)

06 manipulate
məˈnipyəˌlāt
v.

- operate, handle, utilize
- to handle or control something in a skillful way
- The scientist **manipulated** the buttons on the machine.

(사물을 능숙하게) 다루다

v.

- exploit, control, influence
- to control or influence someone or a situation in a clever manner
- The people were tricked and **manipulated** by the politician.

(흔히 교묘하고 부정직하게 사람·사물을) 조종하다

07 substantial
səbˈstan(t)SHəl
adj.

sizeable, meaningful, significant

a considerable size, importance, or worth

*The winner will get a **substantial** amount of cash.*

(양, 가치, 중요성이) 상당한

08 minimal
ˈminəməl
adj.

least, negligible, minimum

of a small amount or degree

*The effort is **minimal** compared to the large profit.*

아주 적은, 최소의

09 tradition
trəˈdiSH(ə)n
n.

custom, practice, convention

a custom or belief that has been passed down for many generations

*The **tradition** is for the bride to wear a white dress.*

전통

10 consist
kənˈsist
v.

comprise, contain, include

to be made up of

*The art gallery **consists** of 100 paintings.*

구성되다

11 timber
ˈtimbər
n.

wood, logs, firewood

wood to be used for building or carpentry

*The trees in this forest are grown to be used for **timber**.*

목재, 재목

12 access
ˈakˌses
n.

entrance, approach, entry

a way of entering a place

*I could not find the **access** to his house.*

(장소로의) 입장(접근)

v.

retrieve, acquire, examine

to obtain or examine

*The information can be **accessed** though the company's webpage.*

접근하다, 들어가다, 이용하다

13 onerous
ˈōnərəs
adj.

troublesome, inconvenient, burdensome

involving the difficulty of a task and how burdensome it is

*The worker found his new job increasingly **onerous**.*

아주 힘든; 부담되는, 짐스러운

SET 14

14 propose
prəˈpōz
v.

suggest, offer, submit

to put forward an idea or plan to be considered or discussed by others

*The United Nations **proposed** a new plan to fight back terrorism.*

(계획, 생각 등을) 제안(제의)하다

15 oppose
əˈpōz
v.

resist, defy, counter

to resist or refuse to follow a person or a system

*The children **opposed** going on a family trip.*

반대하다

16 skeptic
ˈskeptik
n.

cynic, pessimist, doubter

someone who is likely to question or doubt

*After reading the classic book, the **skeptic** frowned and sighed.*

회의론자, 의심 많은 사람

17 burden
ˈbərdn
n.

obligation, liability, trouble

a responsibility or misfortune which might cause hardship or anxiety

*Paying for college was a huge **burden** for the student.*

부담, 짐

18 implement
ˈimpləˌment
v.

execute, apply, administer

to put a decision or plan into effect

*After proposing the plan, it was up to her to **implement** the task.*

시행하다

19 authorize
ˈôTHəˌrīz
v.

sanction, endorse, warrant

to give permission or approve

*The president **authorized** the nuclear warheads to be launched.*

재가(인가)하다, 권한을 부여하다

20 expenditure
ikˈspendəCHər
n.

expense, cost, payment

the amount of money spent

*His ridiculous **expenditure** forced the parents to cancel his credit cards.*

지출; 비용, 경비

21. prophecy
'präfəsē
n.

forecast, prediction, prognosis

a prediction

*The fortune teller gave a **prophecy** that he will become rich.*

예언력

22. reality
rē'alədē
n.

truth, actuality, verity

something that is actually experienced or observed, rather than being ideal

*War veterans have difficulty facing **reality** when they come back home.*

현실(실제 상황)

23. haul
hôl
v.

tug, heave, pull

to pull or drag with effort

*The mule **hauled** the carriage full of vegetables.*

(아주 힘들여) 끌다

n.

booty, loot, plunder

a quantity of something that was taken illegally

*The pirates managed to get a good **haul** from the sunken ship.*

(훔치거나 불법적인 것의) 많은 양

24. skyrocket
'skī ˌräkət
v.

escalate, rise, arise

for a price, rate, or amount to increase very rapidly or steeply

*The cost of cryptocurrency **skyrocketed**.*

급등하다

25. surge
sərj
n.

outburst, rush, blast

a strong rush of an emotion

*The crowd felt a **surge** of pride when the soccer team scored the winning goal.*

(강한 감정이) 치밀어 오름

v.

escalate, leap, jump

to increase suddenly

*Stock prices **surged** when the new technology was announced.*

급증

26. plethora
'pleTHərə
n.

abundance, superfluity, profusion

a large amount of something

*The government has a **plethora** of services to help its citizens.*

과다, 과잉

SET 14

27. prolific
prəˈlifik
adj.

productive, fertile

in regards to a plant or animal, producing much fruit or offspring

*Pigs are **prolific** animals, since they can give birth to several offspring at once.*

다산하는, 열매를 많이 맺는

adj.

abundant, copious, rich

available in large numbers

*Bananas are a staple fruit in Southeast Asia and are exported in **prolific** numbers.*

풍부한

28. breadbasket
ˈbredˌbaskət
n.

a part of a region that produces grain for the rest of the area

*Central United States is the **breadbasket** of the country.*

곡창 지대

29. exponential
ˌekspəˈnen(t)SH(ə)l
adj.

ascending, expanding, mounting

rising or spreading at a steady, rapid pace

*The human population grows at an **exponential** rate.*

기하급수적인

30. commodity
kəˈmädədē
n.

asset, goods, material

something useful or valuable

*Water is the most important **commodity** for any human settlement.*

(유용한) 것

31. expert
ˈekˌspərt
n.

specialist, authority, adept

someone who has comprehensive knowledge or skill in a particular field

*Loki is an **expert** in trickery and mischief.*

전문가

32. refined
rəˈfīnd
adj.

cultured, civilized, stylish

cultured and elegant in appearance or manner

*After living in the city for many years, the farm boy became **refined**.*

교양(품위) 있는, 세련된, 고상한

33. inferior
ˌinˈfirēər
adj.

mediocre, unsatisfactory, deficient

low standard or quality

***Inferior** items were sold at the flea market.*

(…보다) 못한(질 낮은/열등한)

34. endeavor
ənˈdevər
n.

undertaking, attempt, effort

an effort to obtain a goal

*The villain's **endeavor** to conquer the world is pitiful.*

노력, 시도, 애씀

35. conclusive
kənˈklo͞osiv
adj.

incontestable, irrefutable, undeniable

serving to prove a case which cannot be denied

*The lawyer presented **conclusive** evidence which won the case.*

(의심할 여지가 없게) 결정적인(확실한)

36. fatigue
fəˈtēg
n.

tiredness, exhaustion, weariness

tiredness received from mental or physical output

*After working nonstop for 3 days, he was overcome with **fatigue**.*

피로

37. disorient
disˈôrēˌent
v.

astray, adrift, lost

to lose one's sense of direction

*The driver was **disoriented** for a few minutes after the car crash.*

방향 감각을 잃게 하다

38. diurnal
dīˈərnl
adj.

daytime

active during the day

*The lion is a **diurnal** hunter and stalks its prey during daytime.*

주행성의

39. nocturnal
näkˈtərnl
adj.

nighttime

active during the night

*The bat is a **nocturnal** predator and hunts during the night.*

야행성의

SET 14

40 faulty
ˈfôltē
adj.

damaged, defective, malfunctioning
not working properly because of imperfections
The airplane crashed due to a **faulty** landing gear.
흠(결함)이 있는, 불완전한

41 deviate
ˈdēvēˌāt
v.

digress, stray, veer
to depart from a set course
The cyclists had to **deviate** from their course because of an accident.
(일상, 예상 등을) 벗어나다

42 insomnia
inˈsämnēə
n.

sleeplessness, restlessness
inability to sleep
Because he suffers from **insomnia**, my friend takes medicine just to sleep.
불면증

43 disorder
ˌdisˈôrdər
n.

disarray, chaos, mess
a state of confusion
The country was in **disorder** after the civil war.
엉망, 어수선함

44 abuse
əˈbyo͞oz
v.

misuse, exploit, mishandle
to use something for a bad purpose
The police officer **abused** his power to get what he wanted.
남용(오용)하다

45 illusory
iˈlo͞osərē
adj.

delusional, imaginary, unreal
not real
He knew that the oasis he saw in the desert was **illusory**.
(실제가 아니라) 환상에 불과한

46 elastic
əˈlastik
adj.

adaptable, flexible, compliant
able to adjust and change
The **elastic** employee went around different departments to help those in need.
탄성의, 탄력 있는, 신축성 있는

47. revelation
ˌrevəˈlāSH(ə)n
n.

discovery, epiphany, announcement

a surprising and previously unknown information

*Da Vinci encountered several **revelations** which reshaped our way of thinking.*

폭로(된 사실)

48. synchronize
ˈsiNGkrəˌnīz
v.

adjust, harmonize, integrate

to occur at the same time or speed

*Before we begin our mission, let's **synchronize** our watches.*

동시에 발생하게(움직이게) 하다

49. crucial
ˈkro͞oSHəl
adj.

pivotal, key, determining

decisive or critical

*It is **crucial** that we do something about global warming.*

중대한, 결정적인

50. reflect
rəˈflekt
v.

consider, contemplate, review

to think deeply or carefully

*My son **reflected** on what he did wrong.*

고려하다(생각하다)

v.

return, mirror

to throw back heat, light, or sound without absorbing it

*The sun's light **reflected** off the building's windows.*

반사하다, 반향을 일으키다

SET 14 TEST

1. A _____ of basketball shoes were displayed on his wall like trophies.

2. Taking too much medication can create an _____ effect which can trick the person.

3. Archimedes had a _____ while taking a bath and shouted "Eureka!"

4. The currency exchange rate _____ throughout the day.

5. Remodeling a house is an _____ task.

6. A wedding planner will _____ whatever the bride and groom request.

7. The _____ she has on shopping is ridiculous.

8. Salt and pepper were once valuable _____.

9. I developed a _____ taste for meals after I stopped eating fast food.

10. Good luck on your future _____.

---

1. plethora 2. illusory 3. revelation 4. fluctuate 5. onerous 6. implement 7. expenditure 8. commodity 9. refined 10. endeavor

11. We had to return the computer to the store because it was _____.

12. The little boy was _____ after he recieved his gifts.

13. In fact, he recieved a _____ amount of cash.

14. The inspiring speech helped _____ the team to win the match.

15. Storms and hurricanes will _____ ships from their courses.

16. The dancers _____ their movements so that they moved as one.

17. The two players _____ with one another until finally one of them surrendered.

18. The evil queen _____ the king so that he did whatever she requested.

19. The _____ raised his hand when the speaker asked if anyone had questions.

20. The pirates celebrated and returned to shore after their recent _____.

11. faulty 12. buoyant 13. substantial 14. incite 15. deviate 16. synchronize 17. jostle 18. manipulate 19. skeptic 20. haul

SET 14

notes:

LEAD
SET 15
VOCABULARY

SET 15

01 spur
spər
v.

stimulate, encourage, motivate
to give an encouragement or incentive
*The extra allowance money **spurred** the child to study harder.*

원동력(자극제)이 되다, 자극하다

02 insist
inˈsist
v.

assert, protest, claim
to maintain or present a statement assertively
*The family **insisted** that the guest stay for dinner.*

(…해야 한다고) 고집하다(주장하다/우기다)

03 incorporate
inˈkôrpəˌrāt
v.

include, assimilate, integrate
to take in something as part of a whole
*The company has **incorporated** other small businesses under its name.*

(일부로) 포함하다

04 infrastructure
ˈinfrəˌstrək(t)SHər
n.

base, framework, groundwork
the basic structures and facilities needed in a society or business
*Buildings and roads are just some of the **infrastructures** needed in a city.*

사회(공공) 기반 시설

05 favor
ˈfāvər
n.

service, kindness, indulgence
an act of kindness usually beyond normal
*I have a **favor** to ask of you.*

친절한 행위, 은혜, 은전; 청, 부탁

v.

advocate, champion, endorse
to feel or show preference for
*For those who **favor** eating outside, put on your shoes.*

선호하다

06 via
ˈvīə
prep.

through, by, as a means
by means of
*The file was sent **via** email.*

(특정한 사람·시스템 등을) 통하여

07 topography
tə'pägrəfē
n.

contour, shape, layout

the natural and manmade features of an area

*The satellites in space produced an accurate **topography** of the unknown area.*

지형, 지형학

08 preeminent
prē'emənənt
adj.

greatest, foremost, chief

surpassing everything else

*Mr. Geller is the world's **preeminent** expert in dinosaur fossils.*

우위(상위)의; 현저한

09 imminent
'imənənt
adj.

impending, near, approaching

about to happen

*They were in **imminent** danger of being destroyed.*

금방이라도 닥칠 듯한, 목전의, 임박한

10 negligent
'neglǝjənt
adj.

careless, neglectful, lax

failing to properly care for something

*He was **negligent** while writing the essay, so there were many mistakes.*

부주의한, 조심성 없는

11 dimension
dī'men(t)SH(ə)n
n.

measurement, size, extent

a measurement, such as length, depth, or height

*What is the **dimension** of the living room?*

(공간의) 크기

12 estimate
'estə,māt
v.

approximate, guess

roughly calculate or determine the value or number

*The judges **estimate** that the home team will win by three points.*

추산(추정)하다

13 confront
kən'frənt
v.

challenge, defy, oppose

to meet someone or something with hostility or accusation

*The brave citizen **confronted** the robbers as they were leaving the bank.*

(위험한 상황 등에) 정면으로 부딪치다(마주치다)

SET 15

14 barren
'berən
adj.

unproductive, infertile, sterile

for a land to be in poor condition to produce vegetation

*Not having received rain for decades, the land quickly became **barren**.*

열매(씨)가 안 열리는

15 arable
'erəb(ə)l
adj.

fertile, productive, lush

for a land to be used or suitable to grow crops

*The artificial rain made the farmland **arable** again.*

곡식을 경작하는

16 distant
'distənt
adj.

remote, abroad, far

far away in space or time

*There are still undiscovered planets in the **distant** part of our galaxy.*

먼, (멀리) 떨어져 있는

17 increment
'iNGkrəmənt
n.

gain, augmentation, supplement

an increase in fixed proportions

*The employees would receive an **increment** of $100 per month on their salaries.*

(수·양의) 증가

18 obstruct
əb'strəkt
v.

block, barricade, bar

to prevent or hinder someone or something, usually from motion

*The construction crew were **obstructing** the road for several hours.*

(일의 진행 등을) 방해하다

19 sufficient
sə'fiSHənt
adj.

enough, adequate

enough; adequate

*We had **sufficient** time to see everything at the museum.*

충분한

20 fracture
'frak(t)SHər
v.

snap, crack, smash

to break something

*The player **fractured** his leg during the soccer game.*

골절이 되다(되게 하다), 파열(균열)되다(시키다)

21. erode
ə'rōd
v.

abrade, crumble, dissolve

to gradually destroy

*The waves **eroded** the rocky cliffs.*

(서서히) 약화시키다(무너뜨리다)

22. mammoth
'maməTH
adj.

enormous, gigantic, colossal

huge

*The **mammoth** building towered over New York City.*

거대한, 엄청난

23. misery
'miz(ə)rē
n.

suffering, affliction, unhappiness

a state of distress and discomfort

*After breaking up with her boyfriend, the girl cried in **misery**.*

(정신적,육체적으로 심한) 고통

24. distressed
də'strest
adj.

afflicted, agitated, distraught

suffering from anxiety, pain, or sorrow

*He was **distressed** from having to break up with his girlfriend.*

(심리적으로) 괴로워(고통스러워) 하는

25. humanitarian
(h)yoō,manə'terēən
adj.

compassionate, altruistic, generous

concerned with or attempting to promote human well-being

*The UN sent food and medicine with **humanitarian** intention.*

인도주의적인, 인도주의의

26. suffrage
'səfrij
n.

ballot, vote, voice

the right to vote

*For many years, people have worked hard for women's **suffrage**.*

투표권, 선거권, 참정권

27. meddle
'medl
v.

intrude, pry, intervene

to interfere with something that is not their concern

*Do not **meddle** in your neighbor's business.*

(남의 일에) 간섭하다(참견하다/끼어들다)

SET 15

28 promote
prə'mōt
v.

assist, advocate, endorse
to actively support or encourage
*The mayor **promoted** the movie because it was filmed in his city.*

홍보하다

v.

upgrade, elevate, raise
to advance someone to a higher rank
*The floor manager was **promoted** to a store supervisor.*

승진(진급)시키다

29 recognize
'rekəg,nīz
v.

identify, know, remember
to identify someone or something
*I **recognized** her even without the makeup.*

알아보다(알다)

v.

acknowledge, accept, admit
to acknowledge the existence or validity
*The team **recognized** their defeat when the buzzer blew.*

인정(인식)하다

30 contribute
kən'tribyoōt
v.

donate, present, provide
to give something to help
*The rich elderly couple **contribute** money to the orphanage every year.*

기부(기증)하다

31 scope
skōp
n.

range, extent, jurisdiction
the extent of an area or subject matter which is relevant
*The detectives widened the **scope** of their investigation.*

범위

v.

scan, examine, browse
to look at carefully
*The detectives **scoped** the crime scene for any clues.*

샅샅이(자세히) 살피다

32 mask
mask
v.

conceal, cloak, hide
to cover something from view
*She put on makeup to **mask** the scar on her chin.*

가리다(감추다)

33. offspring
'ôf،spriNG
n.

progeny, children, youngsters

a person's child or children

*Sometimes the **offspring** may look nothing like the parents.*

자식

34. aberrant
'abərənt
adj.

deviant, abnormal, atypical

stepping away from a normal standard

*The **aberrant** child had trouble making friends.*

도리를 벗어난, 일탈적인

35. devote
də'vōt
v.

commit, dedicate, allot

to give everything or a large portion of one's time and resource for something

*Korean mothers tend to **devote** themselves to their children.*

(…에) 바치다, 쏟다, 기울이다, 충당하다

36. illegitimate
،ilə'jidəmət
adj.

illegal, illicit, unlawful

not authorized by law

*Separating the migrant parents from their children was an **illegitimate** act.*

불법의

37. loyal
'loi(ə)l
adj.

faithful, devoted, true

giving or showing support or allegiance to a person or a group

*The Roman legion was more **loyal** to their general than the ruler.*

충실한, 충성스러운

38. royal
'roi(ə)l
adj.

regal, sovereign, monarchial

related to the king or queen

*The **royal** palace is heavily secured by guards.*

제왕의, 국왕의

39. delegate
'deləgət
n.

representative, envoy, emissary

someone sent or allowed to represent others

*The **delegate** from Spain presented his case.*

대표

v.

assign, entrust, give

to give a task or responsibility to another

*The team leader **delegated** responsibilities to the rest of the group.*

(권한·업무 등을) 위임하다

SET 15

40 patriot
ˈpātrēət
n.

nationalist, loyalist, chauvinist

one who passionately supports their country

*An Jung-geun is a true **patriot** of Korea.*

애국자

---

41 draft
draft
v.

devise, forge, outline

to prepare a preliminary version of a document

*Thomas Jefferson was asked to **draft** the Declaration of Independence.*

원고, 초안을 만들다

v.

recruit, enlist, enroll

to be recruited for military service

*Young men were **drafted** to fight during the Vietnam War.*

입대하다; 입대시키다, 징집(모병)하다

n.

breeze, current, wind

a current of cool air

*A **draft** entered the room when she opened the window.*

찬바람

---

42 diplomacy
dəˈplōməsē
n.

negotiation, politics, tact

the actions of government officials for negotiations between nations

*Any form of **diplomacy** was scrapped when the opposing nation fired its missile.*

(국가간의) 외교(술)

---

43 reputation
ˌrepyəˈtāSH(ə)n
n.

stature, image, character

a widespread belief that someone or something has a particular characteristic

*Oxford University's **reputation** in education makes it a top school.*

평판, 명성

---

44 quarrel
ˈkwôrəl
n.

dispute, squabble, conflict

an intense argument or disagreement

*A family **quarrel** usually occurs when they meet during lunar new year.*

(말)다툼(언쟁/싸움)

45. liberty
'libərdē
n.

freedom, independence, autonomy

the condition of being free in regards to one's life, behavior or political views

*Every citizen should be entitled to life, **liberty**, and the pursuit of happiness.*

자유

46. repute
rə'pyoōt
v.

thought, rumored, considered

to consider or regard as being a particular thing

*He is **reputed** to earn millions of dollars a year.*

(~을 ~로) 여기다(생각하다)

n.

reputation, name, character

the opinion generally held of someone or something

*His **repute** will decrease if he does not donate to charity when he is rich.*

평판, 명성

47. garment
'gärmənt
n.

outfit, clothing, costume

clothing

*Her **garments** were scattered all over the floor.*

의복, 옷

48. basis
'bāsəs
n.

premise, essence, foundation

the support or foundation of an idea, argument, or process

*What is the **basis** of your accusation?*

기준 (단위)

49. ratify
'radə,fī
v.

sanction, endorse, confirm

to sign or give formal consent to a document

*The treaty was **ratified** when the two nations signed the document.*

비준(재가)하다

50. margin
'märjən
n.

gap, difference, leeway

the amount allowed or available beyond what is required

*The home team won by a ten point **margin**.*

(시간, 득표 수 등의) 차이(차)

SET 15 CROSSWORD PUZZLE

Across

3. to gradually destroy
5. an intense argument or disagreement
8. to break something
11. to take in something as part of a whole
13. about to happen
14. to give a task or responsibility to another
15. failing to properly care for something

Down

1. to look at carefully
2. to consider or regard as being a particular thing
4. an increase in fixed proportions
6. to sign or give formal consent to a document
7. the right to vote
9. a state of distress and discomfort
10. surpassing everything else
12. stepping away from a normal standard

1. scope 2. repute 4. increment 6. ratify 7. suffrage 9. misery 10. preeminent 12. aberrant
3. erode 5. quarrel 8. fracture 11. incorporate 13. imminent 14. delegate 15. negligent

LEAD
SET 16
VOCABULARY

SET 16

01 provision
prəˈviZHən
n.
- services, amenities, equipment
- an amount or thing supplied or provided
- *The government offers minimal social **provisions**.*

공급, 제공

02 patent
ˈpatn
n.
- copyright, license, permit
- a license giving the right or title for a given time
- *He filed a **patent** after he invented the new machine.*

특허권(증)

adj.
- obvious, clear, apparent
- easily recognizable
- *He was smiling with **patent** insincerity when they shook hands.*

분명한(명백한)

03 guide
gīd
n.
- escort, conductor, usher
- someone who advises or leads the way to others
- *He will be our **guide** for the rest of the trip.*

안내(서)(가이드)

v.
- lead, direct, show
- to show or point the way
- *He **guided** the group to the dinosaur exhibit in the museum.*

안내하여 데려가다(보여주다)

04 engrave
inˈgrāv
v.
- carve, inscribe, chisel
- to cut or carve something on the surface of an object
- *The famous athlete **engraved** his name on his statue.*

(나무,돌,쇠붙이 등에) 새기다

05 declare
diˈkler
v.
- proclaim, announce, state
- to say something in a serious manner
- *The leader **declared** that their country would perish soon.*

선언(선포/공표)하다

06 immerse
i'mərs
v.

- submerge, plunge, sink
- to submerge in liquid
- *Immerse the dirty clothes in water for an hour to remove the stain.*

(액체 속에) 담그다

v.
- engross, engage, involve
- to get involved deeply in a particular activity or interest
- *My wife spends day and night immersed in her work.*

~에 몰두하다/몰두하게 만들다

07 inception
in'sepSH(ə)n
v.

- establishment, foundation, initiation
- the starting point of an activity or institution
- *The inception of an idea starts within a dream.*

(단체, 기관 등의) 시작(개시)

08 typical
'tipik(ə)l
adj.

- representative, archetypal, model
- having the distinctive characteristics of a specific person or thing
- *A typical day starts waking up at 8 in the morning.*

전형적인, 대표적인

09 dense
dens
adj.

- thick, heavy, opaque
- closely compacted
- *The dense cloud approached the city with torrential rain.*

짙은(자욱한)

adj.
- stupid, foolish, slow
- being stupid
- *I think you are dense if you cannot understand what I am saying.*

멍청한

10 propagate
'präpə,gāt
v.

- disseminate, distribute, spread
- to spread and promote something widely
- *The Americans propagated the idea that the natives were savages.*

(사상, 신조, 정보를) 전파(선전)하다

11 usher
'əSHər
v.

- escort, assist, accompany
- to show or guide someone to a place
- *The waitress ushered our family to our table.*

안내하다

SET 16

12 interject
ˌin(t)ərˈjekt
v.

interpose, interrupt, interpolate
to say something suddenly in order to interrupt
The student **interjected** the professor's lesson with random questions.

말참견을 하다

13 radical
ˈradək(ə)l
adj.

revolutionary, progressive, reformist
supporting a complete political or social change
His ideas were too **radical** for the conservative group.

급진적인, 과격한

14 fusion
ˈfyo͞oZHən
n.

bonding, joining, merging
the process or result of two or more things joining together
The **fusion** of two elements required a massive amount of energy.

융합, 결합

15 peer
pir
v.

squint, peep, pry
to look carefully or with difficulty
The child **peered** through the crack to see the burglar's face.

유심히 보다

n.

equal, rival, fellow
someone who is the same age or status as another particular person
He received much respect from his academic **peers**.

(나이·신분이 같거나 비슷한) 또래(동배)

16 laud
lôd
v.

extol, acclaim, commend
to praise someone for their accomplishments
The people **lauded** Superman for saving their lives.

칭찬하다

17 synthesis
ˈsinTHəsəs
n.

combination, fusion, merging
the combination of several things to form something else
Plants create energy and oxygen from the **synthesis** of water and carbon dioxide.

종합, 통합

18. unprecedented
/ˌənˈpresəd(ə)n(t)əd/
adj.

uncommon, unusual, abnormal

never done; unaware

*The boy's behavior was **unprecedented**, so his parents became worried.*

전례없는

19. assess
/əˈses/
v.

evaluate, judge, gauge

to evaluate or guess the nature, ability, or characteristic of

*The interviewers must **assess** the abilities of the interviewees.*

(가치, 양을) 평가(사정)하다

20. adherent
/adˈhirənt/
n.

supporter, defender, advocate

one who supports a specific party, person, or ideas

*My father is a strong **adherent** of capitalism.*

(정당, 사상 등의) 지지자

21. obsolete
/ˌäbsəˈlēt/
adj.

outdated, antiquated, archaic

no longer made or used

*The compact disc player is an **obsolete** device.*

더 이상 쓸모가 없는, 한물간, 구식의

22. notion
/ˈnōSH(ə)n/
n.

concept, opinion, idea

an idea or belief about something

*They each had very different **notions** about the roles they had.*

개념, 관념, 생각

23. invaluable
/inˈvaly(oo)əb(ə)l/
adj.

crucial, vital, irreplaceable

extremely useful

*The spy provided an **invaluable** source of information.*

매우 유용한, 귀중한

24. avert
/əˈvərt/
v.

avoid, forestall, preclude

to prevent or stop

*The heroes were able to **avert** the crime.*

방지하다, 피하다

SET 16

25 **dainty**
'dān(t)ē
adj.

delicate, refined, elegant
delicate in build or movement
*The ballerina danced with a **dainty** step during the concert.*
앙증맞은

26 **elaborate**
ə'lab(ə)rət
adj.

complicated, intricate, complex
involving many complex parts or details
*The thieves had an **elaborate** plan to steal the money from the vault.*
정교한, 정성(공)을 들인

27 **sole**
sōl
adj.

only, single, lone
one and only
*My **sole** goal is to eat as much as I can within one hour.*
유일한, 단 하나의

28 **eager**
'ēgər
adj.

anxious, longing, yearning
desire to do or have something
*The father was **eager** to see his son, whom he had not seen for years.*
열렬한, 간절히 바라는, 열심인

29 **embellish**
əm'beliSH
v.

adorn, ornament, furnish
to make something more appealing by adding details or features
*The family **embellished** the tree with lights and decorations.*
장식하다, 꾸미다

30 **relevant**
'reləvənt
adj.

pertinent, applicable, apposite
closely related to what is done or considered
*Is this **relevant** to what we are doing now?*
관련 있는, 적절한

31 **absorb**
əb'zôrb
v.

soak up, suck up
to take in or soak up
*The mop **absorbed** the water on the floor.*
흡수하다(빨아들이다)

v.

assimilate, digest, comprehend
to take in and understand information completely
*The student **absorbed** the lesson taught by the professor.*
(정보를) 받아들이다

32 pace
pās
n.

speed, rate, velocity

consistent and continuous speed at which someone or something moves or works

*Everyone works at their own **pace** in the factory.*

속도

33 forbid
fərˈbid
v.

prohibit, band, outlaw

to not allow something

*Korean fast food restaurants **forbid** diners to throw away their trash mixed with food and plastic.*

금(지)하다

34 divinity
dəˈvinədē
n.

godliness, deity, holiness

the state of being god-like

*Christ's **divinity** is unquestioned in the Christian faith.*

신성

35 heterogeneous
ˌhedərəˈjēnēəs
adj.

diverse, assorted, myriad

various in character or content

*Comic book collectors have a large and **heterogeneous** collection of books.*

여러 다른 종류들로 이뤄진

36 impartial
imˈpärSHəl
adj.

unbiased, neutral, nonpartisan

fair and just

*A judge must be **impartial** in every court case.*

공정한

37 peculiar
pəˈkyoolyər
adj.

distinctive, characteristic, distinguishing

special; particular

*His **peculiar** accent grabbed everyone's attention.*

특유한(고유한/독특한)

38 tolerable
ˈtäl(ə)rəb(ə)l
adj.

bearable, endurable, admissible

able to be endured

*The sound he made while chewing his food was **tolerable**.*

참을 수 있는, 견딜 만한

SET 16

39. taciturn
'tasə,tərn
adj.

uncommunicative, quiet, reticent

reserved in speech; saying little

*Everyone remained **taciturn** while the coffin was being buried in the ground.*

(성격이) 뚱한(말수가 적은/무뚝뚝한)

40. restful
'res(t)fəl
adj.

relaxing, tranquil, soothing

having a quiet and peaceful quality

*A vacation in the Bahamas sounds very **restful**.*

(마음이) 편안한, 평화로운

41. stature
'staCHər
n.

reputation, prestige, status

reputation gained by ability or success

*The politician was a man of important **stature**.*

지명도, 위상

42. adore
ə'dô(ə)r
v.

love, cherish, treasure

to love and respect deeply

*It would be strange if pet owners **adored** their dog more than their children.*

흠모(사모)하다

43. sinister
'sinistər
adj.

menacing, ominous, forbidding

giving the impression that something evil or harmful is about to occur

*The villain gave a **sinister** laugh.*

사악한, 해로운; 불길한

44. convention
kən'ven(t)SH(ə)n
n.

custom, tradition, norm

an act that is considered acceptable to most members of society

*When meeting someone for the first time, the **convention** is to shake hands.*

관습, 관례

assembly, summit, gathering

a large meeting or conference

*A **convention** was held amongst twenty nations.*

대회(협의회)

45. menace
'menəs
n.

danger, peril, threat

someone or something that is likely to cause harm

Dennis the **menace** is a troublemaker in the neighborhood.

위협적인(위험한) 존재

46. gallant
'galənt
adj.

courageous, valiant, valorous

brave; heroic

The **gallant** knight plunged his sword into the dragon's heart.

용감한(용맹한)

47. connate
'känāt
adj.

innate, inborn, inherent

existing in a person or thing from birth

Humanity's violent tendencies are **connate**.

타고난, 선천적인

48. ecumenical
ˌekyəˈmenək(ə)l
adj.

universal, nondenominational, nonsectarian

representing different number of Christian Churches

A **ecumenical** council is made of different leaders to discuss religious matters.

기독교적인, 세계 교회 주의의

49. avocation
ˌavəˈkāSH(ə)n
n.

pastime, recreation, amusement

a hobby or minor job

Although he is a doctor, his **avocation** at night is a bartender.

취미, 여가 활동

50. merchant
'mərCHənt
n.

trader, dealer, wholesaler

a person or company that supplies merchandise to a specific trade

Merchants traveled between Asia and Europe through the Silk Road.

상인, (특히) 무역상

SET 16 TEST

1. The soccer fans were _____ in the match with only one minute left in the game.

2. The bat's screech _____ inside the cave.

3. Once a year, my company _____ the employees and critiques their performance.

4. The pager is an _____ form of communication.

5. The fight was _____ when the teacher walked into the room.

6. The cake was _____ with flowers and ribbons.

7. The father _____ his daughter from going out so late at night.

8. It is important for parents to be _____ when their children get into an argument.

9. The _____ citizen prevented the criminals from escaping.

10. The guest wrote a list of _____ he would require during his stay.

---

1. immerse 2. propagate 3. assess 4. obsolete 5. avert
6. embellish 7. forbid 8. impartial 9. gallant 10. provision

11. The man was so _____ that the group had to explain the rules of the game several times.

12. The hotel employees _____ the guests into their seats.

13. His ideas were _____ and were not welcomed by the conservative group.

14. Soldiers are _____ for their bravery and service with medals.

15. Wearing colorful clothes to a funeral is _____.

16. Many of my friends are _____ of Black Lives Matter.

17. The plastic figure of the robot is _____, so please do not remove it from its case.

18. Lucifer wished to achieve the state of _____ so he was banished from the heavens.

19. The husband was no longer _____ to the sounds his wife made while sleeping.

20. The Joker gave a _____ smile as he was put in prison.

---

11. dense   16. adherent
12. usher   17. dainty
13. radical   18. divinity
14. laud   19. tolerable
15. unprecedented   20. sinister

SET 16

notes:

LEAD
SET 17
VOCABULARY

SET 17

01 vivid
'vivid
adj.

- graphic, realistic, lucid
- creating powerful feelings or strong mental images
- *Memories of the previous night were still **vivid**.*

생생한

adj.
- bright, colorful, glowing
- intensely bright or deep color
- *The color of blood is a **vivid** red.*

선명한, 강렬한

02 derive
də'rīv
v.

- acquire, procure, attain
- to obtain something from a source
- *The family **derived** money from the insurance company.*

~에서 ~을 얻다

03 virtually
'vərCH(oo)əlē
adv.

- practically, almost, essentially
- nearly; almost
- *The company became **virtually** bankrupt.*

사실상, 거의

04 mandatory
'mandə,tôrē
adj.

- obligatory, compulsory, required
- required by rules or laws
- *Wearing helmets is **mandatory** when riding motorcycles.*

법에 정해진, 의무적인

05 viable
'vīəb(ə)l
adj.

- feasible, practical, useable
- able to function successfully
- *The new device was **viable** for time travel.*

실행 가능한, 성공할 수 있는

06 reserve
rə'zərv
v.

- keep, save, hold
- to put aside for future use
- *I cut the bread in two and **reserved** the other half.*

보유하다

v.
- book, order, arrange
- to arrange something to be kept for the use of a specific person in later time
- *My friend helped us **reserve** a table for the weekend.*

예약하다

07 tolerate
'tälə,rāt
v.

endure, bear, stand

to accept or endure someone or something unpleasant

*How are you able to **tolerate** the sound made by your neighbors?*

(불쾌한 일 등을) 참다

08 venture
'ven(t)SHər
n.

pursuit, operation, scheme

a risky undertaking

*The military launched a last minute **venture**.*

모험

v.

travel, journey, move

to go or do something that may be unpleasant

*The military **ventured** into the enemy territory.*

(위험을 무릅쓰고 모험하듯) 가다

09 vertical
'vərdək(ə)l
adj.

upright, erect, perpendicular

at a right angle in relations to a horizontal plane

*The rock climber started to climb the **vertical** wall.*

수직의, 세로의

10 horizontal
ˌhôrə'zän(t)l
adj.

parallel, level, even

parallel to a horizontal plane

*The climber rested on the **horizontal** flat rock.*

수평(선)의, 가로의

11 expose
ik'spōz
v.

uncover, reveal, disclose

to reveal the true nature of someone or something

*The politician was **exposed** as a liar and a cheater.*

(보통 때는 가려져 있는 것을) 드러내다

12 relative
'relədiv
adj.

comparative, respective, correlative

considered in relation or in proportion to something else

*The **relative** effectiveness of the method is not yet known.*

비교상의, 상대적인

13 corroborate
kə'räbə,rāt
v.

endorse, ratify, verify

to confirm or give support to someone or something

*The witness **corroborated** the victim's account of the story.*

제공하다, 확증(입증)하다

SET 17

14 infer
in'fər
v.

deduce, conclude, reason
to deduce or confirm from details and logic
Based on these facts, we can **infer** that he is guilty.
추론하다

15 noxious
'näkSHəs
adj.

toxic, deadly, dangerous
harmful or poisonous
The workers were harmed by the **noxious** fumes.
유독한, 유해한

16 reminiscent
‚remə'nis(ə)nt
adj.

evocative, redolent, nostalgic
tending to remind the person of something
The children playing in the park was **reminiscent** of my childhood.
(특히 흐뭇한 마음으로) 추억에 잠긴 듯한

17 dominate
'dämə‚nāt
v.

influence, command, subjugate
to have a commanding influence over someone or something
Samsung and LG **dominate** the electronic market in South Korea.
지배(군림)하다

18 replica
'repləkə
n.

copy, duplicate, dummy
an exact copy of something
This miniature figure is the exact **replica** of the Statue of Liberty.
복제품, 모형

19 inaugurate
i'nôg(y)ə‚rāt
v.

initiate, institute, launch
to start or introduce something new
The newly elected president **inaugurated** a new policy of trade.
(새로운 발전, 중요한 변화의) 개시를 알리다

v.

instate, induct, ordain
to formally admit someone to public office
The new president will be **inaugurated** next month.
취임하게 하다

20. commemorate
kəˈmeməˌrāt
v.

celebrate, honor, salute

to celebrate an event or person by doing or constructing something

*Their bravery was **commemorated** in a song.*

(중요 인물, 사건을) 기념하다

21. contrary
ˈkäntrerē
adj.

contradictory, conflicting, opposing

opposite in meaning, direction, or nature

***Contrary** to what many people think, he is actually a gentleman.*

~와는 다른(반대되는)

22. denote
dəˈnōt
v.

designate, indicate, signify

to show or indicate

*The symbol of a heart **denotes** love in many cultures.*

의미(뜻)하다, 나타내다

23. ornate
ôrˈnāt
adj.

elaborate, embellished, adorned

to be decorated with complex patterns

*The flag was **ornate** with different symbols and colors.*

화려하게 장식된

24. express
ikˈspres
v.

communicate, convey, demonstrate

to deliver a thought or feeling by words or gestures

*The husband **expressed** his love to his wife by giving her gifts.*

나타내다, 표(현)하다

adj.

rapid, swift, brisk

high speed

***Express** trains will transport passengers while making less stops.*

급행의, 신속한

25. crest
krest
n.

summit, peak, pinnacle

the top of a hill or a mountain

*The climbers reached the **crest** of the mountain.*

꼭대기(정상)

SET 17

26 custom
ˈkəstəm
n.

tradition, practice, convention

a tradition or an accepted behavior that is appropriate for that specific society, place, or time

It is **custom** to greet guests at the door.

관습, 풍습

27 interrelate
ˌin(t)ərəˈlāt
v.

associate, connect, link

to connect or relate to another

Each part of the watch **interrelates** with the other parts, allowing the watch to move.

밀접한 연관을 갖다(갖게 하다)

28 catapult
ˈkadəˌpəlt
v.

launch, hurl, fling

to throw or launch something

The athlete **catapulted** the ball across the field.

내던지다(내던져지다)

29 dislodge
disˈläj
v.

remove, displace, eject

to force out of position

The farmer used a shovel to **dislodge** the rocks on the ground.

(억지로 치거나 해서) 제자리를 벗어나게 만들다

30 persist
pərˈsist
v.

persevere, continue, last

to continue to exist

The adolescent **persisted** in staying awake even past his bed time.

(없어지지 않고) 계속(지속)되다

31 conjecture
kənˈjekCHər
n.

speculation, surmise, guess

an opinion or conclusion made from the basis of incomplete information

Scientists continuously make **conjectures** on everyday phenomena.

추측(한 내용)

32 consensus
kənˈsensəs
n.

concord, consent, agreement

a general agreement

The congressmen reached a **consensus** on the new law.

의견 일치, 합의

33. plumage
'plōomij
n.

feathers

a bird's feathers

*A male peacock's **plumage** is a magnificent showcase of colors.*

깃털

34. freight
frāt
n.

cargo, load, shipment

goods transported in bulk by airplane, ship, train, or truck

*With the development of the airplane, more **freight** have been transported overseas.*

화물, 화물 운송

35. futile
'fyōodl
adj.

fruitless, vain, ineffective

not able to produce a useful outcome

*It is **futile** to expect a hormone-raging teenager to act mature.*

헛된, 소용없는

36. aftermath
'aftər,maTH
n.

repercussions, byproduct, fallout

the results or aftereffects of an unpleasant event

*The **aftermath** of the war saw the people homeless and destitute.*

(전쟁,사고 등의) 여파(후유증)

37. vow
vou
n.

oath, pledge, covenant

a solemn promise

*During a wedding ceremony, the husband and wife exchange **vows**.*

맹세, 서약

38. outrage
'out,rāj
v.

enrage, infuriate, anger

to show anger or shock towards someone

*My father was **outraged** when someone scratched his car.*

격분(격노)하게 만들다

39. obligation
,äblə'gāSH(ə)n
n.

duty, commitment, responsibility

an act to which a person is morally or legally responsible for

*Parents have the **obligation** of taking care of their children until they are of age.*

(법적,도의적) 의무(가 있음)

SET 17 · 209

SET 17

40 humiliate
(h)yoo′mile̵,āt
v.
embarrass, shame, demean
to make someone feel ashamed and foolish
*Standup comedians love to **humiliate** members of the audience.*
굴욕감을 주다

41 abolition
,abə′liSH(ə)n
n.
termination, eradication, annulment
the act of ending a system, practice, or institution
*Abraham Lincoln worked for the **abolition** of slavery.*
(법률,제도,조직의) 폐지

42 permeate
′pərmē,āt
v.
pervade, saturate, imbue
to spread throughout
*The aroma of the perfume **permeated** the air.*
스며들다, 침투하다

43 revenue
′revə,n(y)oo
n.
earning, profit, yield
income
*Apple earns billions in **revenue** each year.*
수익

44 postulate
′päsCHə,lāt
v.
hypothesize, presume, theorize
to suggest or assume the fact or truth of something as a basis for reasoning or arguing
*Darwin's theory **postulate** that animals evolve by adapting to their environment.*
상정하다

45 procreate
′prōkrē,āt
v.
breed, reproduce, multiply
to reproduce
*Most organisms require a male and female subject to **procreate**.*
아이(새끼)를 낳다

46 drift
drift
n.
shift, flow, movement
a steady slow movement from one location to another
*Continents **drift** slowly so that the surface of our planet continuously changes.*
이동(추이)

47 cognizance
ˈkägnəzəns
n.

consciousness, notice, realization

knowledge or awareness

*All living organisms show **cognizance**, even trees and flowers.*

인지, 이해

48 obsess
əbˈses
v.

preoccupy, dominate, engross

to preoccupy the thoughts, feelings, or desires of a person

*Teenagers in Korea are **obsessed** with celebrities.*

사로잡다, … 생각만 하게(…에 집착하게) 하다

49 renounce
rəˈnouns
v.

repudiate, disavow, forsake

to formally announce one's abandonment of something

*The irresponsible prince **renounced** his claim to the throne.*

포기(단념)하다, 포기를 선언하다

50 covet
ˈkəvət
v.

crave, envy, fancy

to desire to have something

*It is healthy to not **covet** what your neighbor has.*

(특히 남의 물건을) 탐내다, 갈망하다

SET 17 TEST

1. If one starts to _____, it may lead to theft.

2. Scientists _____ that the dinosaurs became extinct due to a change in climate.

3. The _____ of child labor is yet to be seen in certain parts of the world.

4. It was _____ to compete in the marathon with his broken toe.

5. The man proposed to the woman at the _____ of the hill.

6. The dress was _____ with various colors and designs.

7. The song playing on the radio was _____ of my college years.

8. Edison _____ his theories with multiple experiments and tests.

9. Lewis and Clark _____ into the uncharted territory of the northwest.

10. NASA came up with a _____ solution to send mankind into space.

---

1. covet   2. postulate   3. abolition   4. futile   5. crest
6. ornate   7. reminiscent   8. corroborate   9. venture   10. viable

11. The dream he had the previous night was still _____.

12. The CEO _____ his position when he was caught evading taxes.

13. It is important to have a steady source of _____ to support a family.

14. Some people consider helping the poor as an _____.

15. The _____ of the war left both sides devastated.

16. The jury reached a _____ on the case.

17. The worker was able to _____ the metal part with a hammer.

18. Countries have different _____ when it comes to greeting a person.

19. The professor _____ the importance of the lesson by putting a star on top.

20. It is _____ for a person to have a driver's license before driving a car.

11. vivid   12. renounce   13. revenue   14. obligation   15. aftermath
16. consensus   17. dislodge   18. custom   19. denote   20. mandatory

SET 17

notes:

LEAD
SET 18
VOCABULARY

SET 18

01 accretion
əˈkrēSH(ə)n
n.

extension, growth, supplement
something formed or added by steady growth or increase
The **accretion** of sediment formed the riverbank.
(서서히 막처럼 생기는) 부착물

02 prevail
prəˈvāl
v.

win, triumph, conquer
to be more powerful than the other
The red team **prevailed** over the blue team in basketball.
승리하다(이기다)

03 propel
prəˈpel
v.

drive, force, prompt
to move into a particular situation
The airplane is **propelled** by two turbine engines.
(몰거나 밀거나 해서) 나아가게 하다

04 assert
əˈsərt
v.

declare, claim, contend
to state a fact or belief forcefully
The company **asserts** that no one will be fired.
주장하다

05 ideal
īˈdē(ə)l
adj.

perfect, exemplary, archetypal
fulfilling one's idea of what is perfect
Please describe your **ideal** boyfriend.
이상적인, 가장 알맞은, 완벽한

06 cessation
seˈsāSH(ə)n
n.

termination, end, suspension
being brought to a stop
There was a **cessation** of battles when the two leaders made peace.
중단, 중지

07 tendency
ˈtendənsē
n.

propensity, likelihood, disposition
an inclination towards a trait or behavior
He had a **tendency** to stutter whenever he gave a presentation.
성향, 기질; 경향

216 · LEAD VOCABULARY

08 simulate
ˈsimyəˌlāt
v.

- imitate, replicate, mimic
- to copy the appearance or trait of something
- Younger siblings tend to **simulate** the behavior of their older sibling.

모방하다, 흉내내다

09 progress
ˈprägres
n.

- progression, advance, headway
- forward movement
- Scientists have made great **progress** in chemical engineering.

진전, (목표 달성완성을 향한) 진척(진행)

10 conduct
ˈkänˌdəkt
n.

- behavior, demeanor, performance
- the way a person behaves
- The student was expelled from school for disorderly **conduct**.

행동

n.

- management, direction, supervision
- the manner of overseeing an activity or organization
- The principal was not happy with the teacher's **conduct** in his classroom.

지휘

11 outcome
ˈoutˌkəm
n.

- result, consequence, effect
- the way something turns out
- Joey's **outcome** in the play was not good.

결과

12 conform
kənˈfôrm
v.

- obey, observe, follow
- to follow the rules or standards
- To stay in the match, I had to **conform** to the rules of the game.

(규칙, 법 등에) 따르다(맞다)

v.

- match, fit, suit
- to be similar in form or type
- I had to **conform** to the outfit of the country.

~에 일치하다

SET 18

13. witness
'witnəs
n.

eyewitness, observer, spectator
a person who sees a crime or accident
*The **witness** swore to tell the truth of what he saw that day.*

목격자

v.

view, observe, behold
to see an event take place
*The pedestrian **witnessed** the car accident.*

목격하다

14. aid
ād
n.

assistance, support, encouragement
help
*The United Nations sent **aid** to the impoverished countries.*

원조, 지원

15. latch
laCH
v.

secure, lock, fasten
to fasten a door
*Kevin **latched** the door as the two burglars made their way to the house.*

걸쇠를 걸다, 걸쇠로 잠그다

16. regurgitate
rəˈgərjəˌtāt
v.

vomit, regorge
to bring up food that was swallowed
*The mother bird would **regurgitate** and feed the hungry chicks.*

(삼킨 음식물을 입 안으로 다시) 역류시키다

v.

recite, reiterate, repeat
to repeat information without understanding it
*The student **regurgitated** her notes in preparation for the exam.*

(듣거나 읽은 내용을 별 생각 없이) 반복하다

17. decompose
ˌdēkəmˈpōz
v.

crumble, disintegrate, fragment
to break down into simpler components
*The chemical compound **decomposed** at room temperature.*

(더 작은 부분들로) 분해하다

18. convert
kənˈvərt
v.

transform, metamorphose, transmute
to change in character, form, or function
*King Midas had the ability to **convert** anything into gold.*

전환시키다(개조하다)

19 nourish
'nəriSH
v.

feed, sustain, maintain

to provide food or other substances required for growth and health

*It is basic instinct for mothers to **nourish** and protect their baby.*

영양분을 공급하다

20 anchor
'aNGkər
v.

affix, bind, fasten

to secure firmly

*The ship **anchored** at the port.*

(움직이지 않게) 고정시키다

n.

announcer, broadcaster, newscaster

a person that broadcasts the news

*The **anchor** sat up straight and organized his notes.*

앵커맨(우먼)

21 facilitate
fə'silə,tāt
v.

simplify, ease, assist

to make an action or process easier

*A wedding planner **facilitates** the ceremony so that the couple can be stress-free.*

가능하게(용이하게) 하다

22 expedite
'ekspə,dīt
v.

accelerate, hasten, hurry

to make the action or process occur sooner

*The restaurant promised to **expedite** the food delivery.*

더 신속히 처리하다

23 origin
'ôrəjən
n.

genesis, dawn, start

the time or place where something begins

*Superman's **origin** starts on the planet of Krypton.*

기원, 근원

24 quarry
'kwôrē
n.

prey, victim, target

someone or something that is chased or sought

*A deer is not an easy **quarry** for a lion.*

사냥감

SET 18

25 **stupendous** st(y)oo'pendəs adj.	amazing, astonishing, remarkable
	very impressive
	The magician's **stupendous** act amazed the audience.
	엄청나게 큰, 거대한

26 **conundrum** kə'nəndrəm n.	quandary, dilemma, enigma
	a difficult problem
	Searching for life in space remains a **conundrum** for scientists.
	수수께끼

27 **degrade** də'grād v.	demean, debase, devalue
	to treat someone with disrespect
	The paparazzi pictures of the celebrity **degraded** him.
	비하(모멸)하다
v.	deteriorate, degenerate, decay
	to break down chemically
	The apple started to **degrade** after a few days.
	(화학적으로) 분해되다(하다)

28 **practical** 'praktək(ə)l adj.	active, applied, empirical
	involving the use of something instead of relying on ideas
	Instead of thinking, let's try some **practical** applications.
	타당한, 현실성 있는, 실현 가능한
adj.	feasible, viable, possible
	the likelihood of an idea or plan to be effective
	Neither of the two methods are **practical** for the research.
	현실(실질/실제)적인

29 **concurrent** kən'kərənt adj.	simultaneous, coinciding, synchronous
	occurring or done at the same time
	There are two **concurrent** birthday parties he must attend.
	공존하는, 동시에 발생하는

30 **rudimentary** ˌroodə'ment(ə)rē adj.	elementary, primary, basic
	involving basic principles
	Addition and subtraction are **rudimentary** mathematics.
	가장 기본(기초)적인

31. poverty
'pävərdē
n.

destitution, deprivation, penury

the condition of being extremely poor

*Southeast Asian countries still suffer from **poverty**.*

가난, 빈곤

32. undertake
ˌəndərˈtāk
v.

devote, contract, commit

to commit oneself to and work on it

*The construction crew **undertook** the building project.*

(책임을 맡아서) 착수하다(하다)

33. grudge
grəj
n.

resentment, bitterness, rancor

a continuous feeling of ill will or resentment from something that happened in the past

*My brother held a **grudge** against his teacher for always making fun of him.*

원한, 유감

34. coerce
kōˈərs
v.

pressure, compel, oblige

persuade someone to do something by force or threat

*The mother managed to **coerce** the children into doing the dishes.*

강압하다(강제하다)

35. vehement
ˈvēəmənt
adj.

passionate, ardent, spirited

showing strong feeling

*Malcom X's voice was low but **vehement**.*

(특히 분노를 담아) 격렬한(맹렬한)

36. protest
ˈprōˌtest
v.

dissent, object, denounce

to show disapproval or objection to something

*The soccer fans **protested** that the goal should not be counted.*

항의(반대/이의) (운동), 시위

37. terminus
ˈtərmənəs
n.

cessation, conclusion, completion

a final point in space or time

*The train had reached the **terminus** so everyone had to get off.*

종점

SET 18

38 entity
ˈen(t)ədē
n.
body, system, institution
something that has a distinct and independent existence
*Preschool is an **entity** composed of two parts: daycare and school.*
독립체

39 injunction
inˈjəNG(k)SH(ə)n
n.
directive, ruling, order
an authoritative warning or command
*The judge gave an **injunction** for the defendant to present his plea.*
명령

40 barge
bärj
v.
push, shove, force
to move forcefully or roughly
*Do not **barge** into my office while I am working.*
밀치고 가다

41 imperil
imˈperəl
v.
endanger, jeopardize, risk
to put at risk of being harmed or injured
*The mounting greenhouse gases in the atmosphere **imperils** our planet.*
위태롭게 하다, 위험에 빠뜨리다

42 erroneous
əˈrōnēəs
adj.
mistaken, inaccurate, incorrect
wrong
*Even the most accurate employee can make **erroneous** calculations.*
잘못된 (정보에 의한)

43 extravagant
ikˈstravəgənt
adj.
wasteful, spendthrift, lavish
lacking restraint in spending money or using resources
*The parents held an **extravagant** birthday party for their son.*
사치스러운

44 pinion
ˈpinyən
v.
restrain, constrain, secure
to tie or hold down the arms or legs of someone
*The professional wrestler **pinioned** the limbs of his opponent.*
(특히 사람의 양 팔을) 묶다(잡다)

45. similitude
siˈmiləˌt(y)o͞od
n.

resemblance, similarity, equivalence

the quality of being similar to something

*There was no **similitude** between the twins.*

유사함

46. temperament
ˈtemp(ə)rəmənt
n.

disposition, character, personality

a person's or animal's nature

*Although he was an engineer, he had an artistic **temperament**.*

기질

47. trace
trās
v.

detect, discover, find

to find or discover by investigation

*Police are trying to **trace** a black minivan in the city.*

추적하다, (추적하여) 찾아내다

n.

vestige, mark, indication

a mark or other indication of something existing or passing by

*There was a **trace** of bread crumbs left by Hansel along the forest grounds.*

자취, 흔적

48. sacred
ˈsākrəd
adj.

holy, consecrated, sanctified

connected with a religious purpose

*Jerusalem is a **sacred** land amongst different ethnic cultures.*

성스러운, 종교적인

49. wrath
raTH
n.

rage, fury, outrage

extreme anger

*The **wrath** of the gods were diminished when the people offered a sacrifice.*

분노, 노여움

50. reproof
rəˈpro͞of
n.

rebuke, reprimand, admonishment

a statement of blame or disapproval

*The employee received a sharp **reproof** for being late.*

책망, 나무람

SET 18 TEST

1. The _____ of the gods shook Mount Olympus and the mortals shook in fear.

2. The _____ of a lamb is peaceful and mellow.

3. The parents made an _____ assumption that their baby would continue to sleep.

4. The couple engaged in a _____ argument that ultimately resulted in a breakup.

5. An office secretary requires _____ skills in using the computer.

6. Archimedes shouted eureka when he solved the _____.

7. The employees worked day and night to _____ the completion of the project.

8. The train was brought to a _____ when a herd of cows crossed the steel tracks.

9. The gladiator _____ over his opponents in a mortal combat.

10. The Aztecs were _____ when the Europeans landed on their shores with new diseases.

---

1. wrath   2. temperament   3. erroneous   4. vehement   5. rudimentary
6. conundrum   7. expedite   8. cessation   9. prevail   10. imperil

11. Ancient Egyptians considered the jackal as an _____ of the afterlife.

12. The child was _____ into taking the medication.

13. Third world countries are characterized by high rates of crime and _____.

14. The waiter was _____ when the customer threw water at his face.

15. Guiness world records are _____ acts performed in various areas.

16. Robot vacuum cleaners _____ cleaning the house.

17. By filling the closet with her clothes, the girlfriend _____ her residence at her boyfriend's house.

18. My son _____ the information I gave him.

19. The poker player has a _____ of blinking nonstop when he has a set of good cards.

20. My friend described her _____ boyfriend.

---

11. entity 12. coerce 13. poverty 14. degrade 15. stupendous 16. facilitate 17. anchor 18. regurgitate 19. tendency 20. ideal

SET 18

notes:

LEAD
SET 19
VOCABULARY

SET 19

01 legacy
'legəsē
n.

fruits, consequence, outcome

something passed down by a predecessor

The **legacy** of his work can be seen in the museum.

유산

02 souvenir
ˌsoovəˈnir
n.

memento, keepsake, memorial

something that is kept to remember a person, place, or event

The sword is a **souvenir** of his days as a knight.

기념품(선물)

03 commission
kəˈmiSHən
n.

task, employment, mission

work or responsibility given to a person or a group

The artist was given a **commission** to paint the wall.

일, 과업, 과제

n.

percentage, share, fee

money that is given to a person, usually a portion from a total value

The car dealer will receive a **commission** for every car he sells.

수수료(커미션)

04 memorial
məˈmôrēəl
n.

monument, shrine, statue

something that was made to remind people of an event or an individual

The **memorial** was built to celebrate the president's achievements.

기념비

05 notable
ˈnōdəb(ə)l
adj.

outstanding, significant, important

worthy of notice

The statue is **notable** for the realistic facial expression.

주목할 만한, 눈에 띄는; 중요한, 유명한

06 former
ˈfôrmər
adj.

bygone, earlier, old

happening in the past or an earlier time

The death penalty was an acceptable punishment in **former** times.

예전(옛날)의

adj.

previous, precursory, antecedent

previously take on a specific role

He was her **former** lover.

(특정한 위치나 지위에 있던) 과거(이전)의

07 unassuming
/ˌənəˈsoomiNG/
adj.

modest, humble, meek

one who is not arrogant

*The priest was an **unassuming** man and always served the needs of others*

잘난 체하지 않는

08 reinforce
/ˌrēinˈfôrs/
v.

fortify, buttress, strengthen

to strengthen or support something

*The armor was **reinforced** with steel.*

강화하다

09 laborious
/ləˈbôrēəs/
adj.

arduous, strenuous, difficult

requiring lots of effort and time

*Construction work is a **laborious** task.*

(많은 시간과 노력을 요하는) 힘든

10 emulate
/ˈemyəˌlāt/
v.

imitate, mirror, echo

to match or surpass someone or an endeavor

*She wishes to **emulate** her favorite pop star.*

모방하다(따라 가다)

11 disinter
/ˌdisənˈtər/
v.

unearth, exhume, discover

to dig up something

*The treasures were **disinterred** and displayed at the museum.*

파내다(발굴하다)

12 lash
/laSH/
v.

flog, beat, thrash

to strike with a whip or stick

*He was **lashed** ten times for the crimes he committed.*

후려치다, 휘갈기다

SET 19

13. scale
skāl
n.

- balance
- an instrument that weighs something
- *The chef used a **scale** to prepare the ingredients.*

저울눈; 잣눈; 비례자, 눈금자

n.
- scope, magnitude, dimension
- the size or extent of something
- *The **scale** of the project requires multiple volunteers.*

규모(범위)

v.
- climb, ascend, mount
- to climb something
- *He succeeded in **scaling** Mount Everest.*

(아주 높고 가파른 곳을) 오르다

14. heed
hēd
v.

- notice, regard, consider
- to pay careful attention
- *The child did not **heed** the warnings ahead of him.*

(남의 충고·경고에) 주의를 기울이다

15. gluttony
ˈglətnē
n.

- greed, overconsumption, overeating
- greed, especially eating excessively
- *In the past, **gluttony** was considered a characteristic of the rich.*

폭식, 과식; 폭음, 과음

16. salutary
ˈsalyəˌterē
adj.

- beneficial, advantageous, productive
- producing good effects
- *The **salutary** environment helped the workers achieve their goal.*

유익한, 효과가 좋은

17. preclude
prəˈklo͞od
v.

- prevent, bar, forbid
- to prevent from happening
- *The heroes **precluded** the crimes set by the villains.*

못하게 하다, 불가능하게 하다

18. inflame
inˈflām
v.

- arouse, provoke, incite
- to intensify the emotions of a person
- *The increasing taxes **inflamed** the citizens.*

흥분(격앙/격분)시키다

19. acclaim
əˈklām
n.

applause, cheers, ovation

passionate and public praise

*The lawyer received **acclaim** for bringing justice to an innocent man.*

찬사(칭찬)

20. respite
ˈrespət
n.

rest, intermission, recess

a short break from something difficult

*The judge took an hour **respite** after being in court for six hours.*

일시적인 중단, 한숨 돌리기

21. pretense
ˈprēˌtens
n.

guise, façade, charade

an inaccurate display of attitude, feelings, or intentions

*The widow's sadness is covered by a **pretense** that she is fine.*

가면, 위장, 허위

22. comply
kəmˈplī
v.

obey, follow, satisfy

to act in accordance with a command

*The company was unable to **comply** with the customer's request.*

따르다(준수하다)

23. reckless
ˈrekləs
adj.

rash, careless, thoughtless

without caring or considering the effects of an action

*His **reckless** driving killed an innocent person.*

무모한, 신중하지 못한; 난폭한

24. equivocal
əˈkwivək(ə)l
adj.

ambiguous, ambivalent, vague

uncertain or questionable

*His response was **equivocal**, so the interrogation had to continue.*

모호한

25. tentative
ˈten(t)ədiv
adj.

provisional, unconfirmed, indefinite

not certain or fixed

*This is a **tentative** schedule of our vacation in Hawaii.*

잠정적인

SET 19

26 demeanor
dəˈmēnər
n.

attitude, appearance, manner
an outward behavior
*The prince's **demeanor** was polite and respectful.*
태도, 몸가짐; 표정

27 acme
ˈakmē
n.

zenith, crest, pinnacle
the point where someone or something is at its best
*Becoming Buddha is the **acme** of the Buddhist religion.*
절정, 정점

28 continence
ˈkänt(ə)nəns
n.

refraining, moderation, abstinence
self-restraint
***Continence** is an important trait everyone must have.*
자제

29 treason
ˈtrēzən
n.

betrayal, disloyalty, treachery
the act of betraying someone or something
*The spy was convicted of **treason** and was exiled from the country.*
반역죄

30 turbulence
ˈtərbyələns
n.

turmoil, tumult, upheaval
conflict
*Before the civil war, the country faced a political **turbulence**.*
격동, 격변

31 proactive
prōˈaktiv
adj.

aggressive, zealous, driven
creating or controlling a situation by letting it happen rather than responding to it after it occurred
*Gotham City is taking **proactive** measures to fight crime by supporting Batman.*
상황을 앞서서 주도하는

32 sham
Sham
n.

pretense, fiction, fraud
something that is not what it is supposed to be
*The recent elections were a total **sham**.*
가짜, 엉터리

33	**molest** məˈlest v.	harass, pester, torment
		to harass someone in an aggressive or continuous manner
		*The drunkard **molested** the neighbors on his way home.*
	폭행하다	

34	**anatomy** əˈnadəmē n.	structure, makeup, construction
		the body structure of an organism
		*A medical doctor should be well-versed in the human **anatomy**.*
	해부학	

35	**dilapidated** dəˈlapəˌdādəd adj.	shabby, battered, unsound
		referring to a construction which is in a state of ruin as a result of age or neglect
		*The old, **dilapidated** cathedral had to be remodeled.*
	다 허물어져 가는	

36	**spare** sper adj.	leftover, surplus, superfluous
		being in excess
		*Do you have some **spare** parts I can use to build my robot?*
	(현재 쓰지 않아서) 남는	
	v.	afford, give, grant
		to give someone an extra of what one has
		*Can you **spare** me some of your time?*
	(시간돈 등을) 할애하다(내다/내어 주다)	

37	**tatty** ˈtadē adj.	faded, disfigured, tattered
		in poor condition
		*The **tatty** furniture needed to be cleaned and fixed before it was to be sold.*
	닳아 해진, 누더기 같은, 지저분한	

38	**hierarchy** ˈhī(ə)ˌrärkē n.	grading, ladder, ranking
		a system of organization in which people or things are ranked according to status or power
		*There is a strict **hierarchy** within any sizeable corporation.*
	계급(계층)	

SET 19

39. pool
pool
v.
merge, blend, amalgamate
to bring together
*Countries should **pool** their resources to solve global warming.*
모으다

40. inextricable
ˌinəkˈstrikəb(ə)l
adj.
inseparable, entangled, raveled
impossible to untangle or take apart
*No matter how hard she tried, her tangled necklace was **inextricable**.*
불가분한, 떼려고 해도 뗄 수 없는

41. tangible
ˈtanjəb(ə)l
adj.
tactile, physical, material
able to be touched
*Although air is not **tangible**, we know that it exists.*
만질(감지할) 수 있는

42. motive
ˈmōdiv
n.
motivation, reason, rationale
a reason for doing something
*What was the **motive** for the murder?*
동기, 이유

43. impediment
imˈpedəmənt
n.
obstruction, barrier, handicap
a hindrance in doing something
*Having a boyfriend or girlfriend can be an **impediment** to academic studies.*
장애(물)

44. neglect
nəˈglekt
v.
disregard, ignore, overlook
to not pay proper attention to
***Neglecting** to do one's homework will result in bad grades.*
도외시하다

45. prosper
ˈpräspər
v.
thrive, multiply, benefit
to be successful or fortunate
*A person who wakes up early will **prosper** in life.*
번영(번창/번성)하다

46 rendition
ren'diSH(ə)n
n.

performance, presentation, interpretation

a performance or interpretation of a music

*We saw a wonderful **rendition** of the Sound of Music.*

(노래, 음악의) 연주(공연)

47 premonition
ˌprēməˈniSH(ə)n
n.

foreboding, suspicion, hunch

a strong feeling that something bad is about to happen

*The boy had a **premonition** of disaster when his friends came over.*

(특히 불길한) 예감

48 fleeting
ˈflēdiNG
adj.

transient, momentary, brief

occurring for a short time

*The crowd looked into the waters, hoping to catch a **fleeting** glimpse of the shark.*

순식간의, 잠깐 동안의

49 impetuous
imˈpeCH(oo)əs
adj.

impulsive, rash, reckless

acting or carried out quickly and with no thought or care

*A daredevil often engages in **impetuous** behavior.*

성급한, 충동적인

50 promulgate
ˈpräməlˌgāt
v.

propagate, spread, publicize

to make widely known

*The important announcement should be **promulgated** across the campus.*

널리 알리다

SET 19 TEST

1. Da Vinci's first _____ as an artist was the Adoration of the Magi.

2. It is _____ that the victor helped the loser stand on his feet and shook his hand.

3. Modern artists have failed to _____ the masterpieces of Renaissance artists.

4. A buffet is a welcoming place for someone with _____.

5. There was a thirty minute _____ after the second act of the play.

6. The search for extraterrestrial life and UFOs has been an _____ field of study.

7. Some people show the _____ of their performance when under pressure.

8. The group reached a _____ when their work was erased from the computers.

9. Emotions are not _____, it can only be described with words.

10. The student _____ to do his homework over the vacation.

1. commission 2. notable 3. emulate 4. gluttony 5. respite 6. equivocal 7. acme 8. turbulence 9. tangible 10. neglect

11. The high school theatre students displayed a _____ of the musical Grease.

12. The couple broke up when the man stated an _____ comment in the heat of the moment.

13. The _____ of his presidency was free health care for the people.

14. The old house was _____ with steel pillars.

15. It is important to _____ to the lessons given by parents.

16. The olympic athletes were met with _____ when they returned to their country with gold medals.

17. The teammate was asked to _____ with the rules or he would be kicked out of the team.

18. He pretended to be _____ while pride and glee swelled within him.

19. Childbirth is a _____ task.

20. The _____ working environment helped the group to finish the task quickly.

---

11. rendition 12. impetuous 13. legacy 14. reinforce 15. heed 16. acclaim 17. comply 18. unassuming 19. laborious 20. salutary

SET 19

notes:

LEAD
SET
20
VOCABULARY

SET 20

01 feeble
'fēbəl
adj.

weak, frail, infirm

to lack physical strength

*He was feeling **feeble** after walking in the rain for hours.*

아주 약한

02 venerate
'venə,rāt
v.

revere, worship, adulate

to give great respect

*Christians **venerate** the cross as a holy object.*

공경(숭배)하다

03 thrash
THraSH
v.

flog, beat, scourge

to beat an animal or a person repeatedly and violently

*The wild animal **thrashed** its prey inside the cage.*

몸부림치다, 허우적거리다, 요동치다

04 lease
lēs
n.

contract, rental, charter

a contract that gives something to another for a set time in return for a payment

*The man put a year long **lease** on the car.*

임대차 계약

v.

rent, borrow, charter

to rent or borrow

*The government **leased** the land to a local farmer.*

임대(임차/대여)하다

05 contraband
'käntrə,band
adj.

smuggled, illegal, banned

exported or imported illegally

*Border patrol has been monitoring for **contraband** drug shipments.*

(수출입) 금지품

06 antiseptic
,an(t)ə'septik
adj.

disinfectant, sterile, aseptic

relating to something that prevents the growth of disease causing bacteria

*Garlic has **antiseptic** properties, so people put lots of it in food.*

소독(살균)이 되는

07 concoct
kənˈkäkt
v.

fabricate, invent, contrive

to create or come up with a plan

*My grandfather **concocted** a bedtime story.*

(이야기, 변명 등을) 지어내다

08 rectify
ˈrektəˌfī
v.

amend, resolve, ameliorate

to correct

*Misconduct can be **rectified** as one ages.*

(잘못된 것을) 바로잡다

09 congenital
kənˈjenədl
adj.

persistent, chronic, regular

having a specific characteristic from birth or from continuous habit

*He has become a **congenital** liar.*

선천적인

10 liberal
ˈlib(ə)rəl
adj.

progressive, modern, radical

willing to honor or welcome behavior or opinions that are different

*The prime minister is a **liberal** person, so he will listen to your ideas.*

자유민주적인

11 elusive
ēˈloōsiv
adj.

evasive, slippery, shifty

difficult to obtain or achieve

*It has become more **elusive** to come up with original ideas.*

찾기(규정하기/달성하기) 힘든

12 sturdy
ˈstərdē
adj.

powerful, robust, hardy

built with dexterity and solidness

*After going to the gym for many years, he achieved a **sturdy** body.*

튼튼한, 견고한

13 detrimental
ˌdetrəˈmen(t)l
adj.

harmful, deleterious, adverse

likely to cause harm

*Eating too much candy will have **detrimental** effect on a person's teeth.*

해로운

SET 20

14. fickle
'fik(ə)l
adj.

capricious, variable, erratic
changing on a regular basis, especially regarding affection or interest
*Mercenaries tend to be **fickle** and fight for whoever pays them more money.*
변덕스러운, 변화가 심한

15. incident
'insəd(ə)nt
n.

occurrence, episode, experience
an event or happening
*Several **incidents** occurred on my way home.*
일(사건)

16. lethal
'lēTHəl
n.

deadly, fatal, mortal
harmful or destructive
*A mechanical pencil can be a **lethal** item since it is very sharp.*
치명적인(죽음을 초래할 정도의)

17. fabricate
'fabrə,kāt
v.

create, construct, assemble
to manufacture something from prepared parts
*The craftsman **fabricated** a chair using leftover pieces of wood.*
제작(조립)하다

v.

forge, counterfeit, falsify
to make up something with the intent to lie
*The lawyer **fabricated** information to win the court case.*
날조하다(조작하다)

18. void
void
adj.

null, revoked, canceled
not valid
*The contract was **void** because he failed to give the payment.*
무효의

adj.

vacant, empty, desolate
completely empty
*The desert is **void**, with no life to be seen anywhere.*
…이 하나도(전혀) 없는

n.

blank, vacuum, chasm
an empty space
*Space is an endless **void**.*
빈 공간, 공동; 공허감

19. cardinal
ˈkärd(ə)nl
adj.

fundamental, chief, principal

of great importance

*The **cardinal** rule of this school is to do your best.*

가장 중요한(기본적인)

20. nascent
ˈnāsənt
adj.

developing, rising, burgeoning

starting to show signs of potential

*The **nascent** clothing brand opened its third offline store.*

발생기의, 초기의

21. implausible
imˈplôzəb(ə)l
adj.

unlikely, doubtful, debatable

not reasonable or probable

*It is **implausible** that humans will live on Mars anytime soon.*

믿기 어려운, 타당해 보이지 않는

22. exquisite
ekˈskwizət
adj.

elegant, graceful, magnificent

very beautiful and delicate

*The **exquisite** sculptures decorated the living room.*

매우 아름다운, 정교한

23. pious
ˈpīəs
adj.

devout, religious, devoted

very religious

*She was a **pious** nun and spent her days in prayer.*

경건한, 독실한

24. malleable
ˈmalyəb(ə)l
adj.

susceptible, compliant, docile

easy to influence

*The dog is a **malleable** creature, as long as you give treats.*

영향을 잘 받는, 잘 변하는

25. discern
dəˈsərn
v.

perceive, detect, discriminate

to perceive or recognize something

*The paleontologist was able to **discern** the shape of the bone.*

알아보다(알아듣다)

SET 20

26 legible
ˈlejəb(ə)l
adj.

readable, clear, comprehensible
recognizable to read
*The original handwriting was not **legible**, so the author had to write again.*
읽을(알아볼) 수 있는, 또렷한

27 portable
ˈpôrdəb(ə)l
adj.

mobile, compact, lightweight
able to carry around or easily move
*He had a **portable** television to watch the game in the bus.*
휴대(이동)가 쉬운, 휴대용의

28 enact
enˈakt
v.

execute, perform, set
to put into effect
*The mastermind **enacted** his plan into motion.*
일어나다, 벌어지다

29 allegiance
əˈlējəns
n.

loyalty, obedience, homage
loyalty or commitment to a group or cause
*He pledged his **allegiance** to the dark side.*
충성

30 attire
əˈtī(ə)r
n.

garment, outfit, clothes
formal clothes
*His **attire** for this evening is a tuxedo.*
의복, 복장

31 capricious
kəˈpriSHəs
adj.

fickle, unstable, erratic
sudden and random changes in mood or behavior
*The manager's **capricious** behavior kept everyone on the edge of their seats.*
변덕스러운

32 municipality
myo͞oˌnisəˈpalədē
n.

district, precinct, borough
a city or town with its own status and government
*Representatives from each **municipality** met in the assembly hall.*
지방 자치제, 지방 자치제 당국

33. keen
kēn
adj.

acute, sharp, sensitive
highly developed sense
*People who cannot see have a **keen** sense of hearing.*

날카로운, 예리한

adj.

enthusiastic, avid, fervent
having or displaying eagerness or excitement
*Different religions around the world have **keen** believers of faith.*

열정적인(열렬한)

34. plague
plāg
v.

afflict, torture, torment
to cause persistent trouble or distress
*Europeans were **plagued** with the Black Death during the 14th century.*

괴롭히다

35. delinquent
dəˈliNGkwənt
adj.

criminal, offending, troublesome
showing or characterized by a likelihood to commit crime
***Delinquent** children should be punished with a beating.*

비행의, 범죄 성향을 보이는

36. deviant
ˈdēvēənt
adj.

abnormal, atypical, divergent
departing from standard behavior
*She had trouble making friends because of her **deviant** personality.*

(정상에서) 벗어난, 일탈적인

37. malicious
məˈliSHəs
adj.

spiteful, malevolent, hostile
intending to cause harm
*The **malicious** software virus shut down my computer.*

악의적인, 적의 있는

38. vice
vīs
n.

immorality, wickedness, wrongdoing
an immoral or evil characteristic
*Kingpin is a person of **vice** and crime in the Spiderman comic book.*

악; 악덕 행위, 비행

SET 20

39 circumspect
ˈsərkəmˌspekt
adj.
- cautious, wary, discreet
- unwilling to take risks
- *Entrepreneurs are very **circumspect** in the decisions they make.*
- 신중한

40 terra
ˈterə
n.
- earth, ground, terrain
- land
- *The **terra** was fertile for farming.*
- 흙, 땅

41 eccentric
ikˈsentrik
adj.
- unconventional, irregular, aberrant
- abnormal and strange
- *Sherlock Holmes is **eccentric** but manages to solve the cases given to him.*
- 괴짜인, 별난, 기이한

42 sterile
ˈsterəl
adj.
- disinfected, aseptic, sanitary
- completely clean
- *Make sure that the tools are **sterile** before performing the surgery.*
- 살균한, 소독한

adj.
- infertile, childless, barren
- unable to produce children or young
- *After working with radioactive wastes, he became **sterile**.*
- 불임의

43 pervasive
pərˈvāsiv
adj.
- pervading, extensive, ubiquitous
- spreading widely amongst people or area
- *The virus was **pervasive** and infected everyone in the country.*
- 만연하는, (구석구석) 스며(배어)드는

44 estrange
əsˈtrānj
v.
- alienate, distance, wean
- to make someone less close or affectionate to someone else
- *The fight **estranged** the two friends.*
- 사이를 멀어지게 하다, 이간하다

45. reverberate
rəˈvərbəˌrāt
v.

resound, resonate, pulsate

to echo

*The bat's screech **reverberated** inside the cave.*

울리다

46. enterprise
ˈen(t)ərˌprīz
n.

firm, venture, business

a business or company

*The multi-billion dollar **enterprise** was given to a teenage boy.*

기업, 회사

47. reliable
rəˈlīəb(ə)l
adj.

dependable, trustworthy, proven

able to be trusted

*A **reliable** partner is necessary in a group project.*

믿을(신뢰할) 수 있는

48. metropolis
məˈträp(ə)ləs
n.

capital, downtown, municipality

the main city of a country or region

*Superman flew over the **metropolis**, looking for crime.*

주요 도시

49. tinker
ˈtiNGkər
v.

toy, play, monkey

to repair or improve something, but in a poor manner

*My grandfather loves to **tinker** with broken electronics.*

어설프게 손보다(고치다)

50. innovate
ˈinəˌvāt
v.

conceive, invent, discover

to introduce new ideas, methods, or products

*Humans **innovated** so much within the past 100 years.*

혁신(쇄신)하다, 획기적으로 하다

SET 20 CROSSWORD PUZZLE

Across

3. to create or come up with a plan
5. starting to show signs of potential
6. difficult to obtain or achieve
8. to lack physical strength
10. built with dexterity and solidness
11. departing from standard behavior
14. of great importance
15. not reasonable or probable

Down

1. easy to influence
2. likely to cause harm
4. to give great respect
7. to make up something with the intent to lie
9. exported or imported illegally
12. not valid
13. intending to cause harm

1. malleable 2. detrimental 3. concoct 4. venerate 5. nascent 6. elusive 7. fabricate 8. feeble 9. contraband 10. sturdy 11. deviant 12. void 13. malicious 14. cardinal 15. implausible

LEAD
SET 21
VOCABULARY

SET 21

01 cogent
ˈkōjənt
adj.

convincing, compelling, sound
clear and logical
*The lawyer gave **cogent** arguments for the court case.*
설득력 있는

02 virtuous
ˈvərCHo͞oəs
adj.

righteous, ethical, upright
having or displaying high moral standards
*The Dalai Lama is a **virtuous** man.*
도덕적인, 고결한

03 fetch
feCH
v.

summon, collect, bring
to go and bring back someone or something
*The dog **fetched** the ball I threw.*
가지고(데리고/불러) 오다

04 submerge
səbˈmərj
v.

immerse, drown, sink
to go underwater
*The submarine **submerged** under the icy waters.*
잠수하다, 물(액체) 속에 잠기다

05 conciliate
kənˈsilēˌāt
v.

appease, placate, pacify
to stop a person from being angry or dissatisfied
*Negotiations were made to **conciliate** both parties.*
달래다, 회유하다

06 snare
sner
n.

trap, noose, net
a trap for catching animals
*The **snare** was set to capture the wild boar.*
(사냥용) 덫(올가미)

07 abominate
əˈbäməˌnāt
v.

detest, loathe, abhor
to dislike strongly
*The pirate **abominated** the idea of working for the royal navy.*
증오하다, 혐오하다

08 substantiate
səbˈstan(t)SHēˌāt
v.

validate, verify, authenticate

to give evidence to support or make valid

*The genuine quality of the handbag was **substantiated** by the expert.*

입증하다

09 inordinate
inˈôrd(ə)nət
adj.

excessive, unreasonable, preposterous

unusually large or disproportionate

*She took an **inordinate** amount of time to get dressed just to go to the market.*

과도한, 지나친

10 coalition
ˌkōəˈliSH(ə)n
n.

union, affiliation, federation

an alliance

*A **coalition** was formed amongst the tribes to fight the invaders.*

연립 정부, 연정

11 inundation
ˌinənˈdāSH(ə)n
n.

overflow, influx, flood

an overflow of people or things

*There was an **inundation** of phone calls when he received the nobel prize.*

범람, 침수; (비유) 충만, 쇄도

12 entreaty
inˈtrēdē
n.

plea, appeal, petition

a humble request

*The tyrant ignored the **entreaties** from the citizens.*

간청, 애원

13 dubious
ˈd(y)o͞obēəs
adj.

doubtful, uncertain, hesitant

hesitating or doubting

*Brian seemed **dubious** when he asked to eat fried chicken.*

의심하는, 미심쩍어 하는

adj.

suspicious, unreliable, untrustworthy

difficult to rely on

*Michelle's methods were **dubious** since she was the only one to benefit.*

수상쩍은

SET 21

14 terminal
ˈtərmənl
adj.

final, ultimate, extreme
at the end or extremity of something
*A **terminal** date was set to finish the project.*

말기의

adj.

incurable, untreatable, fatal
forecast to lead to death
*My father was diagnosed with **terminal** cancer.*

불치의

15 conspicuous
kənˈspikyooəs
adj.

noticeable, obvious, striking
attracting attention or notice
*She wore a **conspicuous** outfit to the party.*

눈에 잘 띄는, 튀는; 뚜렷한

16 catastrophic
ˌkadəˈsträfik
adj.

calamitous, tragic, dire
involving or creating great damage or suffering
*A **catastrophic** earthquake shook San Francisco.*

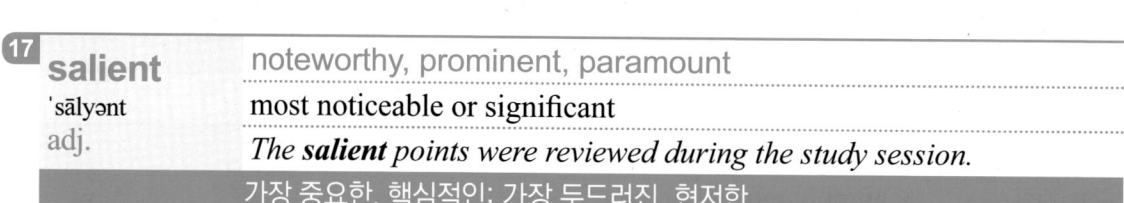

대변동(큰 재앙)의; 파멸의, 비극적인; 대단원의

17 salient
ˈsālyənt
adj.

noteworthy, prominent, paramount
most noticeable or significant
*The **salient** points were reviewed during the study session.*

가장 중요한, 핵심적인; 가장 두드러진, 현저한

18 headstrong
ˈhedˌstrôNG
adj.

unyielding, stubborn, perverse
to be stubborn
*My father is a **headstrong** man and never listens to my mother.*

고집불통의

19 trifle
ˈtrīfəl
n.

inessential, nothing, trinket
something of little value or importance
*The president should not trouble himself with such **trifles**.*

하찮은 것

20. engross
in'grōs
v.

preoccupy, enthrall, beguile
to grab the attention or interest of something
*The animation movie completely **engrossed** the children.*

몰두하게 만들다

21. hype
hīp
n.

publicity, marketing, promotion
an intense publicity
*She did not understand the **hype** of wearing flower dresses.*

(대대적이고 과장된) 광고(선전)

22. affair
ə'fer
n.

event, incident, occurrence
an event or series of events of a particular interest
*Please do not show interest in my personal **affairs**.*

일(사건)

n.

relationship, fling, romance
a romantic relationship between two people outside of their marriage
*The husband is having an **affair** with a coworker at the office.*

불륜 (관계), 정사

23. adage
'adij
n.

maxim, proverb, saying
a short statement revealing a general truth
*The old man gave an **adage** to his grandchildren.*

속담, 격언

24. underlying
ˌəndər'līiNG
adj.

basic, essential, critical
fundamental or basic
*The **underlying** truth is to never lie.*

근본적인(근원적인)

25. placid
'plasəd
adj.

tranquil, imperturbable, composed
not easily excited
*The lion has a **placid** nature, despite its ferocious appearance.*

잔잔한, 차분한

SET 21

26. austere
ô′stir
adj.

- stern, harsh, strict
- strict in attitude, appearance, or manner
- *My father is an **austere** man and no one is allowed to talk during a meal.*
- 엄격한(엄한)

27. intrinsic
in′trinzik
adj.

- inherent, innate, natural
- belonging naturally
- *It is **intrinsic** for a male lion to find its partner during mating season.*
- 본질적인

28. loom
loom
v.

- impend, threaten, menace
- for a threatening event to happen
- *The rumbling volcano **loomed** the small town of Pompeii.*
- (중요하거나 위협적인 일이) 곧 닥칠 것처럼 보이다

29. thrust
THrəst
v.

- shove, plunge, ram
- to push someone or something violently
- *He **thrust** the knife into the meat.*
- (거칠게) 밀다, 밀치다, 찌르다

30. pliable
′plīəb(ə)l
adj.

- flexible, pliant, elastic
- easily bent
- *Plastic is **pliable** at high temperature.*
- 유연한, 잘 휘어지는

adj.
- adaptable, yielding, accommodating
- easily influenced
- *Children have **pliable** attitudes if you give them rewards.*
- 순응적인, 고분고분한

31. ascend
ə′send
v.

- climb, escalate, arise
- to go up or rise
- *The house tied to the balloons started to **ascend**.*
- 오르다, 올라가다

32. trailblazer
'trāl,blāzər
n.

innovator, vanguard, pioneer

a pioneer

Columbus was the **trailblazer** for discovering the Americas.

개척자, 선구자

33. predecessor
'predə,sesər
n.

forerunner, precursor, antecedent

someone or something that arrived or existed before another

The **predecessor** of the current leader had done a horrible job.

전임자

34. pastoral
'pastərəl
adj.

rural, countryside, rustic

related to life in the country

The businessman had several **pastoral** farms outside the city.

시골의, 지방의, 목축의

35. inept
i'nept
adj.

incompetent, unskilled, crude

having or showing no skill

The disfigured wooden doll was obviously made by an **inept** craftsman.

솜씨 없는, 서투른

36. quaint
kwānt
adj.

charming, attractive, picturesque

attractively old-fashioned or peculiar

My grandparents lived in a **quaint** little house in the city.

(매력 있게) 진기한(예스러운)

37. cohesive
kō'hēsiv
adj.

adhesive, united, connected

being connected

Native American tribes live in a **cohesive** community.

화합[결합]하는

38. disseminate
də'semə,nāt
v.

circulate, distribute, disperse

to spread something widely

News regarding the end of the war quickly **disseminated**.

(정보, 지식 등을) 퍼뜨리다(전파하다)

SET 21

39 digress
dīˈgres
v.

deviate, depart, stray

to go off topic in speech or writing

*Children tend to **digress** from the topic when talking with adults.*

주제에서 벗어나다, 다른 말을 하기 시작하다

40 concrete
ˈkänˌkrēt
adj.

conclusive, specific, definitive

definite

*I have **concrete** proof that you cheated on the test.*

사실에 의거한, 구체적인

41 readily
ˈredəlē
adv.

willingly, promptly, eagerly

without hesitation or reluctance

*The athletes gave up **readily** after playing for several hours.*

손쉽게, 순조롭게

42 residue
ˈrezəˌd(y)o͞o
n.

remainder, remnant, leftover

a small amount of something that remains after the main part is removed or used up

*A **residue** of water was left on the table when he picked up the cold ice cup.*

잔여(잔류)물

43 eclectic
əˈklektik
adj.

extensive, comprehensive, multifarious

having ideas or style from a wide and diverse range of sources

*Universities offer an **eclectic** mixture of classes for the students.*

절충적인, 다방면에 걸친

44 immutable
i(m)ˈmyo͞odəb(ə)l
adj.

fixed, set, rigid

not changing as time passes

*The Earth being round is an **immutable** fact.*

변경할 수 없는, 불변의

45 impose
imˈpōz
v.

force, urge, press

to force something to be accepted or carried out

*Dictators often **impose** laws to be followed by the citizens.*

(의견 등을) 강요하다

46 endow
in'dou
v.

provide, supply, present
to give a quality, ability, or asset
*King Solomon was **endowed** with wisdom.*

주다

47 peak
pēk
n.

height, pinnacle, summit
the highest point of something, including an activity or achievement
*The young physicist reached the **peak** of his career with his discovery.*

절정, 정점, 최고조

48 adjoin
ə'join
v.

connected, adjacent, attached
to be next to and connected with
*The living room is **adjoined** to the kitchen.*

인접하다, 붙어 있다

49 inclination
ˌinklə'nāSH(ə)n
n.

tendency, propensity, predisposition
a person's natural tendency
*Edison showed no **inclination** to profit from his inventions.*

(…하려는) 의향(뜻), 성향

50 outskirts
'outˌskərts
n.

fringes, edges, borders
the outer parts of a city or town
*The garbage disposal site lies in the **outskirts** of the city.*

변두리, 교외

SET 21 TEST

1. The son was _____ with superhuman strength from his superhero father.

2. The woman's hobbies were _____, as it ranged from archery to writing poems.

3. The keynote speaker _____ from his speech when the audience started to mock him.

4. The value of gold is considered to be _____.

5. A baby has not yet developed its motor skills, so the infant is _____.

6. A dog baring its teeth when threatened is an _____ behavior.

7. Ghandi left his home to become a _____ man.

8. The mother _____ her baby by offering candy and juice.

9. I _____ the fact that women are still treated unequally in this country.

10. A person's _____ is to help someone when they fall.

---

1. endow 2. eclectic 3. digress 4. immutable 5. inept 6. intrinsic 7. virtuous 8. conciliate 9. abominate 10. inclination

11. The government _____ its citizens to wear face masks.

12. A _____ of the chocolate was smeared on the little boy's mouth.

13. Neil Armstrong is considered a _____ of space exploration.

14. The drill sergeant had to be _____ so that the new cadets would be ready for battle.

15. Chinese fortune cookies are contained with an _____ which are quite helpful.

16. I spend minimal time with _____ since they are inconsequential.

17. It was the most _____ dress from the fashion show.

18. The _____ makeup was rather an eyesore.

19. The poor man made a small _____ to the family.

20. During World War II, America joined the European _____ to stop the Nazis.

---

11. impose   12. residue   13. trailblazer   14. austere   15. adage
16. trifle   17. salient   18. conspicuous   19. entreaty   20. coalition

SET 21

notes:

LEAD
SET
22
VOCABULARY

SET 22

01 primeval
prī'mēvəl
adj.

ancient, antique, primordial

referring to primitive times

The **primeval** land was untouched by human civilization.

원시적인

02 pertinent
'pərtnənt
adj.

appropriate, applicable, relevant

relevant to a particular matter

The student asked **pertinent** questions related to the lecture.

적절한(관련 있는)

03 bombard
bäm'bärd
v.

blitz, shell, batter

to attack repeatedly with bombs or missiles

The city was **bombarded** by missiles from the enemy ships.

(폭격,공격을) 퍼붓다

04 batter
'badər
v.

pummel, pound, thrash

to hit consecutively with hard blows

He was **battered** by the school bully.

두드리다(때리다/구타하다)

05 chronic
'kränik
adj.

persistent, incessant, constant

lasting a long time or reoccurring constantly

My uncle died of lung cancer because he was a **chronic** smoker.

끊임없이 지속(반복)되는

06 rigorous
'rig(ə)rəs
adj.

meticulous, diligent, attentive

extremely accurate and thorough

The editor must be **rigorous** and identify the tiniest errors.

철저한, 엄격한

07 instinct
'instiNG(k)t
n.

inclination, intuition, compulsion

an inborn behavior in animals in response to a stimuli

Moles have a natural **instinct** to dig holes.

본능, 타고난 소질

08 incidentally
ˌinsəˈdent(ə)lē
adv.

accidently, fortuitously, coincidentally

occurring by chance

*The cancer was discovered **incidentally** during his annual health check.*

부수적으로, 우연히

09 extent
ikˈstent
n.

expanse, range, scope

the area covered by something

*The **extent** of Hitler's influence reached all the way to Asia.*

(크기,중요성,심각성 등의) 정도(규모)

10 friction
ˈfrikSH(ə)n
n.

discord, strife, antagonism

conflict created by disagreements

*There was a definite **friction** between the father and his son.*

(사람 사이의) 마찰(알력)

11 exaggerate
igˈzajəˌrāt
v.

overstate, dramatize, overemphasize

to represent something as better or worse than it actually is

*My infant son tends to **exaggerate** his aches and pains.*

과장하다

12 annul
əˈnəl
v.

nullify, void, repeal

to make invalid

*Her speed ticket was **annulled** by the judge due to her emergency.*

(법적으로) 취소하다(무효하게 하다)

13 forebode
fôrˈbōd
v.

foreshadow, portend, presage

to act as a warning of something bad that is about to happen

*The wizard **forebode** of upcoming danger.*

(불길함을) 예감하다

SET 22

14 retreat
rəˈtrēt
v.

withdraw, retire, flee
to withdraw from the enemy
*The Avengers **retreated** to their tower when Ultron attacked.*
후퇴(철수/퇴각)하다

n.

refuge, haven, sanctuary
a quiet and safe place where one can rest
*Asgard is no longer a **retreat** for warriors since it is destroyed.*
피난(처), 피신(처), 도피(처)

15 lament
ləˈment
v.

mourn, wail, grieve
to mourn for a person's death
*The couple was **lamenting** the death of their daughter.*
애통(한탄/통탄)하다

16 deplore
dəˈplôr
v.

abhor, denounce, detest
to show strong disapproval
*South Koreans **deplore** the claim that Dokdo is Japanese territory.*
(특히 공개적으로) 개탄하다

17 entail
inˈtāl
v.

necessitate, prompt, generate
to include something as an important part or consequence
*The battle strategy **entails** multiple sacrifice.*
수반하다

18 enlist
inˈlist
v.

join, recruit, employ
to engage someone to help or support
*The company **enlists** students for their summer projects.*
(협조,참여를) 요청하(여 얻)다

19 onset
ˈänˌset
n.

commencement, start, opening
the beginning of something
*The **onset** of summer starts with the sun going down at a later time.*
시작

20. presentiment
prəˈzen(t)əmənt
n.

premonition, intuition, hunch

an instinctive feeling regarding the future

*I have a **presentiment** that everything will be ok.*

예감

21. lubricious
looˈbriSHəs
adj.

slippery, sleek, oiled

smooth and slippery

*The earthworm is **lubricious** from the mucus it excretes.*

미끄러운, 포착하기 어려운

22. repulsive
rəˈpəlsiv
adj.

revolting, abhorrent, offensive

intense dislike or disgust

*There is a **repulsive** smell coming from the rotten fish.*

역겨운, 혐오스러운

23. myopic
ˌmīˈäpik
adj.

unimaginative, narrow, parochial

lacking imagination or intellectual insight

*The failed scientist had a **myopic** approach when coming up with solutions.*

근시안적인

24. ragged
ˈragəd
adj.

tattered, ripped, worn

old and torn

*The homeless man wore **ragged** clothes.*

누더기가 된, 다 해진

25. bustling
ˈbəsliNG
adj.

crowded, full, hectic

full of activity

*New York City is a **bustling** metropolis.*

부산한, 북적거리는

26. affluent
ˈafloōənt
adj.

wealthy, rich, opulent

having much money

*Elon Musk is now an **affluent** member of the business world.*

부유한

SET 22

27. tranquil
'traNGkwəl
adj.
- serene, placid, peaceful
- without disturbance
- *The ocean water was **tranquil** after the storm passed.*
- 고요한, 평온한

28. serial
'sirēəl
adj.
- sequential, consecutive, successive
- in continuing order
- *Workers carried out their tasks in the same **serial** order.*
- 순차적인

29. wilt
wilt
v.
- sag, droop, languish
- to lose one's energy
- *The flowers seemed to **wilt** under the hot sun.*
- 지치다(처지다/풀이 죽다)

30. apparent
ə'perənt
adj.
- evident, plain, obvious
- clearly seen or understood
- *It became **apparent** that he was nervous about giving his speech.*
- 분명한, 누가 봐도 알 수 있는

31. formation
fôr'māSH(ə)n
n.
- configuration, arrangement, pattern
- a structure or arrangement of something
- *The ducks flew in a v-shaped **formation**.*
- (특정한) 대형(편대)

32. periodic
ˌpirē'ädik
adj.
- regular, recurring, intermittent
- occurring at intervals
- *The monsoon is a **periodic** weather phenomena that occurs every year.*
- 주기적인

33. deposit
dəˈpäzət
n.

- security, stake, installment
- money that is given as security or in part payment
- *We saved enough money for a **deposit** on a house.*
- (지불할 돈의 일부로 처음에 내는) 착수금(보증금)

v.

- place, unload, rest
- to put or set down in a specific place
- *The student **deposited** her textbooks on the table.*
- (특정한 곳에) 두다(놓다)

34. domesticate
dəˈmestəˌkāt
v.

- tame, subjugate, train
- to tame an animal to keep it as a pet or livestock
- *Dogs were **domesticated** so they could guard their masters.*
- (동물을) 길들이다(사육하다)

35. urge
ərj
v.

- advocate, recommend, advise
- to recommend or support strongly
- *General Lee **urged** his troops to continue fighting against the Japanese navy.*
- 강력히 권고(촉구)하다

36. rigor
ˈrigər
n.

- austerity, harshness, difficulty
- severity or strictness
- *Military work is full of **rigor** and haste.*
- 엄격, 준엄

37. ratio
ˈrāSHēˌō
n.

- proportion, correlation, fraction
- the relationship between two things with respect to the number of times one is contained in the other
- *What is the **ratio** of male to female employees in the office?*
- 비율

38. mimic
ˈmimik
v.

- imitate, impersonate, mock
- to copy someone else's actions or words in order to entertain or make fun of
- *Comedians love to **mimic** popular celebrities to entertain their audience.*
- 흉내를 내다

SET 22

39 restore
rəˈstôr
v.

recover, refurbish, revitalize
to bring back to a previous state or situation
*The dirty statue was **restored** to its former aesthetic artwork.*
회복시키다

40 enclose
inˈklōz
v.

surround, circle, encompass
to surround or close off on all sides
*The sheep were **enclosed** with a wooden fence.*
두르다(둘러싸다)

41 revere
rəˈvir
v.

venerate, honor, esteem
to feel respect or admiration for
*The reverend was **revered** for his service to the community.*
숭배하다

42 opaque
ōˈpāk
adj.

obscure, unclear, mysterious
hard or impossible to understand
*The scientific terminology and explanation was **opaque** to the cheerleader.*
불투명(불분명)한, 이해하기 힘든

43 wispy
ˈwispē
adj.

thin, fine, slender
thin and weak
*Mr. Monopoly is famous for his white, **wispy** moustache.*
(촘촘하지 못하고) 몇 가닥(줄기)으로 된, 성긴

44 inhospitable
ˌinhäˈspidəb(ə)l
adj.

uninviting, hostile, desolate
harsh and difficult to live in
*Chernobyl has become an **inhospitable** city due to a nuclear disaster.*
사람이 지내기(살기) 힘든

45 taxing
ˈtaksiNG
adj.

burdensome, arduous, onerous
physically or mentally demanding
*Construction work is a **taxing** job.*
아주 힘든(부담이 큰)

46 crave
krāv
v.

desire, covet, want

to have a strong desire for something

*In this hot weather, I **crave** ice cream.*

갈망(열망)하다

47 ostensibly
äˈstensiblē
adv.

apparently, seemingly, allegedly

the way something appears to be when it is not

***Ostensibly**, the villain is a sweet loving man amongst his family and friends.*

표면상(은)

48 counteract
ˌkoun(t)ərˈakt
v.

thwart, foil, curb

to act against something in order to prevent it

*Countries should decrease their carbon emission to **counteract** global warming.*

(무엇의 악영향에) 대응하다

49 deposition
ˌdepəˈziSH(ə)n
n.

affidavit, affirmation, testimony

the process of providing factual evidence

*Several bystanders gave their **depositions** to help the court case.*

증언(진술) 녹취록

n.

impeachment, removal, dismissal

the action of overthrowing someone

*Several kings in Europe experienced **desposition** from their own subjects.*

물러나게 함(퇴위/폐위(시킴))

50 shed
SHed
v.

discard, scrap, jettison

to throw away something that is not needed

*Trees **shed** their dead leaves during fall.*

(원하지 않는 것을) 없애다(버리다)

SET 22 TEST

1. Taking care of a baby all day long is a _____ job.

2. Children tend to _____ their parents as they get older.

3. Soldiers must show _____ and discipline while in combat.

4. It was _____ to everyone that she liked him.

5. The garden behind the mansion provided a _____ environment.

6. My wife shot a _____ look when she saw a dog without a leash.

7. The birthday party would _____ the opening of presents.

8. My grandmother continues to _____ for her husband who passed away last year.

9. The coupon was _____ after she used it.

10. A _____ drinker is considered an alcoholic.

---

1. taxing   2. revere   3. rigor   4. apparent   5. tranquil   6. repulsive   7. entail   8. lament   9. annul   10. chronic

11. This matter is _____ with the situation at hand.

12. The house my father built in the woods was _____ because it had no water nor gas.

13. Horses were _____ early by Mongolian tribes.

14. The _____ buisnessman parked his Lamborghini.

15. Korean students are _____ since there is no discussion in the classrooms.

16. In the _____ of Spring, trees will turn green and the ice will start to melt.

17. My mother _____ me from getting a tattoo of my girlfriend.

18. The rabbit _____ into its hole when the fox entered the forest.

19. The _____ cave paintings showed that early humans knew how to use fire.

20. _____, the man happened to run into his ex-girlfriend at the store.

---

11. pertinent   12. inhospitable   13. domesticate   14. affluent   15. myopic
16. onset   17. deplore   18. retreat   19. primeval   20. Incidentally

SET 22

notes:

LEAD SET 23 VOCABULARY

SET 23

01 mundane
ˌmənˈdān
adj.

- dull, monotonous, routine
- lacking interest or enthusiasm
- *The old man became tired of his **mundane** life, so he went on a road trip.*

재미없는, 일상적인

02 thrifty
ˈThriftē
adj.

- prudent, economical, frugal
- carefully using money and other resources and not wasting
- *A **thrifty** shopper will never carry a credit card.*

절약(검약)하는

03 salubrious
səˈloobrēəs
adj.

- healthy, beneficial, wholesome
- good for health
- *The **salubrious** diet will surely help me lose weight.*

살기 좋은, 건강에 좋은

04 peremptory
pəˈrem(p)t(ə)rē
adj.

- authoritative, commanding, despotic
- leaving no room for refusal
- *The **peremptory** order from the master sent the servants to do his bidding.*

위압적인, 독단적인

05 prompt
präm(p)t
v.

- cause, induce, lead
- to take course in action
- *A hunger strike from the family **prompted** the mother to learn cooking.*

일으키다, 초래하다

adj.

- instant, immediate, quick
- done with swiftness
- *Do not be **prompt** when solving questions.*

즉각적인, 지체 없는

06 hardly
ˈhärdlē
adv.

- barely, slightly, faintly
- only just
- *He **hardly** works on Mondays because he is too tired from the weekend.*

거의…아니다(없다)

07 seize
sēz
v.

grasp, grab, snatch

to forcefully take hold of something

*Carpe diem translates to **seize** the day.*

와락(꽉) 붙잡다(움켜잡다)

08 evade
əˈvād
v.

elude, deceive, dodge

escape by using cleverness

*The zebra **evaded** the lion by blending in with the grass.*

피하다(모면하다)

09 amplify
ˈampləˌfī
v.

magnify, intensify, augment

to make it more intense

*The speakers will help **amplify** your guitar sound.*

증폭시키다

10 dissect
dəˈsekt
v.

dismember, vivisect, anatomize

to cut up an organism to study its inner parts

*We **dissected** a frog in our science class today.*

해부(절개)하다

v.

scrutinize, inspect, analyze

to analyze something carefully

*A movie critic will **dissect** the film to find irregularities.*

해부(분석)하다

11 irritate
ˈirəˌtāt
v.

antagonize, aggravate, provoke

to make someone annoyed or angry

*The wolf pup **irritated** its mother while she was sleeping.*

짜증나게 하다, 거슬리다

12 proscribe
prōˈskrīb
v.

prohibit, embargo, outlaw

to forbid, typically by law

*The country **proscribed** any imports from the neighboring country.*

(공식적으로) 금하다(금지하다)

SET 23

13 concomitantly
ˌkänˈkämədəntlē
adv.

simultaneously, mutually, together
at the same time
*The two brothers were punished **concomitantly**.*
부수적으로, 수반하여

14 utterly
ˈədərlē
adv.

totally, wholly, thoroughly
completely
*Japanese forces were **utterly** defeated by the atomic bomb.*
완전히, 순전히, 아주, 전혀

15 capitulate
kəˈpiCHəˌlāt
v.

yield, succumb, acquiesce
to give up or surrender
*The Nazis **capitulated** soon after the Americans joined the war.*
항복하다

16 defer
dəˈfər
v.

postpone, adjourn, delay
to put off something to a later time
*The meeting was **deferred** because both parties had not arrived yet.*
미루다, 연기하다

17 fade
fād
v.

dim, dwindle, dissolve
to slowly grow faint and eventually disappear
*The car's backlight **faded** into the night.*
서서히 사라지다, 점점 희미해지다

18 sequence
ˈsēkwəns
n.

course, series, chain
a specific order of events or things
*A good story should follow a logical **sequence**.*
연속적인 사건들

19 philosophy
fəˈläsəfē
n.

ideology, logic, thought
the rational thinking of various truths and principles
*Socrates is an important figure in **philosophy**.*
철학

20 upswing
'əp͵swiNG
n.

boom, growth, increase

an increase in numbers or strength

*There was an **upswing** of factory workers when the labor laws improved.*

호전(상승/증가)

21 startling
'stärdliNG
adj.

astonishing, amazing, surprising

very surprising or remarkable

*Scientists made a **startling** discovery.*

깜짝 놀랄, 아주 놀라운(특이한)

22 minute
'minit
adj.

negligible, minimal, miniscule

very small, almost insignificant

*The driver had made **minute** scratches on the new car.*

극미한, 극히 작은

23 monotonous
mə'nätnəs
adj.

boring, repetitive, routine

lacking in variety and excitement

*Spinning yarn is a **monotonous** task.*

단조로운(변함없는)

24 assure
ə'SHoor
v.

convince, guarantee, promise

to say something to someone with confidence to remove any doubt they may have

*Brian **assured** that they will not be late for the appointment.*

장담하다, 확언(확약)하다

25 triumph
'trīəmf
n.

achievement, conquest, win

a great success or victory

*A parade was held to celebrate the athlete's **triumph** in the Olympics.*

(큰) 업적(승리), 대성공

SET 23

26. revolution
ˌrevəˈlooSH(ə)n
n.

- rebellion, insurrection, revolt
- a forced overthrow to replace an old social order with a new one
- The Soviet Union was formed by a socialist **revolution**.

(정치적인) 혁명

n.

- rotation, whirl, spin
- a turn or a cycle
- The Earth makes one **revolution** around the sun every 365 days.

공전

27. cluster
ˈkləstər
v.

- congregate, assemble, huddle
- to gather in a close group
- The penguins **clustered** together to withstand the cold.

무리를 이루다, (소규모로) 모이다

28. flourish
ˈfləriSH
v.

- thrive, prosper, bloom
- to develop quickly and successfully
- The jellyfish population **flourished** once the number of planktons increased.

번창하다

29. repercussion
ˌrēpərˈkəSHən
n.

- outcome, byproduct, reverberation
- an unintentional consequence
- The **repercussion** of his lie caused many problems in the family.

(어떤 사건이 초래한, 보통 좋지 못한, 간접적인) 영향

30. astound
əˈstound
v.

- startle, confound, stagger
- to shock or surprise
- His sudden death **astounded** everyone.

경악시키다, 큰 충격을 주다

31. conceal
kənˈsēl
v.

- cloak, shroud, screen
- to keep from sight
- The jar of cookies were **concealed** from the obese child.

감추다, 숨기다

32. landmark
'lan(d)ˌmärk
n.

- marker, indicator, signal
- an object or feature of a landscape that is easily seen and recognized from far away
- *The lighthouse is a **landmark** for ships sailing by.*

주요 지형지물, 랜드마크

n.
- milestone, watershed, milepost
- an event or discovery which marks an important stage or turning point
- *The end of racial segregation was a **landmark**.*

획기적 사건

33. fidelity
fə'deləde
n.

- allegiance, loyalty, commitment
- loyal to a person, cause, or belief
- *The judge's public career was marked by **fidelity** to justice.*

충실함

34. insurmountable
ˌinsər'moun(t)əb(ə)l
adj.

- invincible, overwhelming, impossible
- too great to overcome
- *Global warming seems like an **insurmountable** problem to solve.*

대처(극복)할 수 없는

35. aloft
ə'lôft
adv.

- high, skyward, up
- up in the air
- *The gold medalist proudly held the trophy **aloft**.*

하늘(위로) 높이

36. abrasion
ə'brāZHən
n.

- wearing, erosion, corrosion
- the process of scraping something away
- *The bicycle chain is resistant to **abrasion**.*

긁힌 부분, 찰과상

37. percolate
'pərkəˌlāt
v.

- spread, permeate, pervade
- to spread through an area or group of people
- *The most recent gossip started to **percolate** throughout the campus.*

스며들다(퍼지다)

SET 23

38 spelunk
spi-luhngk
v.

to explore caves
Spelunking can be dangerous since one can get lost inside a cave.

동굴을 탐험하다

39 geometric
jēə'metrik
adj.

measurable, structural, symmetrical
characterized by regular lines and shapes
Picasso's artwork can be described with **geometric** shapes.

기하학의

40 virtue
'vərCHoo
n.

goodness, morality, integrity
behavior with high moral standards
An honest man upholds **virtue**.

선, 선행

41 hypothesis
hī'päTHəsəs
n.

theory, conjecture, speculation
a possible explanation based on limited evidence
The **hypothesis** that the Earth is flat was mocked by the scientific community.

가설

42 intrigue
in'trēg
v.

fascinate, captivate, attract
to arouse the interest of
The professor was **intrigued** by the student's novel question.

강한 흥미(호기심)를 불러일으키다

43 merchandise
'mərCHən,dīz
n.

goods, commodities, product
items which are bought and sold
The small corner market offered an impressive variety of **merchandise**.

물품, 상품

44 track
trak
v.

pursue, stalk, trace
to follow the course of someone or something, usually to find them or note their location
The hunter was able to **track** the wounded deer.

추적하다(뒤쫓다)

45. overlook
ˌōvərˈlo͝ok
v.

neglect, disregard, ignore

to ignore or disregard something that is wrong

*Parents are able to **overlook** the mistakes of their children.*

(잘못된 것을) 못 본 체하다(눈감아주다)

46. inherent
inˈhirənt
adj.

intrinsic, ingrained, essential

existing in something as an important, permanent, or characteristic part

*Rock climbing has its **inherent** dangers.*

내재하는

47. comprehensive
ˌkämprəˈhensiv
adj.

inclusive, complete, thorough

including all or nearly all the parts of something

*The instructor has a **comprehensive** knowledge of the lesson.*

포괄적인, 종합적인

48. comprehend
ˌkämprəˈhend
v.

grasp, discern, assimilate

to understand

*The heroes were unable to **comprehend** the power of the supervillain.*

이해하다

49. tacit
ˈtasət
adj.

implicit, implied, hinted

understood or implied without being stated

*His silence was understood to mean **tacit** repentance.*

암묵적인, 무언의

50. cumbersome
ˈkəmbərsəm
adj.

unwieldy, unmanageable, inconvenient

large or heavy and therefore hard to carry or use

*The new hammer was **cumbersome** even for the mighty Thor.*

복잡하고 느린, 번거로운

SET 23 TEST

1. It is important to save money at an early age so that one can be _____ later on.

2. Any _____ command given by someone of higher rank should be carried out.

3. The problem was _____ when more people began to gossip.

4. The state of California _____ citizens from walking outside without wearing face masks.

5. The Japanese forces _____ after the Americans dropped the atomic bombs.

6. Even a _____ dose of the poison can kill you.

7. A _____ of drunk driving can be the death of a pedestrian.

8. The crusader's _____ to the gospel allowed them to triumph over their enemies.

9. The spilled juice slowly _____ on the table.

10. Individuals give up in their pursuit for _____ when they start to lie or steal.

---

1. thrifty   2. peremptory   3. amplify   4. proscribe   5. capitulate   6. minute   7. repercussion   8. fidelity   9. percolate   10. virtue

11. The very first computers were _____, not like the portable ones we have today.

12. Impressionist paintings show _____ scenes of life, but with vivid colors and texture.

13. An apple a day is _____.

14. It is difficult to _____ the situation with so little time.

15. The cockroaches were _____ exterminated once the insecticides were sprayed.

16. College students tend to _____ their studies until the week of their exams.

17. There was an _____ in the number of participants when a prize was announced.

18. The work of a dentist can be a _____ job since they stare into mouths all day long.

19. The friends attempted to _____ their friend by decorating the house with ornaments.

20. The game of hide and seek is to _____ oneself from being discovered.

11. cumbersome 12. mundane 13. salubrious 14. evade 15. utterly 16. defer 17. upswing 18. monotonous 19. astound 20. conceal

SET 23

notes:

LEAD
SET 24
VOCABULARY

SET 24

01 urban
'ərbən
adj.

town, city, metropolitan

characterizing a town or city

The **urban** population far exceeds the rural one.

도시의, 도회지의

02 leisure
'lēZHər
n.

freedom, respite, relief

free time

I watch movies during my **leisure** time.

여가

03 venue
'ven͵yoō
n.

setting, site, place

the place where something occurs

The park could become the **venue** for this year's picnic.

장소

04 lodge
läj
n.

cottage, cabin, house

a small house out in the country

My father has a **lodge** out in the forest.

오두막(산장)

v.

stick, wedge, embed

to put or place something firmly in a particular place

The bullet was **lodged** in his spine.

끼워 넣다(밀어 넣다)

05 reverberation
rəˌvərbə'rāSH(ə)n
n.

resonance, echo, resounding

the lengthening of a sound

The **reverberation** is much better inside a concert hall.

(소리의) 반향(잔향)

06 clever
'klevər
adj.

intelligent, bright, smart

quick to comprehend, learn, and come up with new ideas

Loki was **clever** to have a backup plan.

영리한, 똑똑한

07 designate
'dezigˌnāt
v.

appoint, nominate, delegate

to appoint someone to a particular position

I was **designated** to be the driver during the trip.

(특정한 자리나 직책에) 지명하다

08 reflective
rəˈflektiv
adj.

thoughtful, meditative, contemplative

characterized by insight

*The pope is a quiet, **reflective** man.*

사색적인

09 tedious
ˈtēdēəs
adj.

mindless, insipid, bland

too long or dull

*Cleaning the house is a **tedious** task.*

지루한, 싫증나는

10 thrive
THrīv
v.

bloom, burgeon, succeed

to prosper or flourish

*Celebrities **thrive** from the cheer they receive from their fans.*

번창하다, 잘 자라다

11 centralize
ˈsentrəˌlīz
v.

concentrate, consolidate, unify

to focus under a central authority

*The different businesses were **centralized** under a major corporation.*

중앙집권화하다

12 teem
tēm
v.

overflow, overrun, swarm

to be full of

*The floor **teemed** with ants from the melted ice cream.*

풍부하다

13 rural
ˈroorəl
adj.

country, countryside, rustic

relating to the countryside and not the city

***Rural** areas do not even have a supermarket.*

시골의, 지방의

14 outpace
ˌoutˈpās
v.

eclipse, outrun, exceed

to move or improve faster than

*After much training, Sarah was able to **outpace** Jenny in the race.*

앞지르다, 앞서다

SET 24

15. accommodate
əˈkäməˌdāt
v.

lodge, house, board
to provide housing
*The kind host **accommodated** our family to his home.*

(살거나 지낼) 공간을 제공하다, 수용하다

v.

adjust, adapt, accustom
to adapt to
*My family had to **accommodate** to the miniature size of the room.*

적응하다

16. clumsy
ˈkləmzē
adj.

uncoordinated, ungraceful, awkward
awkward in movement or action
*Jason was **clumsy** and required assistance.*

어설픈, 재바르지 못한

17. lunatic
ˈlooːnəˌtik
n.

maniac, psychopath, loony
someone who is mentally ill
*The **lunatic** decided to rob the bank while the police were inside.*

미치광이 (같은 사람)

18. potent
ˈpōtnt
adj.

powerful, strong, formidable
possessing great power or influence
*Cold medicines happen to be the most **potent** medicine.*

강한(강력한)

19. proportionate
prəˈpôrSH(ə)nət
adj.

corresponding, comparable, relative
similar in amount or size to another
*The number of accidents is **proportionate** to the increase in traffic.*

(~에) 비례하는

20. advent
ˈadˌvent
n.

arrival, appearance, emergence
the arrival of someone or something
*The **advent** of mobile phones increased communication.*

도래, 출현

21 dub
dəb
v.

label, christen, nickname

to give a nickname to someone or something

*A lazy person is **dubbed** "couch potato."*

별명을 붙이다

22 redundant
rəˈdəndənt
adj.

unnecessary, dispensable, disposable

no longer necessary or useful

*The pager has become **redundant** with the invention of the mobile phone.*

불필요한, 쓸모없는

23 authentic
ôˈTHen(t)ik
adj.

original, real, legitimate

genuine

*The painting found in the basement is an **authentic** Monet masterpiece.*

진본(진품)인

24 aesthetic
esˈTHedik
adj.

decorative, ornamental, beautiful

concerned with beauty

*The unbalanced, unfocused painting is considered **aesthetic**.*

심미적, 미학적

25 compromise
ˈkämprəˌmīz
n.

agreement, understanding, settlement

a settlement to a dispute

*The two countries reached a **compromise** in the trade agreement.*

협정, 합의

v.

undermine, weaken, damage

to accept standards that are lower than ideal

*The sudden workload **compromised** his plans for a relaxing night.*

약화시키다, 손상시키다

26 intact
inˈtakt
adj.

whole, unharmed, unscathed

not damaged or weakened

*The porcelain was **intact** even after the long boat ride.*

온전한, 전혀 다치지 않은

SET 24

27 feat
fēt
n.

accomplishment, triumph, attainment

an achievement which requires great skill and strength

*The new space rockets are considerable **feats** of engineering.*

위업, 개가; (뛰어난) 솜씨(재주)

28 diminish
dəˈminiSH
v.

decline, shrink, lessen

to make or become less

*Fossil fuel will **diminish** with the increase in industrial development.*

줄어들다, 약해지다; 줄이다, 약화시키다

29 symbol
ˈsimbəl
n.

sign, character, mark

a mark or character used to represent an object or process

*The exclamation **symbol** along roads stand for danger ahead.*

상징(물)

30 fruitful
ˈfro͞otfəl
adj.

productive, constructive, helpful

producing good results

*Years of hard work produced **fruitful** results.*

생산적인, 유익한

31 replete
rəˈplēt
adj.

teeming, brimful, packed

filled with something

*Her bag was **replete** with candy from the Halloween party.*

가득한(충분한)

32 rival
ˈrīvəl
n.

competitor, contestant, adversary

a person or thing that competes with another for the same goal or superiority

*Coca-Cola and Pepsi will always be **rivals** in business.*

경쟁자, 경쟁 상대

33 woe
wō
n.

misery, sorrow, sadness

great sorrow or distress

*Thor was overcome with **woe** when he witnessed his kingdom being destroyed.*

비통, 비애

34. scrutinize
'skroōtn,īz
v.

inspect, survey, scan

to examine closely and thoroughly

*The professor **scrutinized** the student's essay for any forgery.*

세심히 살피다, 면밀히 조사(검토)하다

35. emergent
ə'mərjənt
adj.

beginning, developing, nascent

in the process of coming into being

*Cryptocurrency is still an **emergent** form of payment.*

신생의, 신흥의

36. voracious
və'rāSHəs
adj.

gluttonous, insatiable, unquenchable

wanting or consuming great amount of food

*I become a **voracious** diner at a buffet.*

(음식에 대해) 게걸스러운

37. pressing
'presiNG
adj.

urgent, desperate, demanding

requiring quick or immediate response

*The President has more **pressing** matters to attend than walking his dog.*

긴급한

38. hallmark
'hôl,märk
n.

mark, sign, indication

a distinctive feature

*The tiny stitches on the bag are the **hallmark** of hand-crafted workmanship.*

특징(특질)

39. shallow
'Shalō
adj.

empty, flat, hollow

of little depth

*Babies can swim in the pool because it is **shallow**.*

얕은

adj.

foolish, superficial, frivolous

not showing, requiring, or capable of seriousness

*Judging a person by their appearance is a **shallow** characteristic.*

얄팍한, 얕은, 피상적인

SET 24

40 suspicion
səˈspiSHən
n.

- intuition, impression, feeling
- a feeling or thought that something is possible or true
- *The astronauts had a **suspicion** that something was wrong with the rocket.*
- (어떤 일이 사실일 것 같은) 느낌

n.
- doubt, skepticism, uncertainty
- cautious distrust
- *I have a **suspicion** that he is lying.*
- 의심, 불신

41 promising
ˈpräməsiNG
adj.

- hopeful, favorable, gifted
- showing signs of success
- *The young Cruella was a **promising** fashion designer, with many novel ideas.*
- 유망한, 촉망되는; 조짐이 좋은

42 shred
Shred
v.

- mince, cut, grate
- to tear or cut into little pieces
- *The cabbage was **shredded** to make the salad.*
- 자르다(찢다), 채를 썰다

43 paltry
ˈpôltrē
adj.

- negligible, inadequate, trifling
- small and insignificant
- *She received a **paltry** 1% raise on her salary.*
- 보잘것없는, 쥐꼬리만한

44 lag
lag
v.

- linger, straggle, delay
- to fall behind in movement or progress
- *The inexperienced team **lagged** behind the other teams in the race.*
- 뒤에 처지다, 뒤떨어지다

45 petition
pəˈtiSH(ə)n
n.

- application, request, suit
- a formal written request
- *The entire class signed a **petition** for the vocabulary test to be easier.*
- (법원에 법률적 처리를 요청하는) 신청서

46. partition
pärˈtiSH(ə)n
v.

divide, separate, split

to divide into parts

*The large conference room was **partitioned** to accommodate the different groups.*

분할하다, 나누다

47. hallow
ˈhalō
v.

consecrate, sanctify, bless

to make holy

*The priest **hallowed** the wine and the bread before serving them.*

신성한 것으로 숭배하다

48. conduit
ˈkänˌd(y)o͞oət
n.

channel, duct, pipe

a pipe or tube to transport water or other fluid

*The sewage water flowed down the **conduit**.*

도관, 전선관

49. impunity
imˈpyoonədē
n.

immunity, indemnity, pardon

exemption from punishment

*The criminal was given **impunity** for his crimes since he helped save the world.*

처벌을 받지 않음

50. alliance
əˈlīəns
n.

union, league, entente

a relationship or association formed for mutual benefits

*America and China have a commercial **alliance** to benefit the economies of both nations.*

동맹, 연합

SET 24 TEST

1. The convict was granted _____ in exchange for important information.

2. The work desks were _____ so that each worker had their individual working space.

3. The homeless shelter gave _____ portions of the thanksgiving meal because of minimal donations.

4. The _____ of any vacation is getting away from one's work or studies.

5. The reporter _____ her notes before writing her article.

6. He was _____ with sorrow when his dog died.

7. Winning a gold medal at the olympics is a remarkable _____.

8. My brother and I reached a _____ on who would get the house.

9. Continuing to play the game would be _____ since there was already a wide gap in the score.

10. The _____ of the steam engine helped usher in the industrial revolution in England.

---

1. impunity 2. partition 3. paltry 4. hallmark 5. scrutinize 6. replete 7. feat 8. compromise 9. redundant 10. advent

11. The witch brewed a _____ love potion for the princess.

12. The lake was _____ with fish since it was fishing season.

13. Organizing the files and folders in a computer is a _____ task.

14. The _____ for the birthday party is on a boat.

15. The young athelete displayed a _____ career ahead of him.

16. The president had to leave his party to respond to a _____ matter.

17. Farming this year was _____ so the family were able to purchase a new tractor.

18. The level of oxygen started to _____ inside the malfunctioning spacecraft.

19. The _____ sculpture of the goddess was auctioned at a record price.

20. My friend is _____ turtle because he is slow in everything.

---

11. potent 12. teem 13. tedious 14. venue 15. promising 16. pressing 17. fruitful 18. diminish 19. aesthetic 20. dub

SET 24

notes:

LEAD
SET 25
VOCABULARY

SET 25

01 superfluous
soo'pərflooəs
adj.

redundant, excess, spare

being more than enough so that it is unnecessary

*Sam fills the cart with **superfluous** items whenever he goes shopping.*

(더 이상) 필요치 않은(불필요한)

---

02 august
ô'gəst
adj.

distinguished, venerable, respected

respected and impressive

*I work for an **august** law firm.*

위엄 있는

---

03 conceive
kən'sēv
v.

inseminate, impregnate, fertilize

to become pregnant with a child

*My wife was **conceived** during our honeymoon.*

(아이를) 가지다(임신하다)

v.

devise, formulate, develop

to make or come up with a plan or idea

*The Mars mission was **conceived** during the late twentieth century.*

(생각,계획 등을) 마음속으로 하다(품다), 상상하다

---

04 genuine
'jenyooən
adj.

real, legitimate, valid

authentic

*The bag is made of **genuine** leather.*

진짜의, 진품의

adj.

honest, truthful, candid

sincere

*The child showed **genuine** interest in science.*

진실한, 진심 어린

---

05 synthetic
sin'Thedik
adj.

artificial, imitation, simulated

not created naturally

*The **synthetic** rubber tire actually helped the car stop better.*

합성한, 인조의

298 · LEAD VOCABULARY

06 exclusive
ik'skloōsiv
adj.

	complete, full, absolute
	not allowing other things
	*My **exclusive** attention is on the professor's lecture.*
	완전한

adj.

	sole, only, unique
	restricted to the area, group, or person
	*The basketball shoe was **exclusive** only in South Korea.*
	혼자(단독)의

07 sustain
sə'stān
v.

	assist, encourage, support
	to support physically or mentally
	*His family **sustained** him during his years in the army.*
	살아가게(존재하게/지탱하게) 하다

v.

	continue, prolong, extend
	to continue or be prolonged
	*The student cannot **sustain** his concentration.*
	계속(지속)시키다

v.

	suffer, endure, experience
	to undergo or suffer
	*They **sustained** some damage from the enemy.*
	(피해 등을) 입다(당하다)

08 defect
'dēfekt
n.

	fault, flaw, imperfection
	an imperfection or lack of a part
	*Children who have genetic **defects** may have problems with their body.*
	결함

v.

	desert, abandon, forsake
	to abandon one's country
	*The soldier **defected** to the other side after being betrayed.*
	(정당·국가 등을) 버리다(떠나다)

09 drawback
'drô͵bak
n.

	disadvantage, downside, catch
	a feature that is problematic
	*The **drawback** to the solution is that he would lose some money.*
	결점, 문제점

SET 25

10 suburb
ˈsəbərb
n.

- suburbia, village
- a residential area
- *There are many **suburbs** in America because there is so much land.*
- 교외(도심지를 벗어난 주택 지역)

11 debut
dāˈbyoo
n.

- launch, premiere, inauguration
- a person's appearance for the first time
- *Her **debut** as a movie star gained immediate attention.*
- 데뷔, 첫 출연(출전)

12 hone
hōn
v.

- whet, sharpen
- to make perfect one's skill over a length of time
- *The athlete **honed** his stamina by running every morning.*
- (특히 기술을) 연마하다

13 grandiose
ˈgrandēˌōs
adj.

- magnificent, imposing, splendid
- excessively grand and impressive
- *The Buckingham Palace is a **grandiose** architecture.*
- (너무) 거창한, (실속 없이) 거창하기만 한

14 hypnosis
hipˈnōsəs
n.

- mesmerism, hypnotism
- a trace-like condition, characterized by susceptibility to suggestion
- *She fell under **hypnosis** conducted by the magician.*
- 최면 (상태)

15 ethereal
əˈThirēəl
adj.

- celestial, heavenly, spiritual
- heavenly or spiritual
- *Her singing was like an **ethereal** performance.*
- 천상의

16 splendor
ˈsplendər
n.

- magnificence, grandeur, glory
- a magnificent appearance
- *The **splendor** of the Hawaiian islands will captivate anyone.*
- 빛남, 광휘, 광채

17 rumor
ˈroomər
n.

- gossip, hearsay, buzz
- a story or report of uncertainty
- *Some people like to spread **rumors**.*
- 소문, 풍문, 풍설, 유언비어

18	**translucent**	semitransparent, glassy, colorless
	tranz'loōsnt	allowing light to pass through, but not detailed shapes
	adj.	*The dirty window became **translucent** after the rain.*
		반투명한

19	**apparition**	ghost, phantom, spirit
	ˌapəˈriSH(ə)n	a ghost or something ghostlike
	n.	*The **apparition** floated down the hall.*
		유령

20	**embolden**	encourage, strengthen, rally
	əmˈbōldən	to give courage to do something
	v.	*The music **emboldened** the athlete to win the game.*
		대담하게 만들다

21	**elicit**	evoke, prompt, provoke
	ēˈlisət	to draw out a response
	v.	*The game host tried his best to **elicit** a response from the contestant.*
		(정보·반응을 어렵게) 끌어내다

22	**exploit**	abuse, swindle, misuse
	ikˈsploit	to benefit from the work of someone else, usually in an unfair way
	v.	*Workers are **exploited** in Vietnam sweatshops by American companies.*
		(부당하게) 이용하다
		feat, stunt, maneuver
	n.	a bold or daring act
		*His **exploits** in the war made him a hero.*
		위업, 공적

23	**hue**	color, tint, shade
	(h)yoō	a color or shade
	n.	*Van Gogh preferred to use dark **hues** in his paintings.*
		빛깔, 색조

24	**chancy**	unpredictable, precarious, uncertain
	ˈChansē	prone to sudden changes and situations
	adj.	*Getting a random airport security check is a **chancy** procedure.*
		불확실한, 위험한

SET 25

25. daunt
dônt
v.
- intimidate, frighten, demoralize
- to intimidate someone
- The drill sergeant **daunted** the new army recruits.
- 겁먹게(기죽게) 하다

26. illuminate
iˈloomə‚nāt
v.
- light, brighten, irradiate
- to make something bright or visible
- The new light bulb **illuminated** the room.
- (…에 불을) 비추다

v.
- clarify, elucidate, reveal
- to make clear
- The professor **illuminated** his lecture by showing video clips.
- (이해하기 쉽게) 밝히다(분명히 하다)

27. avant-garde
‚avänt'gärd
n.
- innovative, original, inventive
- new or unusual ideas
- Michelle's work is very unusual, even **avant-garde**.
- 아방가르드(문학,예술에서 전위적인 사상)

28. compatriot
kəmˈpātrēət
n.
- countryman, countrywoman
- a fellow citizen of a country
- The runner defeated his **compatriot** in the Olympics game.
- 동포

29. coalesce
‚kōəˈles
v.
- unite, merge, fuse
- to come together
- Droplets of oil **coalesce** when mixed with water.
- 합치다

30. tribute
ˈtribyoot
n.
- praise, acclaim, salute
- an act, statement, or gift that is meant to display admiration, gratitude, or respect
- This statue is a **tribute** to the former president.
- 헌사(찬사)

n.
- payment, dues, tax
- payment that is given periodically to someone or an organization
- The people had to give **tribute** each month to receive protection.
- 공물

302 · LEAD VOCABULARY

31. depreciate
/dəˈprēSHēˌāt/
v.

cheapen, devalue, dwindle

to decrease in value over a length of time

*The price of a new car **depreciates** as soon as you drive it out of the lot.*

가치가 떨어지다(절하되다)

32. enrage
/inˈrāj/
v.

anger, infuriate, inflame

to make very angry

*You do not want to **enrage** the Hulk.*

격분하게 만들다

33. verdict
/ˈvərdikt/
n.

judgement, ruling, decision

a decision on a disputed issue

*The head juror delivered the **verdict**.*

평결

34. assault
/əˈsôlt/
v.

strike, hit, beat

to make a physical attack

*He was arrested for **assaulting** a police officer.*

공격

35. constrain
/kənˈstrān/
v.

restrain, contain, curb

to restrict the extent or activity of

*I had to **constrain** my dog from biting the pedestrian.*

제한(제약)하다

36. inexorable
/inˈeksərəb(ə)l/
adj.

relentless, inevitable, persistent

impossible to stop or prevent

*Gossiping is an **inexorable** course of action.*

멈출(변경할) 수 없는, 거침없는

37. uneasy
/ˌənˈēzē/
adj.

anxious, nervous, disturbed

causing or feeling anxiety

*People feel **uneasy** when they leave their house without their mobile phones.*

불안한, 우려되는

SET 25

38. rove
rōv
v.
- roam, meander, wander
- to wander without a fixed destination
- The Mars Rover **roves** the surface of the red planet.
- 방랑하다

39. pity
ˈpidē
n.
- compassion, condolence, sorrow
- the feeling of sorrow and compassion due to the suffering of others
- I felt **pity** for the homeless man.
- 연민, 동정(심), 불쌍히(측은히) 여김

40. abject
ˈab jekt
adj.
- groveling, submissive, obsequious
- without pride or dignity
- A utopia is a place with neither extreme wealth nor **abject** poverty.
- 극도로 비참한, 절망적인

41. intersect
ˌin(t)ərˈsekt
v.
- cross, converge, connect
- when two or more objects pass or lie across each other
- Streets **intersect** on main roads.
- 교차하다(만나다)

42. recurring
rəˈkəriNG
adj.
- persist, repeat, iterate
- occurring again repeatedly
- The **recurring** dream always ended when he fell in the water.
- 되풀이하여 발생하는

43. longevity
lônˈjevədē
n.
- durability, endurance, lastingness
- long existence or service
- Whales can have a **longevity** of more than 100 years.
- 장수, 오래 지속됨

44. balmy
ˈbä(l)mē
adj.
- temperate, mild, gentle
- referring to a pleasantly warm weather
- The **balmy** days of early summer were welcomed after the chilly nights in spring.
- 아늑한, 훈훈한

45. tamper
'tampər
v.

meddle, tinker, manipulate

to make unauthorized changes

*Someone **tampered** with my experiment.*

손대다, 함부로 변경하다

46. meddlesome
'medlsəm
adj.

intrusive, prying, inquisitive

fond of interfering

*Housewives love to be **meddlesome** in another person's affairs.*

간섭(참견)하길 좋아하는

47. depose
də'pōz
v.

overthrow, topple, dethrone

to suddenly and forcefully remove someone from office

*The king was **deposed** after the people won the revolution.*

물러나게 하다(퇴위/폐위시키다)

48. jettison
'jedəsən
v.

ditch, discard, scrap

to abandon or throw away

*The people on the boat had to **jettison** their belongings when the boat started to sink.*

버리다(폐기하다)

49. constrict
kən'strikt
v.

tighten, compress, contract

to make narrower by applying pressure

*The snake **constricted** its prey until it suffocated.*

수축되다(하다), 조이다(죄다)

50. federal
'fed(ə)rəl
adj.

confederate, united, allied

related to a system of government where several states form a unity but maintain their independence

*The postal service in America is administered by the **federal** government.*

연방제의

SET 25 CROSSWORD PUZZLE

Across

1. a decision on a disputed issue
7. to come together
12. to restrict the extent or activity of
13. not created naturally
14. without pride or dignity
15. an imperfection or lack of a part

Down

2. to give courage to do something
3. to intimidate someone
4. excessively grand and impressive
5. to draw out a response
6. impossible to stop or prevent
8. restricted to the area, group, or person
9. a feature that is problematic
10. respected and impressive
11. to make unauthorized changes

LEAD
SET 26
VOCABULARY

SET 26

01 progressive
prə'gresiv
adj.

- continuing, developing, ongoing
- happening step by step
- *There was a **progressive** decline in the bee population.*

점진적인, 꾸준히 진행되는

adj.
- liberal, modern, radical
- in favor of new, liberal ideas
- *The **progressive** politician gained favor from the younger generation.*

진보(혁신)적인

02 profession
prə'feSHən
n.

- career, occupation, vocation
- a paid occupation
- *My **profession** is a teacher.*

직업(직종)

n.
- affirmation, statement, proclamation
- a declaration of a feeling or quality
- *The saint declared his **profession** of faith to the people.*

주장

03 compensate
'kämpən,sāt
v.

- reimburse, recompense, repay
- to give someone something, usually money, for their work, loss, or injury
- *Michelle was **compensated** for her work at the store.*

보상하다

04 deficiency
də'fiSHənsē
n.

- insufficiency, inadequacy, deficit
- a lack or shortage
- *Children who do not eat meat have protein **deficiency**.*

결핍(부족)(증)

n.
- defect, flaw, imperfection
- a weakness
- *The **deficiency** in the car design was quickly fixed.*

결함

05 innovative
'inə,vādiv
adj.

- original, novel, fresh
- original and creative in method and thinking
- *Albert Einstein had many **innovative** ideas.*

획기적인

06 detach
dəˈtaCH
v.

disconnect, separate, disengage

to separate and become removed

*My father **detached** the door to my room so that he could keep an eye on me.*

분리되다

07 layer
ˈlāər
n.

coating, film, covering

a thickness of some material that is put on top or spread over a surface

*There is a **layer** of paint on the wall.*

막(층/겹/켜)

08 transparent
tran(t)sˈperənt
adj.

clear, translucent, crystalline

allowing light to go through

*I can see the fish swimming in the **transparent** blue water.*

투명한

adj.

obvious, lucid, explicit

easy to detect

*It was **transparent** that he did not like her.*

속이 뻔히 들여다보이는, 명백한, 투명한

09 vacancy
ˈvākənsē
n.

void, opening, nothingness

an empty space

*The paralyzed person stared into **vacancy**.*

결원, 공석

10 benevolence
bəˈnevələns
n.

benignity, compassion, decency

kindness

*Mother Theresa's **benevolence** has impacted so many people.*

자비심, 박애

11 affirmative
əˈfərmədiv
adj.

agreeing, concurring, supportive

agreeing with a statement or request

*The wife responded with an **affirmative** answer.*

긍정의 (의미를 나타내는), 긍정(동의)하는

12 hazard
ˈhazərd
n.

peril, threat, danger

a danger or risk

*The **hazards** of smoking are even written on the cigarette box.*

위험 (요소)

SET 26 · 309

SET 26

13 detonate
ˈdetnˌāt
v.

erupt, blast, explode

to explode

*The atomic bomb **detonated** in Hiroshima.*

폭발하다(시키다)

14 rash
raSH
adj.

hasty, reckless, careless

showing or proceeding with minimal consideration of the possible effects of the action

*Do not make any **rash** decisions when investing millions of dollars.*

경솔한, 성급한

n.

spots, breakout, hives

an area of a skin that becomes red or covered with spots, possibly from an allergy or sickness

*Bobby's arm was covered with **rash** after touching the poison ivy.*

발진

15 extant
ˈekstənt
adj.

remaining, enduring, living

still surviving

*The original manuscript from the Middle Ages is no longer **extant**.*

현존(잔존)하는

16 embrace
əmˈbrās
v.

welcome, accept, espouse

to accept or support an idea or change with enthusiasm

*The scientists are **embracing** new approaches to their theory.*

(생각,제의 등을 열렬히) 받아들이다(수용하다)

n.

hug, cuddle, squeeze

an act of holding someone in one's arm

*After receiving the award, the scientists huddled in a group **embrace**.*

포옹

17 renown
rəˈnoun
n.

fame, prominence, prestige

the condition of being well known

*She had great **renown** as an actress so everyone wanted a picture with her.*

명성

18 entitle
inˈtīdl
v.

qualify, authorize, sanction

to give someone a legal authority to receive or carry out an action

*Factory workers are **entitled** to health insurance.*

자격(권리)을 주다

19 critic
'kridik
n.

commentator, reviewer, judge

someone who judges the value of artistic works in a professional manner

The film **critic** praised the director's latest movie.

비평가, 평론가

20 sensation
sen'sāSH(ə)n
n.

consciousness, awareness, feeling

an unexplainable awareness or impression

The woman had a **sensation** that she was being followed.

감각

n.

commotion, uproar, excitement

a widespread reaction of excitement and interest

The new restaurant caused a **sensation** in the neighborhood.

흥분, 신남

21 imperial
im'pirēəl
adj.

sovereign, monarchial, royal

relating to an empire

The **imperial** troops crushed the rebel forces.

제국의, 황제의

22 institute
'instə,t(y)o͞ot/
n.

organization, establishment, foundation

a group or organization having a specific goal or common interest

The research **institute** focuses their efforts on finding life in space.

(특히 교육전문 직종과 관련된) 기관(협회)

v.

launch, found, establish

to set in motion or establish something

The research center was **instituted** in the late twentieth century.

(제도·정책 등을) 도입하다, (절차를) 시작하다

23 reform
rə'fôrm
v.

ameliorate, refine, rectify

to make changes in a social, political, or economic level in order to improve it

With the new leader, there was an opportunity to **reform** the country.

(체제·조직·법률 등을) 개혁(개선)하다

SET 26

24. allocate
'alə‚kāt
v.
- allot, assign, administer
- to distribute resources or jobs
- The government **allocated** the land to the pioneers.
- (특정 목적을 위해 공식적으로) 할당하다

25. enforce
inˈfôrs
v.
- impose, implement, compel
- to follow or comply with the use of force
- The role of a police officer is to **enforce** the law.
- (법률 등을) 집행(시행/실시)하다

26. aristocracy
‚erəˈstäkrəsē
n.
- nobility, nobles, lords
- the highest level in certain societies
- The common people were not even allowed to look at the **aristocracy**.
- (일부 국가의) 귀족 (계층)

27. bureaucratic
‚byoorəˈkradik
adj.
- administrative, ministerial, official
- relating to operating an organization or government
- Third world countries have yet to establish a proper **bureaucratic** system.
- 관료의, 관료주의적인, 요식적인

28. deteriorate
dəˈtirēə‚rāt
v.
- degenerate, decay, degrade
- to become worse
- The two couple's relationship **deteriorated** after their last fight.
- 악화되다, 더 나빠지다

29. erosion
əˈrōZHən
n.
- abrasion, corrosion, weathering
- the slow process of destroying or minimizing something
- The **erosion** of the land was carried out for years by wind and rain.
- 부식, 침식

30. allot
əˈlät
v.
- issue, grant, apportion
- to give or distribute to someone
- Equal play time was **allotted** to each child.
- (시간, 돈, 업무 등을) 할당(배당)하다

31. ancient
ˈān(t)SHənt
adj.

former, bygone, past

from a very long time ago or no longer in existence

The **ancient** Egyptians built the great pyramids using novel techniques.

고대의

32. segment
ˈsegmənt
n.

part, section, division

a portion of a whole

A **segment** of the movie was missing.

부분

33. vitality
vīˈtalədē
n.

liveliness, life, energy

the condition of being strong and active

His **vitality** returned after eating food.

활력

34. assumption
əˈsəm(p)SH(ə)n
n.

supposition, presumption, premise

something that is accepted as truth without proof

The investor made **assumptions** about the stock market.

추정, 상정

n.

acceptance, undertaking, shouldering

the act of accepting responsibility or power

My brother took on the **assumption** as man of the house after my father died.

(권력, 책임의) 인수(장악)

35. mechanism
ˈmekəˌnizəm
n.

apparatus, machine, device

a piece of machinery

Currently, the country has no **mechanism** to harness renewable energy.

기계 장치(기구)

n.

method, technique, system

a process by which something is accomplished

Which **mechanism** do you suggest we use to solve this problem?

방법

36. anxiety
aNGˈzīədē
n.

worry, concern, apprehension

a feeling of nervousness or unease

The student was overcome with **anxiety** when the teacher gave a pop quiz.

불안(감), 염려

SET 26

37. interplay
ˈin(t)ərˌplā
n.

interaction, cooperation, interchange

the way two or more things affect each other

*Someone with schizophrenia experiences an **interplay** of different personalities.*

상호 작용

38. prey
prā
n.

victim, target, dupe

someone or something that is easily injured or taken advantage of

*He was a **prey** of voice phishing.*

희생자(피해자)

39. perceive
pərˈsēv
v.

discern, recognize, sense

to become aware of or conscious of something

*The ability to **perceive** can occur through the senses.*

감지(인지)하다

40. catastrophe
kəˈtastrəfē
n.

disaster, calamity, crisis

an event causing massive damage and suffering

*The asteroid colliding with Earth will cause a **catastrophe**.*

참사, 재앙

41. inorganic
ˌinôrˈganik
adj.

artificial, manmade

not from living matter

*Artificial sweeteners added to coffee are **inorganic** substances.*

무기물의

42. voyage
ˈvoiij
n.

trip, expedition, excursion

a long journey by sea or space

*The Enterprise embarked on a **voyage** to deep space.*

여행, 항해(특히 바다우주로 하는 긴 여행)

43. solidify
səˈlidəˌfī
v.

harden, freeze, stiffen

to make or become hard or solid

*The magma **solidified** into igneous rock.*

굳어지다, 굳히다

44. anoxia
əˈnäksēə
n.

the absence of oxygen

*Some bacteria are heat and cold resistant and can even tolerate **anoxia**.*

산소 결핍(증)의, 무산소증의

45. elongate
ēˈlôNGˌgāt
v.

lengthen, extend, broaden

to make something longer

*Fashion models look like humans that have been **elongated**.*

길어지다, 길게 늘이다

46. accession
akˈseSHən
n.

succession, elevation, inauguration

the obtaining of a position of rank or power

*The mad king's **accession** to the throne horrified the subjects.*

취임, 즉위

47. presume
prəˈz(y)o͞om
v.

suppose, expect, assume

assume that something is the case based on probability

*Do not **presume** that I will give up just because I lost everything.*

추정하다(여기다/생각하다)

48. mutate
ˈmyo͞otāt
v.

metamorphose, evolve, transmute

to change in form or nature

*The turtles **mutated** into human-like ninjas.*

변형되다

49. vicious
ˈviSHəs
adj.

brutal, ferocious, savage

intentionally cruel or violent

*The **vicious** animal was locked in a cage.*

잔인한, 포악한, 악랄한

50. plentitude
ˈplen(t)əˌt(y)o͞od
n.

profusion, wealth, plethora

an abundance

*The zoo boasts a **plentitude** of animals and birds.*

풍부함

SET 26 TEST

1. Undefeated champions _____ they will win their next game.

2. The tracks were _____ to create the path for the transcontinental railroad.

3. Some people are afraid that machines will one day learn to _____ and attack mankind.

4. Jogging everyday will help maintain _____.

5. The king _____ portions of the land to the people.

6. _____ policies are always the headline of the news.

7. The labor office _____ jobs to immigrant workers.

8. Stephen Hawking's _____ as a physicist is unparalleled.

9. The ruins of Pompeii are still _____.

10. The queen's _____ to the people was shunned by the tyrant king.

---

1. presume 2. elongate 3. perceive 4. vitality 5. allot 6. bureaucratic 7. allocate 8. renown 9. extant 10. benevolence

11. The older generation tends to stay away from _____ ideas.

12. Workers are _____ according to the number of hours they work.

13. In the game of poker, it is dangerous for the player to be _____ when they receive good cards.

14. His _____ in the corporate office was celebrated with joy and excitement.

15. The statue started to _____ after the acid rain fell.

16. The newly elected president immediately _____ the members in his cabinet.

17. Korean pop music has become a _____ in the recent decade.

18. This parking permit _____ you to park in the handicapped area.

19. The slaves in the south _____ the Union soldiers who had come to free them.

20. There was no _____ in the hotel.

---

11. progressive 12. compensate 13. transparent 14. accession 15. deteriorate 16. reform 17. sensation 18. entitle 19. embrace 20. vacancy

SET 26

notes:

LEAD
SET 27
VOCABULARY

SET 27

01 productive
prəˈdəktiv
adj.

fertile, fruitful, rich

able to make large amounts of commodities

*The monthly bonus was given to the most **productive** employee.*

(상품, 작물을 특히 대량으로) 생산(산출)하는

02 impact
ˈimˌpakt
n.

collision, crash, smash

the action of one object coming into contact with another forcibly

*An asteroid **impact** most likely killed the dinosaurs.*

충돌, 충격

v.

affect, influence, touch

to have a strong influence on someone or something

*The minister **impacted** the lives of many.*

영향(충격)을 주다

03 drought
drout
n.

aridity, dearth, dehydration

an extended period of low rainfall, leading to a lack of water

*The **drought** brought about a shortage of food.*

가뭄

04 prime
prīm
adj.

chief, central, principal

of main importance

*His **prime** concern is the well-being of his family.*

주된, 주요한; 기본적인

n.

heyday, zenith, pinnacle

the best time or state of a person's life

*He was at the **prime** of his game, breaking his old record.*

한창때, 전성기

05 fertile
ˈfərdl
adj.

prolific, fecund, lush

able to produce abundant vegetation or crops

*The Nile River helped the land near it to be **fertile**.*

비옥한, 기름진

adj.

reproductive, generative

able to conceive young or make seed

*Female lions become most **fertile** during their cycle called heat.*

생식력 있는, 가임의

06 harvest
'härvəst
n.

yield, crop, produce
the farming season's yield or crop
*Because of the monsoon, the farmers had a poor **harvest**.*

수확(추수)(기)

v.

collect, reap, gather
to gather or obtain for future use
*The farmer decided to **harvest** his crops earlier this year.*

수확하다, 거둬들이다

07 textile
'tek͵stīl
n.

fabric, cloth, material
a sort of cloth or fabric
*The Chinese produce **textiles** made of fine silk.*

직물, 옷감

08 epidemic
͵epə'demik
n.

outbreak, plague, scourge
an infectious disease which is widespread in a community at a given time
*A flu **epidemic** swept across the city.*

유행병, 유행성

09 ravage
'ravij
v.

devastate, ruin, destroy
to cause serious and widespread damage to
*The zombie army **ravaged** the city.*

황폐(피폐)하게 만들다, 유린(파괴)하다

10 infectious
in'fekSHəs
adj.

contaminating, virulent, polluting
prone to spread infection
*The common cold is an **infectious** sickness.*

(병이 특히 공기를 통해) 전염되는(전염성의)

11 devastate
'devə͵stāt
v.

wreck, ruin, annihilate
to destroy or ruin something
*The forest fire **devastated** the ecosystem.*

(한 장소나 지역을) 완전히 파괴하다

12 abandon
ə'bandən
v.

renounce, relinquish, disown
to leave someone or something
*The boy **abandoned** his dog and ran home.*

버리다(떠나다/유기하다)

SET 27

13 deserter
dəˈzərdər
n.
- runaway, fugitive, defector
- someone who leaves the group or organization
- The **deserter** was punished for leaving his post.
- 도망자

14 cope
kōp
v.
- handle, tackle, manage
- to deal with something difficult
- The widow had to **cope** with the loss of her husband.
- 대처(대응)하다

15 dilemma
diˈlemə
n.
- quandary, predicament, conundrum
- a difficult problem or situation
- Teenagers face the **dilemma** of obeying their parents or not listening to them.
- 난제

16 concession
kənˈseSHən
n.
- admission, acknowledgement, confession
- the action of surrendering or allowing something
- The **concession** made by the criminal decreased his prison term.
- 인정

17 lax
laks
adj.
- negligent, careless, slack
- not being strict or careful
- The **lax** security allowed the thieves to enter without being noticed.
- 느슨한(일, 규칙, 기준 등에 대해)

18 outright
ˈoutrīt
adv.
- entirely, wholly, totally
- completely
- Drinking alcohol on the streets has been banned **outright**.
- 완전히, 명백히

adv.
- instantly, instantaneously, immediately
- immediately
- The car crash killed the family **outright**.
- 즉시, 즉각

19 reclamation
ˌrekləˈmāSH(ə)n
n.
- recovery, redemption, repossession
- the action of claiming something back
- The Native Americans fought for the **reclamation** of their land.
- 되찾음

20. alien
'ālēən
n.

foreigner, immigrant, nonnative

someone who is not a natural citizen of the country where they live

*The illegal **alien** was deported back to his country.*

외국인 체류자

adj.

unfamiliar, strange, peculiar

not being familiar

*The food was **alien** to him so he did not take a bite.*

색다른

21. legal
'lēgəl
adj.

lawful, legitimate, valid

allowed by law

*The contract was **legal** because it was signed by both sides.*

법이 허용하는(요구하는), 합법적인

22. nationalism
'naSH(ə)nə,lizəm
n.

patriotism, nationality, xenophobia

supporting one's own nation and its interest

*People's **nationalism** can be displayed by putting up their country's flag.*

애국심, 국수주의

23. beneficiary
,benə'fiSHē,erē
n.

inheritor, recipient, receiver

a person who receives benefits from something

*The **beneficiary** received the insurance money and went on a vacation.*

수혜자

24. register
'rejəstər
n.

roster, index, directory

an official record or list

*A membership **register** displays phone numbers and addresses.*

기록(등록/등기)부, 명부

v.

file, enter, record

to enter or record

*Alice **registered** for gym membership.*

등록(기재)하다

SET 27

25 compel
kəmˈpel
v.
- pressure, press, force
- to force to do something
- A sense of duty **compelled** Mark to save the man.
- 강요(강제)하다, (필요에 따라) …하게 만들다

26 encroach
inˈkrōCH
v.
- intrude, trespass, obtrude
- to intrude on someone else's territory or right
- The cockroach **encroached** into the kitchen.
- (남의 시간, 권리, 생활 등을) 침해하다

27 dispute
diˈspyo͞ot
v.
- debate, quarrel, argue
- to argue about a topic
- The two candidates **disputed** which of them should be the leader.
- 반박하다, 이의를 제기하다

28 reclusive
rəˈklo͞osiv
adj.
- solitary, secluded, isolated
- avoiding being with other people
- The man preferred to live a **reclusive** life and moved to the mountains.
- 세상을 버린; 은둔한; 쓸쓸한, 적막한

29 bountiful
ˈboun(t)əfəl
adj.
- abundant, ample, profuse
- large in quantity
- The toy store had a **bountiful** supply of new toys.
- 많은, 풍부한

30 descend
dəˈsend
v.
- drop, fall, sink
- to move or fall down
- The submarine **descended** into deeper waters.
- 내려오다, 내려가다

31 predisposition
ˌprēdispəˈziSH(ə)n
n.
- susceptibility, proneness, tendency
- a likelihood or tendency to act in a particular way
- My grandfather has an annoying **predisposition** to find fault wherever he goes.
- 성향, 경향

32 escalate
'eskə‚lāt
v.

soar, rocket, surge

to increase rapidly

*The price of the antique **escalated** at the auction.*

확대(증가/악화)되다(시키다)

33 interdisciplinary
‚in(t)ər'dis(ə)plə‚nerē
adj.

integrative, associative, incorporative

involving more than one branch of knowledge

*The creation of the universe is an **interdisciplinary** subject which involves physics and astrology.*

학제간의(여러 학문 분야가 관련된)

34 sibling
'sibliNG
n.

brother, sister, kin

a brother or sister

*How many **siblings** do you have?*

형제자매(동기)

35 tenet
'tenət
n.

principle, doctrine, creed

a principle or belief, especially in religion or philosophy

*There are several **tenets** one must follow in Buddhism to achieve Nirvana.*

주의, 교의

36 intuitive
in't(y)ooədiv
adj.

instinctive, innate, inherent

based on what one feels to be true without logical reasoning

*I have an **intuitive** hunch that he will get caught lying.*

직감(직관)에 의한

37 awe
ô
n.

astonishment, amazement, admiration

a feeling of respect mixed with wonder

*The child stood in **awe** as the car transformed into a robot.*

경외감, 외경심

38 untapped
‚ən'tapt
adj.

idle, vacant, untried

referring to a resource that has not been used

*There are **untapped** oil deposits in the Pacific Ocean.*

아직 손대지(사용하지) 않은

SET 27

39 grant
grant
v.

| accord, permit, allow |
| to agree giving or allowing |
| *The genie stated that he will **grant** three wishes.* |
| 승인(허락)하다 |

n.

| endowment, contribution, donation |
| money given by the government or organization for a specific purpose |
| *The university **grant** will help the researchers fund for their experiment.* |
| 보조금 |

40 dissociate
diˈsōSHēˌāt
v.

| detach, sever, divorce |
| to disconnect or separate |
| *My brother decided to **disassociate** himself from the pseudo-religion.* |
| 스스로를/~를 ~와 분리하다(관련이 없음을 분명히 하다) |

41 revere
rəˈvir
v.

| respect, admire, venerate |
| to feel deep respect or admiration for someone or something |
| *King Sejong is **revered** for creating the Korean alphabet.* |
| 존경받는 |

42 coarse
kôrs
adj.

| rough, scratchy, shaggy |
| rough or loose in texture |
| *The wooden chair was too **coarse** to sit on.* |
| 거친 |

adj.

| rude, discourteous, impolite |
| referring to a person's speech as being rude or vulgar |
| *The women in the room were infuriated by his **coarse** speech.* |
| 음탕한 |

43 exacting
igˈzaktiNG
adj.

| demanding, stringent, taxing |
| making great demands |
| *It was difficult for the children to live up to their mother's **exacting** standards.* |
| 힘든, 까다로운 |

44	**soar**	wing, ascend, climb
	sôr	to fly or rise high in the air
	v.	*The majestic eagle **soared** in the cloudless sky.*
		날아오르다(날다)

45	**physiological**	physical, anatomical, bodily
	ˌfizēəˈläjək(ə)l	a branch of biology which deals with the normal functions of living organisms
	adj.	*The Vitruvian Man by da Vinci depicts a human in **physiological** perspective.*
		생리학(상)의, 생리적인

46	**carnivore**	predator, meat-eater
	ˈkärnəˌvôr	an animal that feeds on meat
	n.	*Tyrannosaurus Rex was a **carnivore**.*
		육식 동물

47	**herbivore**	vegan, vegetarian
	ˈ(h)ərbəˌvôr	an animal that feeds on plants
	n.	*A rabbit is a **herbivore**.*
		초식 동물

48	**omnivore**	
	ˈämnəˌvôr	an animal that feeds on both meat and plants
	n.	*A human being is an **omnivore**.*
		잡식 동물

49	**texture**	feel, quality, touch
	ˈteksCHər	the feel, appearance, or consistency of a substance or surface
	n.	*The **texture** of the steak is dependent on which part of the cow it is from.*
		감촉(질감)

50	**mistreat**	maltreat, abuse, misuse
	misˈtrēt	to treat an animal or person badly or unfairly
	v.	*Many animals are **mistreated** at animal shelters.*
		(사람,동물을) 학대(혹사)하다

SET 27 TEST

1. Working at the bank was so _____ that she eventually quit.

2. Mother Theresa is _____ for her kindness to children.

3. There are still _____ sources of energy out in space.

4. It was all thanks to the detective's _____ feeling that the bandit was caught.

5. The level of water _____ throughout the night as the rain continued to fall.

6. Someone who is socially awkward tends to have a _____ lifestyle.

7. The boys quietly _____ into the girl's cabin to set up the trap.

8. Koreans fought against the Japanese forces for the _____ of their freedom.

9. An employee who is _____ in their work will create problems for others.

10. One needs to learn how to _____ with stress, otherwise they will have a meltdown.

1. exacting 2. revere 3. untapped 4. intuitive 5. escalate 6. reclusive 7. encroach 8. reclamation 9. lax 10. cope

11. The villian _____ half the universe with the snap of his finger.

12. The Black Plague was an _____ that killed more than half the population of Europe.

13. Michael Jordan was at the _____ of his career when he was with the Chicago Bulls.

14. His _____ laughter made everyone in the room uncomfortable.

15. The scientists viewed in _____ when the Hubble Telescope sent its first pictures.

16. He became an aetheist after refusing to follow the _____ of the cult.

17. The apprentice slowly _____ towards the dark side of the force.

18. Las Vegas buffets always have _____ meals prepared for its guests.

19. My girlfriend _____ me to shave off my beard.

20. The school _____ did not include the names of the foreign students.

---

11. devastate 12. epidemic 13. prime 14. coarse 15. awe
16. tenet 17. descend 18. bountiful 19. compel 20. register

SET 27

notes:

LEAD
SET 28
VOCABULARY

SET 28

01 determinant
dəˈtərmənənt
n.

crucial, decisive, determining

a factor which determines the outcome

*My son was the **determinant** of where we would eat for dinner.*

결정 요인

02 ephemeral
əˈfem(ə)rəl
adj.

transient, fleeting, momentary

lasting a short time

*Fashion trends tend to be **ephemeral**.*

수명이 짧은, 단명하는

03 retract
rəˈtrakt
v.

withdraw, recede, sheathe

to draw back

*The snail **retracted** itself back into its shell.*

들어가다, 집어넣다

v.

repeal, rescind, revoke

to withdraw a statement or accusation as not true

*The lawyer **retracted** his statement after winning the court case.*

(전에 한 말을) 철회(취소)하다

04 inherit
inˈherət
v.

receive, succeed, acquire

to receive or be left with money or property from the previous owner

*The son **inherited** a fortune from his parents.*

상속받다, 물려받다

05 threat
Thret
n.

warning, ultimatum, intimidation

a statement with the intent of causing hostile actions on someone

*The newly elected leader received death **threats** from his enemies.*

협박, 위협

06 bequeath
bəˈkwēTH
v.

impart, leave, transmit

to pass or leave something to someone else

*The master **bequeathed** his sword to his apprentice.*

물려주다, 유증하다

07 precedent
ˈpresəd(ə)nt
n.

model, example, standard

a previous event or example which serves as an example to be considered in subsequent situations

*There are numerous **precedents** for motorized vehicles, including the chariot.*

전례

08 unravel
ˌənˈravəl
v.

- untangle, unknot
- to undo twisted threads
- *She **unraveled** the yarn.*
- (뜨개질한 것, 엉클어진 것, 매듭 등을) 풀다

v.
- resolve, elucidate, decipher
- to investigate and solve a puzzling situation
- *Sherlock Holmes **unraveled** the mysterious murder.*
- (이해하기 어려운 것, 미스터리 등을(이)) 풀다(풀리다)

09 pave
pāv
v.

- cover, asphalt, surface
- to cover the ground with asphalt, bricks, or concrete
- *The construction workers **paved** the road.*
- (널돌, 벽돌 등으로) 포장하다

10 jurisdiction
ˌjoorəsˈdikSH(ə)n
n.

- authority, power, sovereignty
- the power to make legal decisions and judgements
- *The prime minister has no **jurisdiction** in the neighboring country.*
- 관할권, 사법권

11 tenant
ˈtenənt
n.

- occupant, resident, inhabitant
- someone who rents land or property from a landlord
- *The **tenants** decided to file a complaint to the building manager.*
- 세입자, 임차인, 소작인

12 acute
əˈkyoot
adj.

- critical, severe, drastic
- a severe degree of something that is not pleasant
- *There was an **acute** food shortage after the flood.*
- 격심한, 극심한

adj.
- astute, shrewd, sharp
- possessing or displaying a perceptive understanding or insight
- *A manager should have an **acute** sense of employee management.*
- 예민한, 잘 발달된

SET 28 · 333

SET 28

13. reserved
rəˈzərvd
adj.

private, restrained, remote
hesitant in revealing emotions or opinions
*My father is a **reserved** man and never shows his emotions.*

내성적인

adj.

booked, prearranged, taken
kept for a particular person or purpose
*This is a **reserved** table for a party of five.*

예약된

14. deplete
dəˈplēt
v.

exhaust, drain, sap
to use up the resources
*The blood bank has been **depleted** because there has been no donations.*

대폭 감소시키다

15. sparing
ˈsperiNG
adj.

thrifty, frugal, economical
moderate
*Parents should use **sparing** amounts of sunblock on their children.*

(~을) 조금만 쓰는(아끼는)

16. exhaustive
igˈzôstiv
adj.

complete, thorough, extensive
fully comprehensive
*The rescue team performed an **exhaustive** search for the missing child.*

철저한(완전한)

17. obstinate
ˈäbstənət
adj.

stubborn, headstrong, unyielding
stubborn in refusing to change one's action or opinion
*She was **obstinate** in becoming the next idol star.*

고집 센, 완강한

18. sheer
Shir
adj.

absolute, total, utter
complete
*It was **sheer** luck that he passed his driving test.*

순수한(순전한)

19. variable
ˈverēəb(ə)l
adj.

varying, fluctuating, irregular
not fixed or having a consistent pattern
*The quality of the food served is highly **variable**.*

변동이 심한, 가변적인

20 contrive
kənˈtrīv
v.

engineer, manufacture, orchestrate

to make or bring about by use of skill

*The engineers **contrived** a device to make renewable energy.*

고안하다, 획책하다

21 composed
kəmˈpōzd
adj.

calm, collected, cool

having one's emotion and expression under control

*She was able to stay **composed** while her children ran around the house.*

침착한, 차분한

22 lavish
ˈlaviSH
adj.

opulent, sumptuous, gorgeous

elaborate or luxurious

*The newly wed couple purchased a **lavish** house to start a family.*

풍성한, 호화로운

23 concede
kənˈsēd
v.

admit, acknowledge, recognize

to admit that something is true after first denying it

*I **concede** that my behavior earlier was not pleasant.*

인정하다(수긍하다)

v.

relinquish, cede, surrender

to surrender or yield something

*Germany **conceded** the conquered lands after they lost the war.*

양보하다, 포기하다

24 squander
ˈskwändər
v.

waste, misspend, splurge

to waste in a reckless manner

*Rich people tend to **squander** their money on materialistic things.*

낭비(허비)하다

25 misplace
misˈplās
v.

mislay, lose, forget

to put in the wrong place and lose it temporarily

*My grandmother **misplaced** her ring and spent days looking for it.*

제자리에 두지 않다(그래서 찾지를 못하다)

SET 28

26 obstruction
əb'strəkSH(ə)n
n.

obstacle, barrier, bar
something that prevents or impedes a process or passage
An **obstruction** caused a traffic delay.
방해

27 eclipse
ə'klips
v.

outshine, overshadow, exceed
to surpass someone or something in significance or power
A person's happiness **eclipses** their success.
능가하다

v.

cover, veil, shroud
to block out light
The grey clouds **eclipsed** the sunshine.
가리다

28 radiate
'rādē ˌāt
v.

emit, discharge, scatter
to emit light or heat in the form of rays or waves
Our sun constantly **radiates** solar energy.
(열, 빛, 에너지 등을) 내뿜다(방출하다)

v.

diverge, extend, separate
to depart or spread from a central point
The family of rats **radiated** in all directions when the exterminator walked in.
(사방으로) 퍼지다

29 wield
wēld
v.

flaunt, employ, brandish
to hold and use a weapon or tool
Whoever **wields** this hammer, shall possess the power of Thor.
(무기, 도구를) 휘두르다(들다)

30 convoke
kən'vōk
v.

convene, summon, call
to summon a meeting
King Arthur **convoked** a meeting with his knights of the round table.
(공식적인 회의를) 소집하다

31 record
rə'kôrd
n.

documentation, data, log
something that constitutes a piece of evidence
A journal is a type of written **record**.
기록

32. appreciate
əˈprēSHēˌāt
v.

inflate, rise, increase
to rise in value or price
*The price of the house **appreciated** over the years.*
증가하다

v.

value, prize, admire
to recognize the worth of someone or something
*I **appreciate** your assistance.*
고마워하다, 환영하다

33. confidence
ˈkänfədəns
n.

faith, credence, trust
a firm trust
*I had complete **confidence** in my team that no one would betray one another.*
신뢰

n.

self-assurance, self-confidence, courage
self-assurance that comes from one's own abilities or qualities
*The president was beaming with **confidence** as he stepped up to the podium.*
자신(감)

34. crisis
ˈkrīsis
n.

calamity, disaster, predicament
a time of danger or difficulty
*The police were able to avert the **crisis**.*
위기

35. encompass
inˈkəmpəs
v.

incorporate, embrace, cover
to include all parts
*The premium health insurance **encompasses** all possible health conditions.*
포함(망라)하다, 아우르다

36. deduce
dəˈd(y)o͞os
v.

infer, extrapolate, surmise
to come to a logical conclusion
*Dr. Watson was able to **deduce** who the culprit was from the evidence.*
추론(추정)하다, 연역하다

SET 28 · 337

SET 28

37 pitfall
ˈpitˌfôl
n.

- risk, peril, danger
- a hidden danger or difficulty
- There are many **pitfalls** of starting a new business.

위험(곤란)

38 parallel
ˈperəˌlel
adj.

- analogous, comparable, corresponding
- occurring or existing in a similar way or at the same time
- Collecting comic books and mint coins are **parallel** hobbies.

(둘 이상의 일이) 아주 유사한(병행하는)

39 debate
dəˈbāt
v.

- discuss, argue, dispute
- to argue about a subject
- The two friends **debated** who was better in basketball.

논의(토의/논쟁)하다

40 necessitate
nəˈsesəˌtāt
v.

- involve, require, demand
- to make something necessary
- His severe toothache **necessitated** a visit to the dentist.

…을 필요하게 만들다

41 flexible
ˈfleksəb(ə)l
adj.

- accommodating, adaptable, amenable
- ready to change and adapt to different circumstances
- My roommate was **flexible** with the move in date.

유연한

42 consecutive
kənˈsekyədiv
adj.

- successive, following, continuous
- following continuously
- The Lakers have 3 **consecutive** championship titles in basketball.

연이은

43 augment
ôgˈment
v.

- supplement, enlarge, expand
- to make something bigger by adding to it
- He **augmented** his monthly income by serving tables on the weekends.

늘리다, 증가시키다

44. innumerable
i'n(y)oom(ə)rəb(ə)l
adj.

countless, numerous, manifold

too many to be counted

*The stars in the sky are **innumerable**.*

셀 수 없이 많은, 무수한

45. discrepancy
ˌdis'krepənsē
n.

inconsistency, disparity, variance

a lack of similarity between two or more things

*There was a **discrepancy** between the two testimonies.*

차이(불일치)

46. uptake
'əpˌtāk
n.

utilization, application, employment

the action of making use of something

*The citizens condemned the government's **uptake** of nuclear energy.*

활용

47. negate
nə'gāt
v.

invalidate, nullify, neutralize

to make ineffective

*Drinking alcohol **negates** the effects of the medicine.*

무효화하다, 효력이 없게 만들다

48. misidentify
ˌmisī'dentəˌfī
v.

to identify someone or something incorrectly

*The police **misidentified** the suspect from the crowd.*

오인하다, 잘못 확인하다

49. fluid
'flooid
n.

liquid, solution, gas

a substance that has no fixed shape

*It is recommended to drink lots of **fluid** when one has the common cold.*

유체, 유동체

50. slaughter
'slôdər
v.

massacre, murder, annihilate

to kill in a cruel or violent way

*The soldiers were **slaughtered** on the battlefield.*

대량 학살, 살육

SET 28 TEST

1. Chicken are _____ everyday to make fried chicken for hungry diners.

2. Eating fast food immediately after a workout _____ the excercise.

3. Tony Stark _____ his suit by adding machine guns on both shoulders.

4. In the court of law, working a full time job and taking care of a child are considered _____ work.

5. The father was able to _____ who ate the last cookie by following the trail of crumbs.

6. The building manager _____ a meeting with the building tenants.

7. The construction on the road created an _____ for the drivers.

8. My infant son was able to _____ a robot from the lego pieces.

9. A test taker should be _____ when reading a passage to find the correct answer.

10. Dogs have an _____ sense of hearing.

---

1. slaughter 2. negate 3. augment 4. parallel 5. deduce 6. convoke 7. obstruction 8. contrive 9. exhaustive 10. acute

11. The steam engine became a _____ for future engines.

12. The sweet flavor of a chewing gum is _____.

13. My two children shared a story with many _____ in the content.

14. The undefeated boxing champion has five _____ wins.

15. The new employee was able to avoid the _____ of his first day at work.

16. A typical day at the company retreat _____ workshops as well as fun activities.

17. The apprentice was able to _____ his master in terms of skill.

18. The parable of the prodigal son tells the story of a man who _____ his inheritance.

19. After winning the lottery, the man lived a _____ life.

20. Children are _____ and will resort to screams and tears when they do not get what they want.

---

11. precedent 12. ephemeral 13. discrepancy 14. consecutive 15. pitfall 16. encompass 17. eclipse 18. squander 19. lavish 20. obstinate

SET 28

notes:

LEAD
SET
29
VOCABULARY

SET 29

01 subside
səbˈsīd
v.

abate, moderate, calm

to become less violent or severe

The Hulk **subsided** his anger and turned into Bruce Banner.

가라앉다, 진정되다

02 serenity
səˈrenədē
n.

calmness, composure, tranquility

the condition of being calm and peaceful

A Buddhist monk shows **serenity** even during troubled times.

고요함, 맑음, 화창함, 청명

03 fortify
ˈfôrdəˌfī
v.

secure, protect, reinforce

to add defense to a place in case of an attack

The people **fortified** their camp by adding traps and wooden walls.

요새화하다

04 aptitude
ˈaptəˌt(y)o͞od
n.

talent, skill, knack

a natural ability to do something

Captain America had an **aptitude** to lead the Avengers.

소질, 적성

05 subjugate
ˈsəbjəˌgāt
v.

conquer, vanquish, crush

to bring under control or domination

Thanos did not wish to **subjugate** his enemies; he wanted to wipe them out.

예속시키다, 지배(통제)하에 두다

06 defy
dəˈfī
v.

withstand, resist, confront

to resist obedience

Children tend to **defy** their parents when they become teenagers.

반항(저항/거역)하다

07 delineate
dəˈlinēˌāt
v.

portray, depict, describe

to describe something accurately

The rule clearly **delineates** what not to do.

(상세하게) 기술하다(그리다/설명하다)

v.

outline, trace, draw

to show the exact position of a boundary

The updated map **delineates** the city's boundary.

윤곽을 보여주다

08 posterior
pä'stirēər
adj.

rear, hind, back

to the rear or hind end

Even animals receive vaccine shots in the **posterior** part of their body.

… 뒤의(뒤쪽에 있는)

09 inverse
'invərs
adj.

reverse, inverted, opposite

opposite or reverse in direction, order, or tendency

There is an **inverse** relationship between the populations of predator and prey.

역(반대)의

10 notorious
nō'tôrēəs
adj.

infamous, scandalous, prominent

famous or popular for something bad

Doctor Doom is **notorious** for taking away people's freedom.

악명 높은

11 erratic
ə'radik
adj.

unpredictable, inconsistent, variable

uneven or irregular in pattern or movement

Her heartbeat was **erratic** after running the race.

불규칙한, 일정치 않은, 변덕스러운

12 incessant
in'ses(ə)nt
adj.

ceaseless, constant, continual

continuing without stopping

The **incessant** music can be heard from the night club.

끊임없는, 쉴새없는

13 discrete
di'skrēt
adj.

distinct, individual, separate

individually different

Although they all look similar, the characters have **discrete** differences.

별개의

14 surreal
sə'rēəl
adj.

unreal, unusual, strange

bizarre

Picasso's paintings look **surreal** because they are so geometric.

아주 이상한, 비현실적인, 꿈같은

SET 29

15 medley
ˈmedlē
n.

assortment, mixture, diversity

a various mixture of things or people

A **medley** of costumes walked down the street on Halloween.

(사람,사물이) 여러 가지 뒤섞인 것

16 latent
ˈlātnt
adj.

dormant, inert, potential

existing but dormant or hidden until a given time or situation

His **latent** superpowers appeared when his father died.

잠재하는, 잠복해 있는

17 evident
ˈevədənt
adj.

obvious, apparent, perceptible

clearly seen or understood

It was **evident** who the criminal was.

분명한, 눈에 띄는

18 vagarious
vəˈgerēəs
adj.

arbitrary, erratic, impulsive

random in behavior or movement

Because of his **vagarious** attitude, he never made plans.

상식을 벗어난, 엉뚱한, 기발한, 변덕스러운

19 frivolous
ˈfrivələs
adj.

lighthearted, superficial, pointless

without a purpose or value

Those who did not succeed in life are **frivolous** individuals.

경솔한, 바보 같은; 까부는

20 succinct
sə(k)ˈsiNG(k)t
adj.

concise, condensed, laconic

brief and to the point

My mother's farewell is always **succinct** because she tends to cry if prolonged.

간단명료한, 간결한

21 sparse
spärs
adj.

scant, scare, infrequent

thinly spread out

Rural areas have **sparse** human population.

드문, (밀도가) 희박한

22	**recede** rəˈsēd v.	retreat, withdraw, subside
		to go back from a pervious point
		*The shoreline **receded** at night.*
		물러나다(멀어지다)

23	**folk** fōk n.	humans, individuals, mortals
		people
		*Some **folk** will never change.*
		사람들
	adj.	classic, customary, popular
		regarding traditional art or culture of a group or country
		*African American's **folk** music are based on biblical stories.*
		민속의, 전통적인

24	**acrid** ˈakrəd adj.	pungent, bitter, sour
		possessing a strong and unpleasant smell or taste
		*Some traditional Korean food are **acrid**.*
		(냄새나 맛이) 매캐한(콕 쏘는 듯한)

25	**poignant** ˈpoin(y)ənt adj.	touching, saddening, pitiful
		bring out a sense of sadness or regret
		*The scar on his body is a **poignant** reminder of his escape from prison.*
		가슴 아픈(저미는)

26	**equivalent** əˈkwiv(ə)lənt adj.	identical, analogous, parallel
		equal in value, function, or meaning
		*One token is **equivalent** to one dollar.*
		동등한(맞먹는)

27	**supplement** ˈsəpləmənt v.	augment, amplify, enlarge
		to add an extra amount or part
		*I work as a waitress on the weekends to **supplement** my income.*
		보충(추가)하다

28	**colleague** ˈkälēg n.	coworker, associate, partner
		an individual someone works with at a job
		*My **colleague** and I ride the same bus to work.*
		(같은 직장이나 직종에 종사하는) 동료

SET 29

29 redeem
rəˈdēm
v.

justify, vindicate, redemptive

to compensate for the mistakes or bad traits of something

*His tardiness to game practices was **redeemed** by an outstanding performance.*

(결함 등을) 보완(벌충/상쇄)하다

v.

retrieve, reclaim, recover

to gain something in exchange for a payment

*I **redeemed** my bike from the school bullies.*

만회하다

30 implore
imˈplôr
v.

beg, beseech, urge

to beg someone to do something

*The victim **implored** the jury to reconsider their decision.*

애원(간청)하다

31 mammal
ˈmaməl
n.

vertebrate

an organism with a vertebrate, possessing hair, feeding the young with milk from glands, and giving birth

*Monkeys, dogs, and elephants are all **mammals**.*

포유동물

32 irrefutable
ˌirəˈfyo͞odəb(ə)l
adj.

undeniable, unquestionable, indisputable

impossible to deny or prove false

*The evidence given by the lawyer was **irrefutable**.*

반박할 수 없는

33 oncoming
ˈänˌkəmiNG
adj.

approaching, advancing, coming

moving toward

*The **oncoming** traffic scared the deer standing on the road.*

다가오는

34 repugnance
rəˈpəgnəns
n.

revulsion, abhorrence, repulsion

intense disgust

*The amateur doctor showed **repugnance** as the dead body lay on the table.*

반감(혐오감)

35	**epoch** ˈepək n.	era, age, period
		a period of time in history, usually marked with notable events
		*The Renaissance **epoch** saw a rebirth of old classical ideas.*
		시대

36	**sublime** səˈblīm adj.	elevated, awesome, extreme
		of such excellence or beauty as to inspire admiration or awe
		*The tourists stood on top of the Grand Canyon, amazed at the **sublime** scenery.*
		절묘한; 숭고한, 지고한

37	**canonize** ˈkanəˌnīz v.	beatify, consecrate, saint
		officially declare a dead person to be a saint
		*The pope was declared a saint and was **canonized** on his deathbed.*
		(…를) 성인으로 공표하다(시성하다)

38	**ascertain** ˌasərˈtān v.	confirm, verify, check
		to find out for certain
		*In order to **ascertain** the truth, the police searched the crime scene several times.*
		(옳은 정보를) 알아내다(확인하다)

39	**chronological** ˌkränəˈläjək(ə)l adj.	sequential, ordered, serial
		starting with the earliest time and following the order they occur
		*The lessons in history class follow a **chronological** order.*
		발생(시간) 순서대로 된, 연대순의

40	**decipher** dəˈsīfər v.	decode, decrypt, interpret
		to change a code into normal language
		*Archaeologists must **decipher** ancient languages in order to understand the past.*
		판독(해독)하다

41	**unanimous** yo͞oˈnanəməs adj.	united, concordant, undivided
		fully in agreement
		*The classmates were **unanimous** when they voted for no quiz.*
		만장(전원)일치의

SET 29

42 fanciful
'fansəfəl
adj.

whimsical, impractical, imaginative

over imaginative and unrealistic

*The origin of Korea tells a **fanciful** story of a bear and a tiger.*

상상(공상)의

43 fiction
'fikSH(ə)n
n.

novels, stories, fable

literature that tells imaginative events and people

*Harry Potter is a work of **fiction** that has captivated many readers.*

소설

44 epic
'epik
n.

saga, legend, myth

a long poem that narrates the adventures of heroes and legends or the history of a nation

***Epics** from ancient Greece tell stories of demi-gods triumphing over evil.*

서사시

45 recount
ri'kount
v.

depict, portray, tell

to tell someone about something

*My grandfather **recounted** the story of when he had to trek through snow to go to school.*

이야기하다(말하다)

46 juxtapose
'jəkstə,pōz
v.

mix, compare, collocate

to put close together for contrasting effects

*Andy Warhol is famous for **juxtaposing** his artworks in different colors.*

(특히 대조,비교를 위하여) 병치하다(나란히 놓다)

47 oral
'ôrəl
adj.

spoken, verbal, vocal

by word or mouth

*Instead of taking shots, patients prefer **oral** medication.*

구두(구어/구술/구전)의

48 impel
im'pel
v.

compel, oblige, demand

to force or urge someone to do something

*Lack of finance **impelled** the family to sell their boat.*

…해야만 하게 하다.

49. resurge
ri-surj
v.

to rise again

*His water bills **resurged** when he started to take baths again.*

재기(부활)하다, 다시 나타나다

50. dearth
dərTH
n.

scarcity, shortage, deficiency

a lack of something

*There is a **dearth** of natural resources on our planet.*

부족(결핍)

SET 29 TEST

1. A _____ of water spells out disaster for farmers.

2. The young cub _____ its mother to play with him.

3. Native American elders _____ stories of their ancestors in the firecamp.

4. The _____ vote for a four day work week proved that everyone was tired.

5. Lawyers hire law school students to _____ the facts before they go to court.

6. The rotten food was more than enough to show _____.

7. It is an _____ fact that the Earth is round, not flat.

8. I exchanged my game tickets to _____ the prize.

9. The mellow music was a _____ reminder of his sad breakup.

10. His hairline _____ each year.

---

1. dearth 2. impel 3. recount 4. unanimous 5. ascertain 6. repugnance 7. irrefutable 8. redeem 9. poignant 10. recede

11. The lawyer's argument in court was _____ and to the point.

12. It is _____ that he will not pass the exam since he did not study for it.

13. A _____ of songs played in the jukebox.

14. His _____ nagging finally caused the mother to explode and yell at him.

15. The _____ rapper was arrested again, this time for the use of drugs.

16. The teacher _____ the instructions by writing them on the board.

17. Ancient civilizations _____ its prisoners by teaching them the culture and ideology of their nation.

18. The angry mob _____ when the governor's dead body was thrown at their feet.

19. Computer analysts _____ programs left by hackers.

20. The steak dinner can be _____ with a lobster tail.

---

11. succinct   12. evident   13. medley   14. incessant   15. notorious
16. delineate   17. subjugate   18. subside   19. decipher   20. supplement

SET 29

notes:

LEAD
SET
30
VOCABULARY

SET 30

01 maim
mām
v.
- disable, incapacitate, impair
- to injure someone where the body part cannot be healed
- The criminal **maimed** the legs of his victim so that he could never walk again.
- 불구로 만들다

02 enjoin
in'join
v.
- press, prompt, urge
- to order someone to do something
- The new traffic law **enjoined** citizens to drive safely.
- (무엇을 하도록) 명하다(이르다)

v.
- ban, inhibit, prevent
- to prohibit someone from doing an action by giving an injunction
- The father was **enjoined** from seeing his son.
- (법령, 명령으로) ~가 ~하는 것을 금하다

03 profuse
prə'fyoos
adj.
- copious, prolific, ample
- too much
- I received **profuse** complements for changing my hairstyle.
- 많은, 다량의

04 clout
klout
n.
- leverage, influence, power
- an influence or power
- The president carries a lot of **clout**.
- 영향력

v.
- strike, beat, smack
- to hit using one's hand or an object
- The bully **clouted** the student with the books he was carrying.
- 때리다

05 hybrid
'hī,brid
n.
- cross, mixture, blend
- something made by mixing two different elements
- A car that runs on gasoline and battery power is a **hybrid**.
- 혼성체, 혼합물

06 vogue
vōg
n.
- trend, fad, fashion
- the fashion or style that is generally accepted at a particular time
- The **vogue** in fashion is to wear over-fit sizes.
- 유행

356 · LEAD VOCABULARY

07 satire
'sa͵tī(ə)r
n.

mockery, ridicule, derision

the use of humor or irony to make fun of people's stupidity or vices

*Saturday Night Live does an excellent **satire** on American politics.*

풍자

08 creed
krēd
n.

faith, order, religion

a set of beliefs; faith

*People today believe in different **creeds**.*

교리; 신념, 신조

09 insinuate
in'sinyoo͵āt
v.

imply, suggest, hint

to suggest something bad in an indirect way

*My wife was **insinuating** that I was lazy.*

(불쾌한 일을) 암시하다(넌지시 말하다)

10 drag
drag
v.

haul, tug, pull

to pull someone or something with force or difficulty

*Egyptian slaves had to **drag** gigantic stones to build the pyramid.*

(힘들여) 끌다(끌고 가다)

11 protrude
prə'trood
v.

project, jut, obtrude

to extend out of a surface

*The bone was **protruding** out of the skin.*

튀어나오다, 돌출되다

12 devout
də'vout
adj.

dedicated, devoted, loyal

completely committed

*I am a **devout** Christian and I go to church every Sunday.*

독실한

13 vulgar
'vəlgər
adj.

unrefined, gross, tasteless

lacking good taste or sophistication

*His **vulgar** comments chased away his female friends.*

저속한, 천박한

SET 30

14 indict
inˈdīt
v.

charge, prosecute, incriminate
to accuse with a serious crime
*The student was **indicted** for cheating on his test.*

기소하다

15 compile
kəmˈpīl
v.

assemble, compose, collate
to collect information to produce something
*Santa Claus **compiles** a list of children who behaved well that year.*

(여러 출처에서 자료를 따와) 엮다, 편집(편찬)하다

16 affront
əˈfrənt
n.

insult, indignity, offense
an action or comment that produces anger or offense
*The visitor's joke was a complete **affront** to the host.*

모욕, (마음의) 상처

17 dissipate
ˈdisəˌpāt
v.

vanish, dissolve, evaporate
to disappear, especially in terms of emotions
*The nervousness he had **dissipated** when he received the test.*

소멸되다, 소멸하다(시키다)

18 incise
inˈsīz
v.

etch, carve, inscribe
to mark an object with a cut
*The ancient scribes **incised** lines onto clay tablets using wooden stylus.*

(글자, 무늬 등을) 새기다

19 capsize
ˈkapˌsīz
v.

overturn, upset, invert
to overturn in water
*The boat **capsized** during the storm.*

(배가) 뒤집히다, (배를) 뒤집다

20 adjourn
əˈjərn
v.

retire, retreat, withdraw
to go somewhere, usually for a break
*The jury members **adjourned** for a lunch break.*

(재판, 회의 등을) 중단하다, 휴정(휴회)하다

21	**retire** rəˈtī(ə)r v.	surrender, resign, secede
		to leave one's work, mainly because of reaching an age for leaving employment
		*My father **retired** when he turned sixty-five and went on a long vacation.*
	은퇴(퇴직)하다, 은퇴(퇴직)시키다	

22	**testimony** ˈtestəˌmōnē n.	testament, attestation, witness
		a written or spoken work to prove the existence or appearance of something
		*The **testimony** she gave to the jury seemed to support the defending side.*
	증언(보통 법정에서 하는 것)	

23	**predicament** prəˈdikəmənt n.	difficulty, plight, dilemma
		a difficult or embarrassing situation
		*The company was in a **predicament** after the CEO suddenly quit.*
	곤경, 궁지	

24	**consort** ˈkänsôrt v.	mingle, mix, associate
		to associate with someone, in spite of the disapproval of others
		*He was seen **consorting** with his ex-girlfriend at the restaurant.*
	(남들이 좋지 않게 생각하는 사람들과) 어울리다	

25	**surpass** sərˈpas v.	excel, exceed, transcend
		to be greater than
		*The apprentice **surpassed** his master in terms of skill.*
	능가하다, 뛰어넘다	

26	**expediency** ikˈspēdēənsē n.	usefulness, effectiveness, pragmatism
		the trait of being convenient and practical
		*Today, my secretary showed his **expediency** when everything was hectic.*
	편의, 형편 좋음; 방편, 편리한 방법	

27	**scrupulous** ˈskroopyələs adj.	meticulous, thorough, assiduous
		diligent and attentive to details
		*The experiment was done with **scrupulous** attention to measurements.*
	세심한, 꼼꼼한	

SET 30

28. recurrent
rəˈkərənt
adj.
- repetitive, periodic, regular
- occurring often
- *I keep having these **recurrent** nightmares.*
- 되풀이되는, 반복되는, 재발되는

29. inquisitive
inˈkwizədiv
adj.
- intrigued, interested, curious
- curious or questioning
- *My son has an **inquisitive** mind and asks questions nonstop.*
- 탐구심(호기심)이 많은

30. slender
ˈslendər
adj.
- slim, lean, skinny
- referring to a person's body as being thin
- *Fashion models tend to be **slender**.*
- 날씬한, 호리호리한

31. vector
ˈvektər
n.
- course, direction, route
- a course taken by an airplane
- *The plane followed the **vector** along the shorelines.*
- 진로

32. efficacy
ˈefəkəsē
n.
- effectiveness, success, usefulness
- the ability to create a wanted or intended result
- *The **efficacy** of the treatment will be seen in a few days.*
- (특히 약이나 치료의) 효험

33. net
net
adj.
- final, remaining
- remaining after deductions
- *The **net** worth of the house after tax deduction is close to a million dollars.*
- (돈의 액수에 대해) 순

34. avian
ˈāvēən
adj.
- aerial, flying, soaring
- related to birds
- *The **avian** influenza was transmitted by aquatic birds.*
- 새(조류)의

360 · LEAD VOCABULARY

35 revise
rəˈvīz
v.

amend, alter, edit

to review and make changes

*The professor gave back my essay to be **revised**.*

변경(수정)하다

36 ironic
īˈränik
adj.

paradoxical, incongruous, odd

occurring in the opposite way to what is expected

*It was **ironic** that she had the money but could not buy the purse because it was sold out.*

아이로니컬한, 역설(모순)적인

37 spectrum
ˈspektrəm
n.

range, scope, scale

a scale of two extreme or opposite points

*Fictional books cover a wide **spectrum** of topics.*

범위(영역)

38 toxic
ˈtäksik
adj.

venomous, virulent, noxious

poisonous

*Factories often produce **toxic** wastes.*

유독성의

39 pronounced
prəˈnounst
adj.

conspicuous, striking, marked

very noticeable or marked

*The tusk of a mammoth has a **pronounced** curvature, compared to the elephant.*

확연한; 단호한, 천명된

40 justify
ˈjəstəˌfī
v.

validate, vindicate, warrant

to show or prove to be correct or reasonable

*The criminal was given a chance to **justify** his wrongdoing.*

정당화시키다(하다), 해명(옹호)하다

41 formulate
ˈfôrmyəˌlāt
v.

plan, contrive, devise

to create or devise systematically

*The government should **formulate** a plan to stop the disease from spreading.*

만들어 내다

SET 30

42. barrier
'berēər
n.

obstacle, hurdle, bar

an obstacle that prevents communication or progress

*Language **barrier** usually prevents immigrants from living a comfortable life.*

장애물(장벽)

43. fend
fend
v.

guard, secure, shield

look after oneself without receiving help from others

*I can **fend** for myself without my parent's help.*

받아넘기다, 피하다, 다가서지 못하게 하다

44. resort
rəˈzôrt
n.

measure, alternative, option

the action, usually disagreeable or undesirable, carried out to solve a difficult situation

*Her only **resort** was surgery after having tried other options.*

제1/마지막/최후의 수단

45. atypical
ˌāˈtipək(ə)l
adj.

unusual, untypical, unconventional

not normal or standard

*It is **atypical** for a younger man to eat first before the older person.*

이례적인

46. ventilate
ˈven(t)əˌlāt
v.

express, air, debate

to discuss an issue or complaint in pubic

*Larry King was famous for **ventilating** common issues in his radio show.*

(감정,의견을) 표명하다

47. dormant
ˈdôrmənt
adj.

sleeping, slumbering, resting

having normal functions suspended or slowed down for a given time

*The bear becomes **dormant** during winter due to lack of food.*

휴면기의, 활동(성장)을 중단한

48. impending
imˈpendiNG
adj.

approaching, imminent, looming

referring to an event that is about to happen

*The **impending** punishment scared the little boy.*

곧 닥칠, 임박한

49. herald
ˈherəld
v.

signal, indicate, announce

to indicate that something is about to happen

*The candidate's win **heralded** a change in policies.*

예고하다(도래를 알리다)

50. monitor
ˈmänədər
v.

observe, watch, track

to observe and check the progress or quality of something

*The principal **monitors** his school through security cameras.*

추적 관찰하다

SET 30 CROSSWORD PUZZLE

Across

7. the trait of being convenient and practical
9. lacking good taste or sophistication
10. curious or questioning
11. to disappear, especially in terms of emotions
13. remaining after deductions
14. not normal or standard
15. completely committed

Down

1. to discuss an issue or complaint in pubic
2. very noticeable or marked
3. diligent and attentive to details
4. to accuse with a serious crime
5. a difficult or embarrassing situation
6. a set of beliefs; faith
8. too much
12. referring to an event that is about to happen

1. ventilate 2. pronounced 3. scrupulous 4. indict 5. predicament 6. creed 7. expediency 8. profuse 9. vulgar 10. inquisitive 11. dissipate 12. impending 13. net 14. atypical 15. devout

LEAD
SET
31
VOCABULARY

SET 31

01 prosaic
prəˈzāik
adj.

- usual, conventional, everyday
- common and ordinary
- His daily routine was **prosaic**, something everyone his age would do.

따분한, 세속적인

02 valiant
ˈvalyənt
adj.

- courageous, fearless, intrepid
- having or showing courage
- The **valiant** knight went inside the dragon's cave.

용맹한, 단호한

03 contingent
kənˈtinjənt
n.

- group, party, delegation
- a group of people with a common feature
- A **contingent** of scientists performed the experiment.

대표단

adj.

- accidental, fortuitous, possible
- subject to chance
- The **contingent** nature of the plan required several backup plans.

(~의) 여부에 따라

04 inhibit
inˈhibit
v.

- impede, hamper, discourage
- to hinder or prevent an action
- The stormy weather **inhibited** the children from playing outside.

억제(저해)하다

05 endorse
inˈdôrs
v.

- favor, advocate, champion
- to publicly declare one's approval or support
- The politician **endorsed** the new law.

(공개적으로) 지지하다

06 veto
ˈvēdō
v.

- reject, dismiss, forbid
- to vote against a decision
- The president has the authority to **veto** any potential law.

(거부권을 행사하여) 거부(기각)하다

07 inflation
inˈflāSH(ə)n
n.

- an overall increase in costs and decrease in the purchasing of money
- The recent **inflation** in the country caused difficulty amongst the citizens.

인플레이션율, 물가 상승율

08	**prolong**	extend, lengthen, elongate
	prə'lôNG	to extend the duration of
	v.	*Ponce de Leon's life was **prolonged** by drinking the fountain of youth.*
		연장시키다, 연장하다

09	**foresee**	anticipate, forecast, envision
	fôr'sē	to predict
	v.	*Doctor Strange was able to **foresee** the possible outcomes of the fight.*
		…일 것이라고 생각하다, 예견하다

10	**criticism**	censure, disapproval, condemnation
	'kridə,sizəm	the disapproval of someone or something based on faults or mistakes
	n.	*Most people do not like to receive **criticism**.*
		비판, 비난

11	**charitable**	philanthropic, humanitarian, altruistic
	'CHerədəb(ə)l	in regards to helping others in need
	adj.	*The Red Cross performs **charitable** actions across the world.*
		자선을 베푸는, 궁핍한 사람들을 돕는

12	**recruit**	hire, enroll, employ
	rə'kroot	to enroll someone as a member of an organization or work force
	v.	*The company **recruits** only from the best candidates.*
		모집하다(뽑다)

13	**resolve**	settle, solve, rectify
	rə'zälv	to find a solution to a problem
	v.	*A lawyer was hired to **resolve** the lawsuit.*
		(문제 등을) 해결하다
		determination, resolution, tenacity
	n.	strong determination to carry out a task
		*Captain America always has the **resolve** to do what is right.*
		(단호한) 결심(결의/의지)

14	**replenish**	restore, renew, recharge
	rə'pleniSH	to fill up on supplies to its former level or status
	v.	*The electric car **replenished** its battery after being charged overnight.*
		(원래처럼) 다시 채우다, 보충하다

SET 31

15. shun
SHən
v.
- evade, eschew, ignore
- to avoid or reject someone or something
- The boy was **shunned** by his friends after he betrayed them.
- 피하다

16. swerve
swərv
v.
- veer, skew, deviate
- to suddenly change direction
- The car **swerved** off the road while trying to avoid a deer.
- 방향을 바꾸다(틀다)

17. presage
ˈpresij
v.
- portend, foreshadow, bode
- to be a warning that something bad will happen
- The fortune teller **presaged** the unfortunate accident.
- (보통 불길한 일의) 전조가 되다

18. acoustic
əˈkoostik
adj.
- audio, auditory, phonic
- relating to sound
- Concert halls have better **acoustic** range than most auditoriums.
- 음향의, 청각의

19. cavity
ˈkavədē
n.
- chamber, hole, pocket
- a hollow space in a solid object
- The **cavity** in the rock was filled with rain water.
- 구멍(빈 부분)

20. probe
prōb
v.
- examine, prod, check
- to explore or examine something physically, using hands or instruments
- The doctor **probed** the inside of his esophagus using a small camera.
- (특히 길고 가느다란 기구로) 살피다(탐사/탐색하다)

21. amendment
əˈmen(d)mənt
n.
- revision, alteration, modification
- a small change or addition to improve a text, mostly law
- The Supreme Court made an **amendment** to an outdated law.
- (법 등의) 개정(수정)

22. suspend
səˈspend
v.

debar, remove, expel
to prohibit someone from work or carrying out their role
*The employee was **suspended** for giving out confidential information.*
(공식적으로) 유예(중단)하다

v.

hang, sling, drape
to hang something
*The picture frame was **suspended** on the wall.*
걸다, 매달다

23. template
ˈtemplət
n.

figure, guide, mold
something that acts as a model for others to follow
*Use the **template** shown earlier to write your essay.*
형판

24. typify
ˈtipəˌfī
v.

epitomize, exemplify, represent
to be an example of
*A dry, sandy area **typifies** a desert.*
전형적(대표적)이다

25. induce
inˈd(y)o͞os
v.

instigate, prompt, cause
to bring about or cause
*The television commercial **induced** my mother to purchase the mop.*
설득하다, 유도하다

26. slumber
ˈsləmbər
n.

sleep, nap, doze
sleep
*The dragon awoke from his deep **slumber**.*
잠, 수면

27. resound
rəˈzound
v.

echo, reverberate, resonate
to fill a place with sound
*His scream **resounded** inside the cave.*
울려 퍼지다

28. upsurge
ˈəpˌsərj
n.

upswing, boom, rise
an increase in strength or quantity
*There was an **upsurge** in the number of voters compared to last year.*
급증

SET 31

29 vestige
ˈvestij
n.
- remnant, fragment, relic
- a small amount of something that is disappearing or is no longer available
- The last **vestiges** of slavery are seen in Asia.

자취, 흔적

30 suppress
səˈpres
v.
- subdue, repress, crush
- to forcefully put an end to
- The rebellion was **suppressed** quickly by the military.

진압하다

31 summit
ˈsəmət
n.
- acme, pinnacle, zenith
- the highest level of achievement
- My mother reached the **summit** of her career just before retiring.

정상, 산꼭대기; 절정, 정점

32 tremor
ˈtremər
n.
- tremble, quiver, shake
- an involuntary shaking movement
- Did you feel the **tremor** just now?

(약간의) 떨림

33 rim
rim
n.
- brim, edge, lip
- the outer edge of a circular object
- There was a lipstick mark on the **rim** of the wine glass.

가장자리(테두리/테)

34 remote
rəˈmōt
adj.
- distant, isolated, secluded
- situated far away
- The **remote** island never had contact with human civilization.

외진, 외딴

35 anomaly
əˈnäməlē
n.
- oddity, peculiarity, abnormality
- something that is different from the norm
- There were several **anomalies** in the experiment.

변칙, 이례

36 emanate
ˈeməˌnāt
v.

- emit, exude, radiate
- to issue or spread out something abstract
- Warmth **emanated** from the radiator.

(어떤 느낌, 특질 등을) 발하다(내뿜다)

37 inflate
inˈflāt
v.

- overstate, dramatize, exaggerate
- to exaggerate
- The number of deaths were **inflated** by the local news.

부풀리다(과장하다)

v.
- aerated, filled, swell
- to fill with air or gas
- The party clown **inflated** the balloons.

부풀리다(부풀다)

38 deflate
dəˈflāt
v.

- subdue, humble, humiliate
- to cause someone to lose confidence
- The Nobel prize winner was **deflated** when an amateur scientist corrected him.

기를 꺾다(죽이다)

v.
- collapse, flatten, puncture
- let air or gas out
- First, you must **deflate** the tires before changing them.

공기를 빼다

39 cue
kyo͞o
n.

- signal, sign, indication
- a signal for action
- The anchor received the **cue** to deliver the news.

신호

40 rift
rift
n.

- division, split, disagreement
- a break in relationships
- There was a **rift** between the two friends after their fight.

균열(틈)

41 evacuate
iˈvakyəˌwāt
v.

- remove, clear, vacate
- to remove people from a place of danger
- The shoppers were asked to **evacuate** the building when the fire alarm rang.

대피 시키다

SET 31

42. pending
ˈpendiNG
adj.

unresolved, undecided, unsettled
waiting for a decision or settlement
*Several cases were still **pending** while the judge was on vacation.*
(어떤 일이) 있을 때 까지, …을 기다리는 동안

43. retention
rəˈten(t)SH(ə)n
n.

holding, memory, recall
the ability to keep something in one's memory
*Someone with a photographic memory has excellent **retention**.*
보유(유지)

44. strata
ˈstrādəm
n.

level, layer, class
a layer or series of layers
*The Earth's crust is divided into several **strata**.*
층, 지층, 단층

45. crevice
ˈkrevəs
n.

crack, fissure, cleft
a narrow opening in a rock or wall
*Rock climbers look for **crevices** to have a better footing.*
(바위나 담에 생긴) 틈

46. saturate
ˈsaCHəˌrāt
v.

permeate, suffuse, pervade
to fill with something until it can no longer fill
*North Korean children are **saturated** by lies from the government.*
포화시키다, 포화 상태를 만들다

47. stationary
ˈstāSHəˌnerē
adj.

motionless, parked, immobile
not moving
*It is important to stay **stationary** when confronted by a bear.*
움직이지 않는, 정지된

48. effluence
ˈeflo͞oəns
n.

outflow, discharge, gush
a substance that flows out of something
*Our water supplies are being polluted from industrial and human **effluence**.*
내뿜음, 발산, 방출, 흘러나옴

49. ebb
eb
v.

diminish, dwindle, wane

for an emotion or quality to decrease

*The comedy film was helpful in **ebbing** away my depression.*

약해지다, 점점 쇠하다

50. intrude
in'trood
v.

encroach, trespass, infringe

to enter without permission and cause disruptive and negative effect

*The burglar **intruded** into our house while we were away.*

자기 마음대로 가다(침범하다)

SET 31 TEST

1. Only time will _____ the sadness from a breakup.

2. The sponge was _____ with the soap water.

3. Children have a short _____ span.

4. Nuclear waste is dangerous because it continuously _____ radiation.

5. The fight was _____ by the police.

6. The seven course lunch _____ me to sleep.

7. An annual checkup is recommended so that doctors can _____ to see if there is anything wrong.

8. The ugly duckling was _____ from his flock because of his appearance.

9. He continued to run the marathon after gaining the _____ to finish the race.

10. The city _____ the mayor's decision to create more parks.

---

1. ebb 2. saturate 3. retention 4. emanate 5. suppress 6. induce 7. probe 8. shun 9. resolve 10. endorse

11. The _____ boy crushed the bug to impress the girl.

12. The files were _____ from being downloaded because too many people were using the internet.

13. A family feud results in a _____ between family members.

14. There was an _____ in the computer program.

15. After reaching the _____ of her game, the athlete announced her retirement.

16. There was an _____ in electricty during the thunderstorm.

17. Someone who works nonstop is _____ as a workaholic.

18. The dark clouds in the distance _____ a thunderstorm.

19. I have to go to the supermarket to _____ my refridgerator.

20. Drinking coffee in the morning is a _____ routine for most people.

---

11. valiant 12. pending 13. rift 14. anomaly 15. summit
16. upsurge 17. typify 18. presage 19. replenish 20. prosaic

SET 31

notes:

LEAD
SET
32
VOCABULARY

SET 32

01 exhibit
ig'zibət
v.

- manifest, display, reveal
- to display a behavior or quality on purpose
- The child **exhibited** signs of high intelligence.
- (감정·특질 등을) 보이다(드러내다)

n.
- exhibit, parade, presentation
- an object or collection of artwork put on public display
- The art **exhibit** in France displays the last painting of da Vinci.
- 전시품

02 flora
'flôrə
n.

- vegetation, plants
- the plants in a particular habitat
- The **flora** in the Amazon rainforest is the most diverse in the world.
- 식물군

03 cripple
'kripəl
v.

- impair, ruin, destroy
- to cause severe damage
- The advanced weaponry **crippled** the enemy forces.
- 심각한 손상을 주다, 제대로 기능을 못 하게 만들다

v.
- paralyze, immobile, disable
- to disable a person from walking
- The car accident **crippled** the racer.
- 불구로 만들다

04 transition
tran'ziSH(ə)n
n.

- conversion, transformation, change
- the process of changing from one state to another
- Students go through a **transition** when they become high school students.
- (다른 상태, 조건으로의) 이행, 변화

05 subsist
səb'sist
v.

- endure, continue, persist
- to maintain or support
- The rescued dogs **subsist** on donations from pet lovers.
- 존속되다, 유효하다

06 leach
lēCH
v.

- drain, percolate, leak
- to drain away from the ground by water
- The nutrients in the ground were **leached** from the recent rain.
- 침출되다

07 forage
'fôrij
v.

hunt, search, seek

to search for food or necessities

*Early humans did not farm, so they had to **forage** for food.*

먹이를 찾다

08 camouflage
'kamə,flä(d)ZH
v.

conceal, veil, mask

to hide or disguise by blending in with the environment

*The stick bug is able to **camouflage** effectively since it looks like a stick.*

위장하다, 감추다

09 disperse
də'spərs
v.

scatter, disseminate, distribute

to spread over a large area

*During Spring, flower seeds **disperse** by wind.*

흩어지다, 해산하다

10 bulky
'bəlkē
adj.

sizeable, huge, big

taking up much space

*My **bulky** friend had trouble going through the door.*

덩치가 큰, 부피가 큰

11 stifle
'stīfəl
v.

suppress, impede, curb

to prevent or constrain an action or showing emotion

*I had to **stifle** my tears when we said our goodbyes.*

(감정 등을) 억누르다, 억압하다

12 aggravate
'agrə,vāt
v.

annoy, irritate, exasperate

to bother someone persistently

*Younger siblings always seem to **aggravate** their older brother or sister.*

짜증나게 만들다

13 counterbalance
'koun(t)ər,baləns
v.

offset, balance, nullify

to neutralize or cancel by inputting an opposite influence

*My mother's strictness is **counterbalanced** by my father's fun nature.*

균형을 잡아 주다

SET 32

14. arrest
əˈrest
v.

- apprehend, seize, detain
- to seize someone with legal authority and bring into custody
- *The criminal was **arrested** for stealing money.*
- 체포하다

v.
- stop, halt, end
- to stop or check the progress or process
- *Her heart **arrested** for a minute before it started beating again.*
- (무엇의 진행을) 막다

15. befuddle
bəˈfədl
v.

- confuse, bewilder, disorient
- to prevent someone from thinking clearly
- *Drinking too much alcohol seems to have **befuddled** him.*
- 정신을 잃게 하다, 어리둥절하게 하다

16. proclaim
prəˈklām
v.

- declare, pronounce, announce
- to announce publicly or officially
- *The pope **proclaimed** her to be the next queen.*
- 선언(선포)하다

17. regain
rəˈgān
v.

- recover, recoup, retrieve
- to get something back or use again after losing it
- *Iron Man **regained** his power when he created a new energy source.*
- 되찾다(회복하다)

18. refrain
rəˈfrān
v.

- abstain, withhold, forgo
- to stop oneself from doing something
- *I had to **refrain** from saying something cruel.*
- 삼가다

19. lapse
laps
n.

- downturn, deterioration, regression
- a decline from high standards
- *The criminal traced his **lapse** to repeated lies.*
- 감소(하락/축소)

n.
- interval, intermission, hiatus
- a short break in time
- *There was a 10 minute **lapse** in the middle of the musical.*
- 경과

380 · LEAD VOCABULARY

20. flee
flē
v.

run, escape, split

to run away from a place or from danger

*Let's **flee** before the cops arrive.*

달아나다, 도망하다

21. grind
grīnd
v.

pound, granulate, crush

to crush something into small particles

*The barista **grinds** the coffee beans after roasting them.*

갈다(빻다)

22. aptly
ˈaptlē
adv.

appropriately, suitably, accordingly

in an appropriate manner

*America is **aptly** named the land of opportunity.*

적절히

23. dodge
däj
v.

evade, duck, veer

to avoid someone or something with a quick movement

*The chosen one **dodged** the bullets without breaking a sweat.*

재빨리(휙) 움직이다(비키다/피하다)

24. susceptible
səˈseptəb(ə)l
adj.

gullible, naïve, vulnerable

easily influenced or likely to be harmed

*A child is **susceptible** to anything he or she hears.*

민감한

25. firm
fərm
adj.

resistant, unyielding, hardened

having a solid surface or structure

*The mattress was **firm**, but not too hard.*

딱딱한, 단단한

n.

company, business, venture

a business

*The **firm** is looking to hire new employees.*

회사

26. fatal
ˈfādl
adj.

lethal, mortal, deadly

causing death

*The gunshot was a **fatal** wound.*

죽음을 초래하는, 치명적인

SET 32 · 381

SET 32

27 profound
prə'found
adj.

intense, extreme, great
very great or intense
*She showed **profound** interest in cooking.*

엄청난(깊은)

28 circulate
'sərkyə,lāt
v.

flow, course, rotate
to move continuously in a system or area
*The fan helped **circulate** the air in the room.*

순환하다, 순환시키다

v.

spread, disseminate, propagate
to pass between places or people
*News of the victory **circulated** in the city.*

(소문 등이(을)) 유포되다(유포하다)

29 local
'lōk(ə)l
adj.

community, district, neighborhood
belonging to a specific area
*Tourists should know about **local** customs before traveling there.*

지역의, 현지의

adj.

confined, restricted, limited
(used technically) relating to a specific area
*The virus was only a **local** infection and was able to be controlled.*

일부에 대한

30 credit
'kredət
n.

acclaim, commendation, merit
recognition given for an act or quality
*She deserves **credit** for the project.*

인정, 표창

n.

balance, loan, tab
the ability of a buyer to get items or services before payment
*She was able to purchase the bag with her excellent **credit**.*

신용 거래

31 nutrition
n(y)oō'triSH(ə)n
n.

food, sustenance, nutrients
food or nourishment
*A fetus is given **nutrition** through the umbilical cord.*

영양

32. launch
lôn(t)SH
v.

- initiate, begin, activate
- to start or set in motion
- The government **launched** a new program to help recycling.

시작(개시/착수)하다

33. clamor
ˈklamər
n.

- racket, uproar, tumult
- a loud and confused noise
- There was much **clamor** when the people started to protest.

시끄러운 외침, 떠들썩함

34. rugged
ˈrəgəd
adj.

- rough, bumpy, rocky
- having a rocky and uneven surface
- The **rugged** terrain caused trouble for the hikers to walk on.

바위투성이의, 기복이 심한

adj.

- austere, tough, spartan
- characterized by toughness and determination
- The **rugged** Spartans fought against their natural enemy.

강인하게(다부지게) 생긴

35. subsidence
səbˈsīdns
n.

- collapse, sinking, crash
- the slow caving in or sinking of land
- The road had to be fixed due to the **subsidence** of the path.

침하(침강)

36. moral
ˈmôrəl
adj.

- virtuous, ethical, righteous
- concerned with the principles of right and wrong and the goodness or badness of human behavior
- Scientific undertakings often encounter **moral** dilemmas.

도덕과 관련된, 도덕상의

37. furnish
ˈfərniSH
v.

- supply, equip, provide
- to provide something
- Napa Valley **furnishes** the best wine in the country.

제공(공급)하다

38. repeal
rəˈpēl
v.

- rescind, cancel, nullify
- to revoke or annul a law or act
- The outrageous law was **repealed** within a few weeks.

(법률을) 폐지하다

SET 32

39. confer
kənˈfər
v.

consult, negotiate, converse
to have a discussion
*The thieves wanted to **confer** before they turned themselves in to authority.*
상의하다

award, allot, donate
to grant or bestow
*The wealthy family **conferred** half of their estate to the homeless.*
수여(부여)하다

40. rampant
ˈrampənt
adj.

unrestrained, unbridled, unchecked
to spread without being controlled
*The virus spread **rampant** all throughout Asia.*
걷잡을 수 없이 자라는(무성한)

41. sever
ˈsevər
v.

discontinue, suspend, end
to cut off a connection or relationship
*The country **severed** its tie with the rest of the world when it received no help.*
(관계, 연락을 완전히) 끊다(단절하다)

42. underpin
ˌəndərˈpin
v.

derive, establish, ground
to support or form the basis of something
*It is important to **underpin** the ideas of serving and protecting amongst police officers.*
(주장 등을(의)) 뒷받침하다(근거를 대다)

43. antagonistic
anˌtagəˈnistik
adj.

hostile, opposed, inimical
showing or feeling opposition or hostility toward someone or something
*The **antagonistic** group threw eggs at the embassy.*
적대적인

44. mushroom
ˈmeSHˌroom
v.

proliferate, burgeon, spread
to increase, spread, or develop rapidly
*The prairie dog population **mushroomed** when their predators left the land.*
급속히 커지다, 우후죽순처럼 늘어나다

45. thermal
'THərməl
adj.

- warm, heated, hot
- relating to heat
- *Thermal energy created by friction can be felt when rubbing both hands.*

열의

46. hassle
'hasəl
n.

- bother, nuisance, inconvenience
- irritating inconvenience
- *Packing up for a vacation can be a hassle.*

귀찮은(번거로운) 상황(일)

47. deed
dēd
n.

- exploit, performance, feat
- an action that is performed consciously
- *Performing good deeds will help you go to heaven.*

행위(행동)

n.

- contract, certificate, document
- a legal document regarding the ownership of property or legal rights
- *I signed over the deed to my house.*

(보통 주택,건물의 소유권을 증명하는) 증서

48. foliage
'fōl(ē)ij
n.

- leaves, greenery, vegetation
- plant leaves
- *The foliage turned orange and brown with the arrival of autumn.*

나뭇잎

49. harbor
'härbər
n.

- dock, port, marina
- a place on the coastline where ships may rest
- *Several boats were in the harbor.*

항구

v.

- protect, shield, shelter
- to shelter or hide a criminal
- *It is considered a crime to harbor a fugitive.*

(죄인 등을) 숨겨 주다

50. symbiosis
ˌsimbī'ōsəs
n.

- an interaction between two different organisms, with mutual benefit
- *A clown fish and a sea anemone form a symbiosis.*

공생

SET 32 TEST

1. _____ a wanted criminal is also a crime.

2. The classmate's _____ behavior resulted in afterschool detention.

3. The zoo animals became _____ after the zookeeper forgot to lock the gates.

4. The new tax was _____ after a riot broke out to protest.

5. Abraham Lincoln deserves _____ for the emancipation of slavery.

6. The finding of water on Mars was a _____ discovery.

7. A person who is indecisive is very _____.

8. Please _____ from touching the paintings.

9. Do not _____ the tiger or it will attack you.

10. In the suburbs, raccoons will _____ inside trash cans to look for food.

---

1. harbor 2. antagonistic 3. rampant 4. repeal 5. credit 6. profound 7. susceptible 8. refrain 9. aggravate 10. forage

11. It is a _____ to clean up after eating take out food.

12. Serving the community is _____ when performing community service.

13. The team decided to _____ before announcing their answer.

14. Hotel rooms are _____ with amenities for a pleasant stay.

15. The _____ cowboy rode his horse.

16. The Pentagon is _____ named because the structure has five sides.

17. The court decided to take a short _____ during the trial.

18. Abruptly waking up _____ the mind.

19. The prank was _____ when the parents caught their children setting up the trap.

20. The old building was able to _____ thanks to the steel pillars.

| 11. hassle | 12. underpin | 13. confer | 14. furnish | 15. rugged |
| 16. aptly | 17. lapse | 18. befuddle | 19. stifle | 20. subsist |

SET 32

notes:

LEAD
SET 33
VOCABULARY

SET 33

01 swift
swift
adj.

prompt, instant, sudden

happening quickly

*His **swift** recovery amazed everyone.*

신속한(재빠른)

02 initiate
iˈniSHēˌāt
v.

commence, institute, being

to cause a process or action to start

*The committee **initiated** the plan to save their country.*

개시되게 하다, 착수시키다

n.

novice, beginner, newcomer

someone who has been accepted into an organization recently

*The **initiates** of the university sorority moved into the sorority house.*

가입(입회)자

03 dismantle
disˈman(t)l
v.

disassemble, deconstruct, destroy

to take apart a machine or structure

*The robot was **dismantled** to locate the problem.*

(기계,구조물을) 분해(해체)하다

04 lend
lend
v.

loan, borrow

to allow someone to use something under the condition that it be returned

*John asked me to **lend** him my mobile phone.*

빌려주다

05 explicit
ikˈsplisit
adj.

plain, straightforward, clear

stated clearly and thoroughly

*The instructions were **explicit**, so Jenny had no trouble arriving at the house.*

분명한, 명쾌한

06 shock
SHäk
n.

surprise, upset, disturbance

a feeling of surprise from a disturbing event

*The family were in **shock** when they found out that their dog was run over.*

충격, 충격적인 일

n.

trauma, stupor, collapse

a medical condition related to a decrease in blood pressure

*My grandfather went into **shock** when he forgot to take his medicine.*

(의학적인) 쇼크

	n.	vibration, shake, reverberation
		a violent shaking caused by an explosion or tremor
		*Earthquake **shocks** are common in Los Angeles.*
		격동, 진동, 지진

07	**downturn**	dip, plunge, slump
	ˈdounˌtərn	a decline in an activity, usually economic or business
	n.	*There was a **downturn** in the stock market during the Great Depression.*
		감소(하락), (경기) 하강(침체)

08	**restrain**	hinder, impede, hamper
	rəˈstrān	to prevent someone or something from performing an action
	v.	*I had to **restrain** my dog from jumping out the window.*
		저지(제지)하다
	v.	suppress, moderate, subdue
		to stop from displaying a strong urge or emotion
		*My mother **restrained** her anger when my sister came home past midnight.*
		(감정 등을) 억누르다(참다)

09	**dynamic**	energetic, lively, vigorous
	dīˈnamik	showing positive attitude, full of energy and new ideas
	adj.	*The **dynamic** employee was a key player in the group project.*
		정력적인, 활발한
	n.	a force that encourages change or progress in a system or process
		*The **dynamics** in the workplace allowed the company to grow.*
		동력학, 역학

10	**strewn**	dispersed, littered, scattered
	stroon	scattered in an unorganized manner
	adj.	*Michelle's clothes were **strewn** all over her room.*
		흩다, 흩뿌리다

11	**resonate**	echo, reverberate, vibrate
	ˈreznˌāt	to produce a deep, reverberating sound
	v.	*The wolf's howl **resonated** in the forest.*
		(깊게, 낭랑하게) 울려 퍼지다

SET 33

12. core
kôr
n.

- chief, fundamental, principal
- the central or the most critical aspect of something
- *The **core** of any advertisement campaign is the consumers.*
- 중심부

n.
- center, nucleus, interior
- the dense central area of an object.
- *Earth's **core** is mainly composed of iron.*
- 속

13. imitate
ˈiməˌtāt
v.

- emulate, mimic, echo
- to copy or follow as a model
- *Japan **imitated** China's infrastructure during its development as a nation.*
- 모방하다, 본뜨다

14. makeup
ˈmākˌəp
n.

- composition, configuration, constitution
- the parts of something
- *The **makeup** of ocean sediments include minerals and dead matter.*
- 조립, 구성, 구조

15. swivel
ˈswivəl
v.

- spin, rotate, pivot
- to turn around a point
- *The villain **swiveled** his chair to reveal his identify.*
- 돌리다, 회전시키다

16. inquire
inˈkwīr
v.

- probe, inspect, scrutinize
- to investigate
- *Doctor Watson **inquired** the suspect before his partner arrived.*
- 묻다, 알아보다

17. succession
səkˈseSHən
n.

- sequence, series, chain
- a number of people or things following one after the other
- *A **succession** of models walked down the street during the show.*
- 연속, 잇따름

n.
- descent, lineage, heritage
- the right of inheriting a position or title
- *The **succession** to the throne was argued amongst the children.*
- 승계, 계승; 승계권

18 evolve
ē'välv
v.

advance, develop, progress

to develop slowly, from a simple to a more advanced form

*The amateur photographer **evolved** into a professional artist over the years.*

발달(진전)하다(시키다)

19 tend
tend
v.

incline, veer, favor

regularly behave in a particular way or show a certain trait

*My sister **tends** to bite her lips when she is lying.*

(…하는) 경향이 있다, (…을) 하기 쉽다(잘 하다)

v.

nurse, nurture, manage

to care for or look after

*The farmer **tended** the cows.*

돌보다, 보살피다

20 encircle
in'sərk(ə)l
v.

surround, enclose, circle

to form a circle around a subject

*The pack of wolves **encircled** the reindeer, ready to devour their prey.*

(둥글게) 둘러싸다(두르다)

21 annual
'any(oo)əl
adj.

yearly, anniversary

happening once every year

*We decided to make the camping trip an **annual** event.*

매년의, 연례의

22 moderate
'mäd(ə)rət
adj.

average, ordinary, common

average in amount, degree, or intensity

*The final exam was of **moderate** difficulty.*

보통의, 중간의

v.

chair, arbitrate, mediate

to preside over an argument

*The homeroom teacher **moderated** the discussion amongst my classmates.*

(평가에서 채점이 공정하게 이뤄지도록) 조정(관리)하다

23 severe
sə'vir
adj.

grave, critical, dire

involving a serious issue

*There was a **severe** lack of food in the farm.*

극심한, 심각한

SET 33

adj.		harsh, stern, serious
		stern in behavior or appearance
		*The father looked at his son with a **severe** face.*
		엄한, 엄격한

24 **fortune** ˈfôrCHən n.

	coincidence, chance, accident
	chance or luck
	*It was **fortune** that he won the lottery.*
	운(행운)

	wealth, riches, property
n.	a large amount of money or assets
	*The family **fortune** was locked up in a vault.*
	재산, 부; 거금

25 **boost** bo͞ost v.

	augment, magnify, improve
	to help something to improve
	*The government created lots of attractions to **boost** tourism.*
	신장시키다, 북돋우다

	lift, raise, hoist
v.	to push from below
	***Boost** me up so I can go over the fence.*
	올려주다

26 **manure** məˈn(y)o͝or n.

	dung, droppings
	animal dung used to fertilize land
	***Manure** is added to the ground to improve soil quality.*
	거름(천연 비료)

27 **fauna** ˈfônə n.

	animals
	the animals in a particular habitat
	*Different **fauna** are seen grazing in the Serengeti.*
	동물상

28 **den** den n.

	lair, burrow, cave
	an animal's lair or home
	*The lion was sleeping in its **den**.*
	굴

29 hibernate
'hībər,nāt
v.

sleep, winter, vegetate

to spend time in a dormant state

Bears **hibernate** all winter long.

동면하다

30 partial
'pärSHəl
adj.

limited, restricted, fragmentary

existing only in part

Even the smartest person was able to give **partial** answers.

부분적인, 불완전한

adj.

biased, prejudiced, partisan

favoring one side

Certain news stations give a **partial** view of the situation.

(~을) 편애하는, (~에 대한 지지가) 편파적인

31 parasitism
'perəsə,tizəm
n.

a relationship where the host suffers while the parasite benefits

A hookworm living inside a host is an example of **parasitism**.

기생 (생활)

32 commensalism
kə'mensə,lizəm
n.

a relationship where one organism benefits while the other receives no benefit nor harm

A remora hitching a ride with a shark is an example of **commensalism**.

공서, 공생

33 hijack
'hī,jak
v.

seize, snatch, commandeer

to steal a transport and force it to go to a different destination

The terrorists **hijacked** the plane and crashed it into a building.

(차량, 특히 비행기를) 납치하다

34 penchant
'pen(t)SH(ə)nt
n.

fondness, preference, partiality

a strong liking for something or tendency to do something

She has a **penchant** for adopting homeless cats.

애호

35 bolster
'bōlstər
v.

reinforce, fortify, strengthen

to support or strengthen

The coach gave a speech that helped **bolster** the athletes' confidence.

북돋우다, 강화(개선)하다

SET 33

36. avaricious
/ˌavəˈriSHəs/
adj.

covetous, greedy, materialistic

having or showing greed for wealth or material gain

The **avaricious** rapper bought another car to add to his collection.

탐욕스러운, 욕심 많은

37. erudite
/ˈer(y)əˌdīt/
adj.

scholarly, learned, knowledgeable

having or showing knowledge or learning

The **erudite** discussion bored the cheerleader.

학식 있는, 박식한

38. respective
/rəˈspektiv/
adj.

separate, individual, appropriate

belonging or relating separately to each of two or more people or things

The two scientists discussed about their **respective** research.

각자의, 각각의

39. rot
/rät/
v.

decay, decompose, disintegrate

to decay by the action of bacteria and fungi

The food began to **rot** after a few days.

썩히다, 부식(부패)시키다

40. condense
/kənˈdens/
v.

compress, compact, abridge

to make something more dense or concentrated

The documentary was **condensed** into a two hour film.

압축하다

v.

precipitate, liquefy, deliquesce

to change from a gas or vapor to a liquid

The water vapor was **condensed** into rain.

(기체가) 응결되다, 응결시키다

41. scholar
/ˈskälər/
n.

academic, intellectual, professor

a specialist in a specific branch of study

The **scholar** gave a lecture on mutation.

학자

42. accredit
/əˈkredət/
v.

recognize, license, authorize

to give authority to someone or something

Schools that have not been **accredited** by the government tend to be private institutions.

승인하다, 인가하다

43	**bestow** bəˈstō v.	confer, grant, bequeath
		to give an honor or gift
		My grandfather **bestowed** the family wristwatch to me.
		수여(부여)하다

44	**maleficent** məˈlefəs(ə)nt adj.	antagonistic, baneful, destructive
		causing harm or destruction
		The **maleficent** witch cursed the royal family.
		해로운, 나쁜 짓을 하는

45	**enigmatic** ˌenəɡˈmadik adj.	mysterious, puzzling, mystifying
		difficult to understand or translate
		The **enigmatic** artifact puzzled the archaeologists.
		수수께끼 같은, 불가사의한

46	**remedy** ˈremədē n.	medication, antidote, cure
		a medicine or treatment
		The best **remedy** for any sickness is sleep.
		처리 방안, 해결(개선)책

47	**perpetrator** ˈpərpəˌtrādər n.	criminal, culprit, violator
		a person who commits a crime
		The **perpetrator** was sentenced to ten years in prison.
		가해자(범인)

48	**incarcerate** inˈkärsəˌrāt v.	imprison, jail, detain
		to imprison or confine
		The criminal was **incarcerated** for robbing a bank.
		감금(투옥)하다

49	**medicate** ˈmedəˌkāt v.	sedate, treat, anesthetize
		to administer a drug
		Someone with a common cold can be **medicated** without going to the hospital.
		약을 투여하다

50	**euphoria** yo͞oˈfôrēə n.	elation, delight, glee
		a feeling of intense excitement and happiness
		The man was full of **euphoria** when he won the lottery.
		행복감, 희열

SET 33 TEST

1. The fan girls shouted with _____ when they saw their favorite celebrity.

2. The doctor prescribed a _____ for the patient.

3. The _____ old man taught the young man important life lessons.

4. Children have a _____ for sweet snacks.

5. The chef served a _____ portion of the meal to each diner.

6. The _____ of phone calls drove the receptionist insane.

7. The mother gave _____ instructions to the babysitter.

8. Ford _____ three of his cars and put them back together with exchanged parts.

9. The war was brought to a _____ close when the army brought out the big guns.

10. The traitors were _____ in the dungeon.

---

1. euphoria 2. remedy 3. erudite 4. penchant 5. moderate 6. succession 7. explicit 8. dismantle 9. swift 10. incarcerate

11. How the ancient Egyptians were able to build the pyramid is still an _____ process.

12. The king _____ the sword to the brave knight.

13. The _____ woman walked into the store and purchased the entire Fall colletion.

14. A judge should not be _____ when deciding the verdict.

15. Chinese cookies do not give _____ to the diner.

16. A _____ punishment was given to the criminal.

17. The reporters _____ the man to interview him.

18. The detective _____ the suspects.

19. The _____ of a computer includes a monitor, keyboard, and desktop.

20. The _____ of a successful buisness starts with a buisness plan.

---

11. enigmatic   12. bestow   13. avaricious   14. partial   15. fortune
16. severe   17. encircle   18. inquire   19. makeup   20. core

SET 33

notes:

LEAD
SET 34
VOCABULARY

SET 34

01 expansive
ikˈspansiv
adj.

- extensive, sweeping, broad
- covering a wide area
- *The Great Plains is an **expansive** grassland in the middle of the United States.*
- 툭 트인, 광활한

adj.
- sociable, friendly, outgoing
- pertaining to a person's open and communicative manner
- *Some people are **expansive**, while others tend to be quiet.*
- 속이 트인(말을 잘 하는)

02 variety
vəˈrīədē
n.

- assortment, range, array
- a range of things that are different from one another
- *There is a **variety** of ice cream flavors at the restaurant.*
- 여러 가지, 갖가지, 각양각색

03 foster
ˈfôstər
v.

- promote, stimulate, further
- to encourage the development of something
- *The mentor's role is to **foster** learning amongst the children.*
- 조성하다, 발전시키다

v.
- rear, raise, nurture
- to raise a child, usually not one's own by birth
- *The family **fostered** the homeless child as best as they could.*
- (수양부모로서) 아이를 맡아 기르다

04 seethe
sēTH
v.

- fume, rage, burn
- for a person to be filled with unexpressed anger
- *The man was **seething** when his son broke his favorite guitar.*
- (마음속으로 분노 등이) 부글거리다, 속을 끓이다

05 harsh
härSH
adj.

- barbarous, savage, despotic
- cruel or severe
- *The **harsh** words left a scar in his heart.*
- 가혹한, 냉혹한

06 reckon
'rekən
v.

	calculate, compute, number
	to calculate
	*The total cost was **reckoned** at $100.00.*
	계산하다

v.

	consider, judge, view
	to consider to think in a specific way
	*I **reckon** that he will come back, begging for forgiveness.*
	(…라고) 생각하다

07 enrich
in'riCH
v.

	enhance, augment, supplement
	improve the quality or value of
	*Adding salt **enriched** the flavor of the meat.*
	질을 높이다, 풍요롭게 하다

08 ignite
ig'nīt
v.

	kindle, spark, burn
	to catch fire
	*The fire in the forest was **ignited** by a camper's cigarette.*
	불이 붙다, 점화되다

09 shudder
'SHədər
v.

	shake, shiver, quiver
	to tremble out of fear or revulsion
	*He **shuddered** with horror when he saw the ghost.*
	(공포·추위 등으로) 몸을 떨다, 몸서리치다

10 alleviate
ə'lēvē,āt
v.

	reduce, ease, relieve
	to make a problem less severe
	*The medicine helped **alleviate** the pain.*
	완화하다

11 hasten
'hās(ə)n
v.

	accelerate, expedite, quicken
	to cause something to happen sooner
	*We **hastened** back to the house when we realized we forgot our passports.*
	서둘러 하다

12 conservative
kən'sərvədiv
adj.

	traditional, orthodox, conventional
	hesitant to change and holding onto traditional values
	*My grandmother's **conservative** ideals prevented her from understanding pop culture.*
	보수적인

SET 34

13	**perceive**	discern, detect, recognize
	pərˈsēv	to become aware of something
	v.	Her eyes widened when she **perceived** the truth.
		감지(인지)하다

14	**banality**	predictability, dullness, staleness
	bəˈnalədē	empty of freshness or originality
	n.	The **banality** of his daily life forced him to go on an adventure.
		따분함, 시시한 말(일)

15	**extravagance**	luxury, indulgence, excess
	ikˈstravəgəns	something where too much money was spent or used up lots of resources
	n.	Caviar is considered an **extravagance** even amongst diners.
		사치(품)

16	**envelop**	cover, surround, blanket
	ənˈveləp	to wrap up or surround completely
	v.	The grim reaper was **enveloped** in a black cloak.
		감싸다, 뒤덮다

17	**ostentatious**	pretentious, conspicuous, flamboyant
	ˌästənˈtāSHəs	designed to impress or receive attraction
	adj.	Certain books have **ostentatious** covers, however the content is mediocre.
		(남에게 과시하기 위해 만든 것처럼) 대단히 비싼(호사스러운)

18	**grandeur**	splendor, magnificence, greatness
	ˈgranjər	impressive in appearance or style
	n.	The Rocky Mountains is a showcase of America's **grandeur**.
		장엄함

19	**brand**	make, line, label
	brand	a type of product made by a specific company under a label
	n.	This is a new **brand** of athlete apparel.
		상표, 브랜드
		denounce, discredit, vilify
	v.	to mark as having a bad quality
		The company was **branded** for polluting the environment.
		(특히 부당하게) 낙인을 찍다

20	**genre** 'ZHänrə n.	category, group, class sort; style
		Which **genre** of movies do you like to watch?
		장르

21	**defining** dəˈfīniŋ adj.	characterizing, determining, representative critically important
		A **defining** feature of Picasso's art is the rectangular shapes.
		본질적인 의미를 규정하는

22	**rigid** ˈrijid adj.	stiff, hard, firm unable to bend or change shape
		The rice cake turned **rigid** after being left out for a day.
		뻣뻣한, 단단한, 잘 휘지(구부러지지) 않는
	adj.	stern, stringent, rigorous strict or severe
		Children must follow **rigid** rules in classrooms.
		엄격한, 융통성 없는

23	**confine** kənˈfīn v.	enclose, cage, incarcerate to restrict someone or something within certain boundaries
		The animals are **confined** in cages at the zoo.
		(활동,주제,지역 등을) 국한시키다

24	**agitate** ˈajəˌtāt v.	upset, perturb, fluster to make someone nervous or troubled
		The passenger **agitated** the cab driver with numerous questions.
		(마음을) 뒤흔들다(불안하게 만들다)

25	**mediate** ˈmēdēˌāt v.	arbitrate, moderate, conciliate to intervene in an argument to bring about an agreement
		America tends to **mediate** between any two countries in dispute.
		(해결책을 찾기 위해) 중재(조정)하다

26	**clergy** ˈklərjē n.	clerics, priests, the church a group of people ordained for religious responsibilities
		The **clergy** oversees the affairs of the Catholic Church.
		(특히 기독교의) 성직자들

SET 34

27 ecclesiastical
əˌklēzēˈastək(ə)l
adj.

clerical, ministerial, priestly

relating to the Church or its clergy

*There exists a **ecclesiastical** hierarchy within the Catholic Church.*

기독교의

28 esoteric
ˌesəˈterik
adj.

obscure, arcane, abstruse

likely to be comprehended by only a small group of people

***Esoteric** philosophical discussions can only be engaged by philosophy majors.*

소수만 이해하는(즐기는), 비전의

29 secular
ˈsekyələr
adj.

temporal, worldly, nonreligious

not having to do with religion nor spiritual realm

*Those who are devoted to faith are not to indulge in **secular** things.*

세속적인

30 adorn
əˈdôrn
v.

embellish, decorate, furnish

to make more attractive

*The Christmas tree was **adorned** with lights.*

꾸미다, 장식하다

31 therapy
ˈTHerəpē
n.

treatment, remedy, cure

treatment meant to heal or relieve a disorder

*The most common **therapy** to a minor cold is to drink warm water with lemon.*

치료, 요법

32 deny
dəˈnī
v.

contradict, repudiate, refute

to refuse or admit the truth or existence of

*I will not **deny** that what I did was wrong.*

(무엇을) 인정하지(받아들이지) 않다, 부인하다

33 enlightenment
inˈlītnmənt
n.

insight, awareness, illumination

the state of having received greater knowledge and understanding concerning a subject or situation

*Gandhi strived to achieve **enlightenment** throughout his life.*

깨우침, 이해

34 vibrant
'vībrənt
adj.

spirited, lively, energetic

full of energy and enthusiasm

*The **vibrant** city life attracted people from the country.*

활기찬, 생기가 넘치는

35 valid
'valəd
adj.

authentic, proper, genuine

legally or officially acceptable

*He had a **valid** contract to own the land.*

유효한(정당한)

adj.

sound, rational, logical

having a basis in logic or fact

*The opponent gave some **valid** arguments against the case.*

(논리적으로) 타당한(근거 있는)

36 archetypal
ˌärkəˈtīp(ə)l
adj.

representative, standard, conventional

very typical

*The **archetypal** dental checkup still scared the little boy.*

전형적인

37 deference
'def(ə)rəns
n.

respect, consideration, reverence

humble submission and respect

*The women wore dark veils in **deference** to their religion.*

존중(경의)(을 표하는 행동)

38 myth
miTH
n.

legend, tale, fable

a traditional story usually involving supernatural beings and events

*Hercules is a famous character in Greek **myth**.*

신화

39 legitimize
ləˈjidəˌmīz
v.

validate, warrant, sanction

to make lawful

*The government **legitimized** cutting down trees in the rainforest.*

정당화하다

SET 34

40. infuse
in'fyooz
v.

pervade, permeate, saturate

to fill and spread

*His acting was **infused** with charisma so it captivated the audience.*

불어넣다(스미게 하다)

41. quintessential
ˌkwin(t)ə'sen(t)SHəl
adj.

typical, archetypal, classic

representing the most typical or perfect example of a characteristic or class

*He was the **quintessential** nice guy, always putting others before him.*

정수의, 본질적인

42. terse
tərs
adj.

abrupt, brief, curt

short in the use of words

*The queen gave a **terse** greeting before the prime minister gave his speech.*

간결한(간단한)

43. sumptuous
'səm(p)(t)SH(oo)əs
adj.

luxurious, opulent, resplendent

splendid and expensive

*The five-course-meal at the hotel was the most **sumptuous** meal she had ever had.*

호화로운

44. despicable
də'spikəb(ə)l
adj.

loathsome, detestable, abhorrent

deserving hatred and contempt

*The **despicable** villain had a change of heart and adopted the three girls.*

비열한, 야비한

45. decoy
'dēˌkoi
n.

lure, bait, temptation

a person or thing used to mislead a person or animal into a trap

*The teddy bear acted as a **decoy** while the hunters waited for the lion.*

유인하는 사람(물건), 바람잡이; 유인

46. tease
tēz
v.

mock, satirize, ridicule

to make fun of or attempt to provoke

*The children **teased** the new student until he started to cry.*

놀리다(장난하다), 지분(집적)거리다

47. uphold
ˌəpˈhōld
v.

preserve, protect, sustain

to maintain a custom or practice

*The immigrant parents wanted to **uphold** their traditions even in the new land.*

유지시키다(옹호하다)

48. recast
rēˈkast
v.

reassemble, renovate, fix

to organize in a different style or form

*The engineers decided to **recast** the machine to improve its performance.*

재구성하다, 다르게 제시하다

49. lucrative
ˈlookrədiv
adj.

profitable, fruitful, rewarding

to make a lot of profit

*Real estate can be a **lucrative** business.*

수익성이 좋은

50. abide
əˈbīd
v.

obey, observe, follow

to accept or follow a rule

*Citizens must **abide** by the laws of the country.*

(법률, 합의 등을) 따르다

v.

tolerate, bear, endure

to tolerate something

*I cannot **abide** living in a dirty house.*

참다, 견디다

SET 34 TEST

1. Students must _____ by the rules set up in the classroom.

2. The massacre of the Jewish people was a _____ act commited by the Nazis.

3. The best farewells are _____.

4. Christians wear cross accessories in _____ to their religion.

5. The _____ teammate encouraged the rest of the team to try harder.

6. The wedding cake is _____ with flowers and ribbons.

7. The message was so _____ that only a few would understand.

8. Neil Armstrong landing on the moon was a _____ moment in human history.

9. The millionaire's mansion is a _____ showcase of his wealth.

10. The _____ of the designer's work got him fired.

---

1. abide 2. despicable 3. terse 4. deference 5. vibrant
6. adorn 7. esoteric 8. defining 9. grandeur 10. banality

410 · LEAD VOCABULARY

11. Continuous physical therapy helped _____ her back problems.

12. Adding manure to the soil _____ the ground.

13. Crypto currency at one point was a _____ business.

14. The feeble soldier acted as the _____ while the rest of the troops snuck up on the enemy.

15. The comment he made to the girl for the first time was very _____.

16. During the crusades, anyone with _____ thoughts were punished by the Church.

17. _____ the dragon will only result in a terrible misfortune.

18. Certain companies are _____ as notorious buisnesses for taking advantage of cheap labor in Asia.

19. South Korea is a _____ nation with traditions that date back a thousand years still being followed.

20. I _____ that he will soon give up.

---

11. alleviate 12. enrich 13. lucrative 14. decoy 15. archtypal 16. secular 17. agitate 18. brand 19. conservative 20. reckon

SET 34

notes:

LEAD
SET
35
VOCABULARY

SET 35

01 literate
ˈlidərət
adj.

educated, erudite, scholarly
being able to read and write
Nowadays, public education has allowed almost everyone to be **literate**.
글을 읽고 쓸 줄 아는

02 entrench
inˈtren(t)SH
v.

establish, root, install
to establish so firmly that any sort of change would be difficult or improbable
Gender gap is deeply **entrenched** in our society.
(변경이 어렵도록) 단단히 자리 잡게 하다

03 motif
mōˈtēf
n.

theme, concept, subject
a marked feature or idea in art or literature
A repeating **motif** in Mark Twain's books is adventure.
(문학,음악 작품 속에서 반복, 전개되는) 주제

04 ornament
ˈôrnəmənt
v.

decorate, embellish, garnish
to make something more attractive by adding decoration
The family **ornamented** their house for the Christmas party.
장식하다

05 illusion
iˈlo͞oZHən
n.

mirage, hallucination, apparition
something that is or is probably wrong in perception or interpretation
Without rest and water, the man started to see **illusions** in the desert.
환상, 환각

06 stark
stärk
adj.

sheer, absolute, total
complete
Tony Stark displayed a **stark** difference in behavior after escaping captivity.
극명한, 완전한

07 tension
ˈtenSHən
n.

stress, anxiety, pressure
mental or emotional burden
During the Cold War, the **tension** between Americans and Soviets were high.
긴장 상태

08 symmetric
səˈmetrik
adj.

equal, proportional, balanced
a mirror image of each other or around an axis
*The building is completely **symmetric**.*

대칭적인

09 discard
diˈskärd
v.

reject, scrap, dump
to get rid of someone or something after losing usefulness or desire
*My son **discarded** the toys he no longer played with.*

버리다, 폐기하다

10 meticulous
məˈtikyələs
adj.

diligent, scrupulous, thorough
very careful and precise
*My boss is very **meticulous** and keeps his desk and files organized.*

꼼꼼한, 세심한

11 disfigured
disˈfigyər
adj.

scarred, blemished, impaired
not attractive
*The hunchback of Notre Dame is a **disfigured** man.*

흠이 있는

12 exemplify
igˈzempləˌfī
v.

typify, epitomize, represent
to be an example of
*The colorful clothes **exemplify** the nature of the hippy era.*

전형적인 예가 되다

13 recoil
rəˈkoil
v.

flinch, cower, wince
to suddenly draw back or flinch in fear or disgust
*The boy **recoiled** when the dentist started to treat his cavity.*

(무섭거나 불쾌한 것을 보고) 움찔하다(흠칫 놀라다)

14 conscientious
ˌkän(t)SHēˈen(t)SHəs
adj.

diligent, industrious, dedicated
wishing to do what is right related to one's work or responsibilities
*The employee of the month was a **conscientious** worker.*

양심적인, 성실한

SET 35

15. weighty
ˈwādē
adj.
- important, significant, consequential
- of great seriousness
- He put aside the **weighty** decisions to be made at the end.
- 중대한

16. provoke
prəˈvōk
v.
- enrage, irritate, insult
- to make someone annoyed or angry on purpose
- The mouse **provoked** the cat by stealing its food.
- 화나게(짜증나게) 하다, 도발하다

17. mere
mir
adj.
- trifling, meager, trivial
- being nothing more than nor better than
- **Mere** mortals cannot stand against the gods of Olympus.
- 겨우 …의, (한낱) …에 불과한

18. manifest
ˈmanəˌfest
v.
- exhibit, express, demonstrate
- to display a trait or emotion by one's actions or appearance
- The clown **manifested** signs of happiness in his act.
- (특히 감정,태도,특질을 분명히) 나타내다

19. clemency
ˈklemənsē
n.
- leniency, pity, sympathy
- mercy
- The queen showed **clemency** towards the thieves and offered food and shelter.
- (처벌 대상에 대한) 관용, 관대한 처분

20. prestige
preˈstēZH
n.
- status, reputation, esteem
- reputation or respect from one's success, rank, or achievement
- The warrior gained more **prestige** after defeating his enemies.
- 위신, 명망

21. overturn
ˌōvərˈtərn
v.
- rescind, revoke, repeal
- to abolish or reverse a system or decision
- The judge **overturned** the jury's decision to vindicate the man.
- (판결 등을) 뒤집다(번복시키다)

416 · LEAD VOCABULARY

22. prodigal
ˈprädəgəl
adj.

- spendthrift, reckless, wasteful
- wasting money and resources
- The **prodigal** son returned to his father after spending his wealth.
- (돈,시간,에너지,물자를) 낭비하는

23. vagary
ˈvāgərē
n.

- peculiarity, eccentricity, caprice
- an unexpected change in someone's behavior or situation
- The **vagaries** of the weather made it difficult to plan the vacation.
- (날씨 등의) 예측 불허의 변화(변동)

24. regard
rəˈgärd
v.

- consider, assess, gauge
- to consider someone or something in a specific way
- I **regard** South Korea as my home.
- …을 … 으로 여기다(평가하다)

n.

- greetings, felicitations, compliments
- best wishes
- Give my **regard** to your parents.
- 안부의 말(인사)

25. solemn
ˈsäləm
adj.

- earnest, sincere, serious
- deep sincerity
- It is respectful to be **solemn** at a funeral.
- 엄숙한

26. superficial
ˌso͞opərˈfiSHəl
adj.

- exterior, outer, peripheral
- existing on the surface
- The car had some **superficial** damage.
- 피상(표면)적인

adj.

- shallow, artificial, meaningless
- not having any depth of character or comprehension
- American movies tend to show high school girls as **superficial**.
- 깊이 없는, 얄팍한

27. sincere
sinˈsir
adj.

- wholehearted, genuine, honest
- having to do with genuine feelings
- Her **sincere** apology helped me to forgive her.
- 진실된, 진정한, 진심 어린

SET 35

28. jubilant
ˈjo͞obələnt
adj.

joyful, rejoicing, exuberant
feeling or showing great happiness
There is always the **jubilant** family member who keeps the family happy.

승리감에 넘치는, 득의만면한, 의기양양한

29. instigate
ˈinstəˌgāt
v.

initiate, kindle, launch
to bring about or start an action or event
The terrorists **instigated** fear amongst the citizens.

부추기다, 선동하다

30. grieve
grēv
v.

mourn, lament, sorrow
to suffer from grief
Korea has three days for families to **grieve** before burying their loved one.

(특히 누구의 죽음으로 인해) 비통해 하다

31. resolute
ˈrezəˌl(y)o͞ot
adj.

resolved, decided, adamant
determined and unwavering
He was **resolute** to break up with his girlfriend this time.

단호한, 확고한

32. offset
ˈôfˌset
v.

counterbalance, cancel, neutralize
to counteract something by giving an opposing effect or force
The profit from this month **offset** the deficit from the previous month.

상쇄(벌충)하다

33. emigrate
ˈeməˌgrāt
v.

migrate, relocate, resettle
to leave one's country to settle permanently in another
My family **emigrated** to the United States when I was eight-years-old.

이민을 가다, (다른 나라로) 이주하다

34. surveillance
sərˈvāləns
n.

scrutiny, monitoring, observation
close observation, especially for criminals or spies
The important witness was put under a twenty four hour **surveillance**.

감시

35 seldom
'seldəm
adv.

rarely, infrequently, scarcely

not often

*The same people **seldom** show up twice to get a sample of the food at Costco.*

좀처럼(거의) …않는

36 tame
tām
v.

train, master, subjugate

to domesticate an animal

*It was difficult for the zoo keepers to **tame** the lions.*

길들이다, 다스리다

37 kindle
'kindl
v.

stimulate, rouse, inspire

to arouse or inspire an emotion or feeling

*Martin Luther King Jr's speech **kindled** justice and equality within the minorities.*

(관심, 감정 등을(이)) 불붙이다(불붙다)

38 falter
'fôltər
v.

hesitate, stall, stumble

to be hesitant and unsteady

*It is important to be confident when giving a speech and not **falter**.*

불안정해지다, 흔들리다

39 delude
də'lo͞od
v.

deceive, fool, dupe

to give a misleading idea upon someone

*Loki **deluded** himself into thinking that he was the rightful heir to the throne.*

속이다, 착각하게 하다

40 listless
'lis(t)ləs
adj.

lethargic, lifeless, spiritless

lacking energy or enthusiasm

*A sloth is a **listless** mammal that spends most of its time on a tree.*

힘(열의)이 없는, 무기력한

41 pecuniary
pə'kyo͞onē,erē
adj.

financial, monetary, fiscal

relating to money

*After he won the lottery, his **pecuniary** troubles ended.*

금전상의

SET 35

42 insulate
ˈinsəˌlāt
v.

- encase, enclose, envelop
- to prevent the loss of heat or intrusion of sound
- *The recording room was **insulated** with foam.*

절연(단열/방음) 처리를 하다

43 explicate
ˈekspləˌkāt
v.

- explain, clarify, elucidate
- to make plain or clear
- *There are some concepts in this world that cannot be **explicated**.*

설명(해석)하다

44 blunt
blənt
adj.

- flat, rounded, dull
- having a flat or rounded end
- *The sword had not been used for ages, so it was **blunt** and needed sharpening.*

무딘, 뭉툭한

adj.
- straightforward, frank, candid
- plain and direct in manner
- *Children are **blunt** and do not consider the feelings of others.*

직설적인

45 indecent
inˈdēs(ə)nt
adj.

- obscene, rude, vulgar
- not fitting with the standards of behavior or speech
- *The latest film by the popular director was **indecent** for the public.*

외설적인

46 auxiliary
ôgˈzilyərē
adj.

- supplementary, additional, reserve
- providing additional help and support
- *The security system operated through an **auxiliary** power when the main power went out.*

보조의

47 extemporaneous
ikˌstempəˈrānēəs
adj.

- impromptu, spontaneous, unscripted
- done or spoken without preparation
- *The president was asked to give a **extemporaneous** speech.*

즉석의; 준비 없이 하는

48 brunt
brənt
n.

force, impact, shock
the main impact of a specific action
*His torso took the **brunt** of the tackle from the linebacker.*

(공격 등의) 예봉

49 rationale
ˌraSHəˈnal
n.

logic, reasoning, sense
a set of reasons or a logical basis for an action or belief
*The manager explained the **rationale** behind the change.*

이유(근거)

50 sojourn
ˈsōjərn
n.

visit, stopover, stay
a temporary stay
*His **sojourn** in Seoul was only for the summer.*

체류

SET 35 CROSSWORD PUZZLE

Across

3. of great seriousness
6. mercy
7. wasting money and resources
10. determined and unwavering
11. to bring about or start an action or event
13. to arouse or inspire an emotion or feeling
14. lacking energy or enthusiasm
15. to be hesitant and unsteady

Down

1. deep sincerity
2. existing on the surface
4. feeling or showing great happiness
5. very careful and precise
8. complete
9. to abolish or reverse a system or decision
12. not often

1. solemn   2. superficial   3. weighty   4. jubilant   5. meticulous   6. clemency   7. prodigal   8. stark   9. overturn   10. resolute   11. instigate   12. seldom   13. kindle   14. listless   15. falter

LEAD
SET
36
VOCABULARY

SET 36

01 whittle
'(h)widl
v.

- shave, peel, carve
- to carve into an object by continuously cutting small slices from it
- The hunter **whittled** a hook from a tree branch.

(나무 등을) 깎아서 만들다

02 complimentary
kämplə'mentrē
adj.

- flattering, appreciative, admiring
- expressing a compliment
- The headmaster was very **complimentary** about Mark's academic work.

칭찬하는

adj.

- free, courtesy, gratis
- given free of charge
- Enjoy a **complimentary** bottle of wine from our restaurant.

무료의

03 delusion
də'loōZHən
n.

- deception, misleading, trickery
- the action of misleading or the condition of being misled
- Television dramas portray a **delusion** of reality to its viewers.

착각, 오해

04 emphasis
'emfəsəs
n.

- prominence, attention, significance
- special attention or importance given to something
- Martin Luther King Jr. placed great **emphasis** on non-violence.

강조, 역점, 주안점

05 distort
də'stôrt
v.

- misrepresent, twist, skew
- to give a false account or impression of someone or something
- My friend **distorted** about the girl I was supposed to meet for a blind date.

(사실, 생각 등을) 왜곡하다

06 astonish
ə'stäniSH
v.

- amaze, startle, astound
- to impress someone greatly
- My wife never fails to **astonish** me.

깜짝(크게) 놀라게 하다

07 inhabit
in'habət
v.

- settle, populate, occupy
- to live in or occupy a place
- The very first humans supposedly **inhabited** Africa.

살다(거주/서식하다)

08 desiccate
'desəˌkāt
v.

dehydrated, dry, powdered

to become completely dry

Years of no rain **desiccated** the farmland.

건조시키다, 탈수하다

09 endemic
enˈdemik
adj.

local, regional, native

native to a certain place

Kangaroos are **endemic** to Australia.

(특정 지역, 집단) 고유의

10 refuge
ˈrefˌyo͞oj
n.

protection, asylum, sanctuary

a place that acts as a shelter

The kingdom of Wakanda became a **refuge** to the heroes.

보호 시설, 쉼터

11 constraint
kənˈstrānt
n.

restriction, restraint, check

limitation

Time **constraints** prevented the tourists from seeing everything.

제한, 통제

12 deter
dəˈtər
v.

avert, impede, thwart

to prevent something from happening

The crew of the Enterprise were able to **deter** the alien invasion.

단념시키다, 그만두게 하다

13 speciation
ˌspēSHēˈāSHən
n.

the formation of a new species

In order for **speciation** to occur, the particular animal group needs to be divided.

종 형성

14 colonize
ˈkäləˌnīz
v.

occupy, seize, subjugate

for a country to send people to settle somewhere and establish political dominance

Europeans **colonized** different parts of America.

식민지로 만들다

SET 36 · 425

SET 36

15. pioneer /ˌpīəˈnir/ n.
- settler, colonist, explorer
- someone who is the first to explore or settle in a new area
- *Lewis and Clark are **pioneers** who explored the lands west of the Mississippi.*
- 개척자

n.
- developer, innovator, trailblazer
- someone who researches and develops something new
- *Steve Jobs was a **pioneer** in computer electronics.*
- (특정 지식문화 부문의) 개척자(선구자)

16. stable /ˈstābəl/ adj.
- secure, steady, firm
- firmly established
- *My colleagues and I have a **stable** work relationship.*
- 안정된, 안정적인

17. congregate /ˈkäNGgrəˌgāt/ v.
- assemble, rally, crowd
- to gather into a large crowd
- *In a flash mob dance, people will **congregate** to dance to a song.*
- 모이다

18. inevitable /inˈevidəb(ə)l/ adj.
- unavoidable, inescapable, certain
- certain to occur
- *The appearance of a hero is **inevitable** with the coming of a villain.*
- 불가피한, 필연적인

19. segregate /ˈsegrəˌgāt/ v.
- separate, quarantine, partition
- to isolate or divide from a group
- *Different ethnic groups were **segregated** in America's early history.*
- 분리(차별)하다

20. morphology /môrˈfäləjē/ n.
- physiology, biology
- the study of organisms and their body structures
- ***Morphology** looks into why birds have different shaped wings.*
- 형태학

21. agile /ˈajəl/ adj.
- nimble, acrobatic, graceful
- able to move fast and with ease
- *Ninjas are **agile** and move without being detected.*
- 날렵한, 민첩한

426 · LEAD VOCABULARY

22	**ingest**	consume, devour, digest
	in'jest	to take in food or drink into the body
	v.	*The first thing I want to **ingest** are tacos when I go to California.*
		(음식, 약 등을) 삼키다(먹다)

23	**sustenance**	nourishment, nutrition, diet
	'səstənəns	food or drink
	n.	*All living organisms require **sustenance** to live and reproduce.*
		(음식, 물 등) 생명을 건강하게 유지시켜 주는 것

24	**requisite**	necessity, precondition, prerequisite
	'rekwəzət	something that is necessary to achieve a goal
	n.	*Addition and subtraction are **requisites** before learning multiplication and division.*
		(어떤 목적에 필요한) 필수품, 필요조건

25	**myriad**	countless, unlimited, infinite
	'mirēəd	extremely great in number
	adj.	*The **myriad** stars light up the night sky.*
		무수한

26	**overcome**	conquer, vanquish, defeat
	ˌōvərˈkəm	to defeat an opponent
	v.	*Rocky Balboa was unable to **overcome** Apollo in the final match.*
		(남을) 이기다
		solve, control, best
	v.	to succeed in dealing with a problem
		*He was able to **overcome** his fear of heights.*
		극복하다

27	**alternate**	rotate, oscillate, fluctuate
	'ôltərˌnāt	to occur in turn periodically
	v.	*The dance moves **alternate** every twenty steps.*
		번갈아 나오게 만들다

28	**sympatric**	occurring in the same geographic area
	simˈpatrik	*There is less genetic diversity when **sympatric** species interbreed.*
	adj.	동지역성

SET 36 · 427

SET 36

29. volatile
ˈvälədl
adj.

unpredictable, erratic, turbulent

likely to show rapid changes in emotion

*My girlfriend becomes **volatile** once a month.*

변덕스러운

30. bemoan
bəˈmōn
v.

lament, deplore, mourn

to express discontent or sorrow

*There was no reason to **bemoan** for getting fired.*

한탄하다

31. elucidate
ēˈloōsəˌdāt
v.

illuminate, clarify, explicate

to make something clear and understandable

*Einstein **elucidated** his theory of relativity to the class.*

(더 자세히) 설명하다

32. spouse
spous
n.

partner, mate, consort

a husband or wife

*I am happily married to my **spouse**.*

배우자

33. conglomerate
kənˈglämərət
n.

combination, mixture, mingling

a number of different parts that are put together but still remain distinct entities

*The salad was a **conglomerate** of fruits and vegetables.*

(잡다한 물건의) 집합(복합)체

34. bypass
ˈbīˌpas
v.

avoid, evade, dodge

to go around

*The cab driver **bypassed** the accident and continued to our destination.*

우회하다

35. deceit
dəˈsēt
n.

deception, duplicity, fraud

the act or practice of hiding or misrepresenting the truth

*The dictator's **deceit** tricked everyone in the country.*

속임수, 사기, 기만

36 linger
'liNGgər
v.

loiter, dawdle, wait

stay in place longer than needed

*The bear **lingered** around the bee hive, waiting for the bees to go away.*

(예상보다 오래) 남다(계속되다)

37 dogma
'dôgmə
n.

teaching, tenet, principle

a set of principles set down by an authority as undeniable truth

*The anarchists rejected the political **dogma** that had governed the nation.*

(독단적인) 신조, 도그마

38 assuage
ə'swāj
v.

relieve, alleviate, mitigate

to make an unpleasant feeling less intense

*The mother helped **assuage** her son's anger.*

(안 좋은 감정을) 누그러뜨리다(달래다)

39 resuscitate
rə'səsə,tāt
v.

revive, restore, revitalize

to revive someone from unconsciousness

*The life guard was able to **resuscitate** the drowned man.*

(인공호흡법 등으로) 소생시키다

40 apportion
ə'pôrSH(ə)n
v.

allocate, allot, distribute

to divide and distribute

*The medical kits were **apportioned** to each village.*

나누다, 배분(할당)하다

41 petite
pə'tēt
adj.

dainty, tiny, small

attractively small and dainty

*Even as an adult, she wears **petite** size clothes.*

자그마한

42 provident
'prävədənt
adj.

prudent, judicious, shrewd

making preparations for the future

*A **provident** individual will have a savings account.*

앞날에 대비하는

SET 36

43. impersonate
im ˈpərsə ˌnāt
v.

imitate, mimic, parody

to imitate someone in order to entertain or deceive

*James Bond **impersonated** a scientist to go inside the laboratory.*

가장하다, 흉내내다

44. ruse
rooz
n.

ploy, trick, tactic

an action meant to trick someone

*She came up with a **ruse** to get out of the house and go to the party.*

계략, 책략

45. champion
ˈCHampēən
n.

victor, winner, titlist

a person who has defeated all the rivals in a competition

*The boxing **champion** walked around the ring with his championship belt.*

챔피언, 선수권 대회 우승자

v.

advocate, promote, defend

to support the cause of something

*The new district attorney **championed** justice in the crime ridden city.*

…을 위해 싸우다, …을 옹호하다

46. disparity
dəˈsperədē
n.

discrepancy, inconsistency, incongruity

a noticeable difference

*Economic **disparities** have always existed within society.*

차이

47. vanguard
ˈvan ˌgärd
n.

front, pioneer, trailblazer

the forefront of new ideas

*Space engineers are in the **vanguard** of technological development.*

선봉(선두)

48. commend
kəˈmend
v.

compliment, congratulate, praise

to praise formally

*The commander **commended** his men by awarding them the medal of bravery.*

칭찬하다

49 rebuke
rəˈbyoōk
v.

reprimand, scold, admonish

to express disapproval or criticism because of one's action or behavior

*The teacher **rebuked** the student for not completing the project.*

힐책(질책)하다, 꾸짖다

50 pacify
ˈpasəˌfī
v.

placate, appease, calm

to relieve an emotion

*The exchange for a new computer helped **pacify** the angry customer.*

진정시키다(달래다)

SET 36 TEST

1. The hotel offered _____ breakfast for making the guests wait so long.

2. Students are under the _____ that they will ace the test without studying for it.

3. The witness _____ his testimony because he was bribed.

4. The deceased are _____ before they are wrapped and turned into mummies.

5. There was a _____ on his budget after last night's spending.

6. People tend to _____ around a fight or an accident.

7. Deer are _____ creatures that are able to run swiftly inside a forest.

8. A _____ of attending a birthday party is to bring a gift.

9. A _____ of flavors were available at the ice cream store.

10. The mother searched frantically for the toy to _____ her crying child.

---

1. complimentary 2. delusion 3. distort 4. desiccate 5. constraint 6. congregate 7. agile 8. requisite 9. myriad 10. pacify

11. The brave firemen were _____ by the mayor for putting out the dangerous fire.

12. A _____ was employed by the seniors to trick the new freshmen.

13. The _____ civilization stocked up in their grain supply before the famine came.

14. The wise ruler _____ the food to the inhabitants.

15. Lobbyists _____ around government buildings, waiting to talk with an official.

16. The slap in the face helped me to _____ what was going on.

17. A teenager going through puberty tends to be _____.

18. Babies need more _____ than adults because they are growing continuously.

19. African Americans were _____ from the rest of the community because of their ethnicity.

20. It was _____ that the old building would collapse after the earthquake.

---

11. commend 12. ruse 13. provident 14. apportion 15. linger
16. elucidate 17. volatile 18. sustenance 19. segregate 20. inevitable

SET 36

notes:

LEAD
SET 37
VOCABULARY

SET 37

01 ordain
ôrˈdān
v.

- appoint, anoint, induct
- to make someone a priest or minister
- He was **ordained** a minister after finishing his seminary school.
- (성직자로) 임명하다

v.
- decree, rule, order
- to order something officially
- A jail sentence of three years was **ordained** for his crime.
- 명하다, (미리) 정하다

02 protract
prəˈtrakt
v.

- prolong, extend, lengthen
- to lengthen the time
- The time it takes to get ready to go out always **protracts** when my wife is involved.
- 오래 끌다, 길게 하다, 연장하다

03 invasive
inˈvāsiv
adj.

- intrusive
- tending to spread wide with a harmful intent
- Cancer is an **invasive** sickness which eventually kills the host.
- 급속히 퍼지는, 침습성의

04 hinder
ˈhindər
v.

- hamper, obstruct, inhibit
- to delay or block by creating difficulties
- Poor Wi-Fi connection **hindered** my internet access.
- 저해(방해)하다, …을 못하게 하다

05 spoil
spoil
v.

- damage, blemish, disfigure
- to decrease the value or quality of something
- Please do not **spoil** this surprise party by telling the birthday girl.
- 망치다, 못쓰게 만들다

v.
- overindulge, pamper, coddle
- to harm the character of a child by being too lenient
- Parents tend to **spoil** their child especially if they have no other siblings.
- (아이를) 응석받이로(버릇없게) 키우다

n.
- booty, loot, plunder
- goods stolen from a person or place
- The warriors indulged in the **spoils** of war.
- 전리품

06 piteous
'pidēəs
adj.

sad, pitiful, heartbreaking

deserving compassion

*The female dog howled a **piteous** cry when her pup died.*

애처로운, 가련한

07 vex
veks
v.

irritate, enrage, agitate

to make someone annoyed or worried

*Teenagers are constantly **vexed** by their parents because of their constant nagging.*

성가시게(짜증나게)하다

08 enliven
in'līvən
v.

uplift, rouse, invigorate

to make someone more cheerful

*The war hero was **enlivened** when his family greeted him at the airport.*

더 재미있게(생동감 있게) 만들다

09 imprudent
im'proodnt
adj.

incautious, rash, reckless

not caring for the results of an action

*It was **imprudent** for my dad to make a promise and not keep it.*

현명하지 못한, 경솔한

10 abstruse
ab'stroos
adj.

arcane, enigmatic, esoteric

hard to understand

*A reward was to be given to anyone who solved the **abstruse** mathematical problem.*

난해한

11 isolate
'īsə,lāt
v.

separate, segregate, detach

to cause someone or something to be alone or apart from others

*The Amish are people who have **isolated** themselves from technology.*

격리하다, 고립시키다

12 manifold
'manə,fōld
adj.

multifarious, diverse, myriad

having various forms or elements

*The reasons for the Gulf War was **manifold**.*

(수가) 많은, 여러 가지의

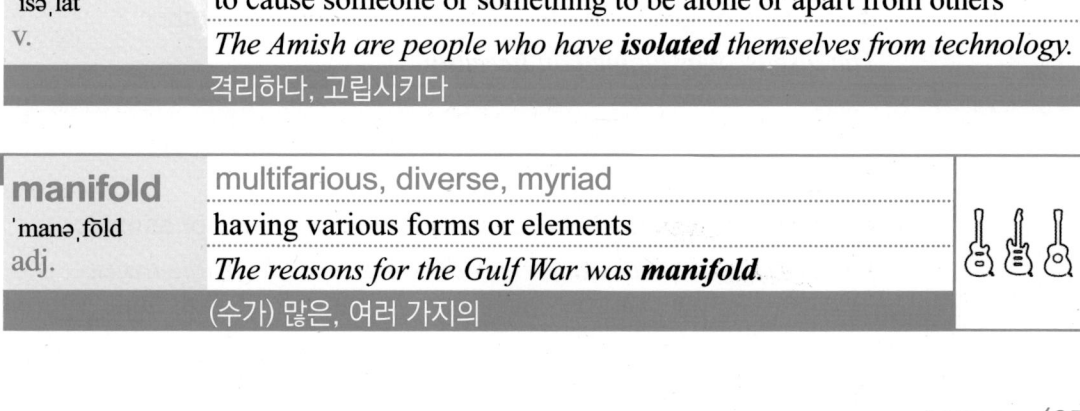

SET 37

13. roam
rōm
v.
- wander, rove, meander
- to move around aimlessly over a wide area
- Lions **roamed** the vast plains of the Serengeti.
- (이리저리) 돌아다니다, 배회(방랑)하다

14. virtual
ˈvərCH(oo)əl
adj.
- essential, practical, effective
- almost or nearly as mentioned, but not completely
- The **virtual** absence of security made it easy to steal the jewelry.
- 사실상의, 거의 …과 다름없는

adj.
- not physically existing
- **Virtual** reality is a popular game subject amongst game developers.
- (컴퓨터를 이용한) 가상의

15. dwindle
ˈdwindl
v.
- diminish, wane, decay
- to decrease in size, strength, or number
- Thor's power started to **dwindle** when his hammer was taken away.
- (점점) 줄어들다

16. peril
ˈperəl
n.
- jeopardy, hazard, threat
- serious and immediate danger
- The Earth was in **peril** from an alien invasion.
- (심각한) 위험

17. sanctuary
ˈsaNGk(t)SHə‚werē
n.
- haven, oasis, shelter
- a place of refuge or safety
- Abandoned animals are placed in animal **shelters**.
- 피난처, 안식처

18. heredity
həˈredədē
n.
- genetics, parentage, ancestry
- the passing of genetic traits from one generation to another
- The disease was blamed on **heredity**.
- 유전(적 특징)

19. inbred
ˈinbred
adj.
- congenital, inborn
- produced by breeding between closely related people or animals
- **Inbred** dogs are necessary to produce the most desirable traits.
- (동식물을) 근친(동계) 교배한

20 **vulnerable** ˈvəln(ə)rəb(ə)l *adj.*	endangered, exposed, defenseless
	susceptible to harm
	Without any weapons, the army was in a **vulnerable** position.
	(~에) 취약한, 연약한

21 **prehistoric** ˌprē(h)iˈstôrik *adj.*	primitive, ancient, primal
	referring to a time before written records
	Prehistoric men did not farm nor did they practice politics.
	선사 시대의

22 **contagious** kənˈtājəs *adj.*	infectious, transmissible, transferable
	spreading from one to another by direct or indirect contact
	Viruses are **contagious** so it is advised to always wear face masks.
	전염되는, 전염성의

23 **shrink** SHriNGk *v.*	contract, diminish, lessen
	to become smaller in size or numbers
	The number of employees **shrunk** after the disaster.
	줄어들다(오그라지다)

24 **petty** ˈpedē *adj.*	trivial, insignificant, inconsequential
	of little importance
	We should not break up because of **petty** problems.
	사소한, 하찮은

25 **brief** brēf *adj.*	short, momentary, transient
	of short duration
	For a **brief** time in history, Japan ruled over Korea.
	짧은, 잠시 동안의

26 **precipitate** prəˈsipəˌtāt *v.*	trigger, provoke, instigate
	to cause something bad to happen
	The assassination of the archduke **precipitated** a global war.
	(특히 나쁜 일을) 촉발시키다

SET 37

27. exterminate
ikˈstərməˌnāt
v.

- slaughter, massacre, eliminate
- to destroy completely
- The dodo birds were **exterminated** by the Europeans who settled on the island.

몰살(전멸)시키다

28. decimate
ˈdesəˌmāt
v.

- obliterate, execute, destroy
- to kill or remove a large portion of something
- The construction would **decimate** the historical landmark.

심하게 훼손하다(약화시키다)

29. maximize
ˈmaksəˌmīz
v.

- exaggerate, overestimate, magnify
- to make as great as possible
- Samsung is attempting to **maximize** their profits this year.

극대화하다

30. ease
ēz
n.

- facility, simplicity, mastery
- absence of difficulty
- My father built the table with **ease**.

쉬움, 용이함, 편의성

v.

- subside, weaken, abate
- to make less serious
- Tensions began to **ease** on both sides with the passing of time.

(고통·불편 등이(을)) 덜해지다(덜어 주다)

31. glamour
ˈglamər
n.

- allure, charm, enchantment
- an attractive or exciting quality
- The **glamour** of Las Vegas can be seen from the night sky.

화려함(매력)

32. nurture
ˈnərCHər
v.

- rear, support, raise
- to care for
- Mother birds **nurture** their chicks until they are ready to fly out of the nest.

양육하다(보살피다)

33. figurative
ˈfiɡyərədiv
adj.

- metaphorical, symbolic, representative
- departing from the literal usage of words
- He was imprisoned in his room, in a **figurative** sense.

비유적인

34	**aborigine** ˌabəˈrijənē n.	native, local, indigene
		a person, animal, or plant that has been in that area since the beginning
		*Kangaroos and Koalas are just some of the **aborigines** of Australia.*
	원주민	

35	**precede** prəˈsēd v.	herald, antedate, predate
		to come before
		*The shrimp appetizer **preceded** the steak and lobster dinner.*
	…에 앞서다(선행하다)	

36	**cynical** ˈsinək(ə)l adj.	skeptical, doubtful, suspicious
		distrustful of human sincerity or integrity
		*The students were **cynical** when the strict professor gave them free time.*
	냉소적인	

37	**hindsight** ˈhīn(d)ˌsīt n.	retrospect, recollection
		understanding the situation only after it occurred
		*I now understand with **hindsight**, what I did wrong.*
	사정을 다 알게 됨, 뒤늦은 깨달음	

38	**infringe** inˈfrinj v.	violate, transgress, breach
		to break the terms of the law or agreement
		*His human rights were **infringed** when they sold him as a slave.*
	위반하다	

39	**copious** ˈkōpēəs adj.	ample, profuse, abundant
		abundant in supply or amount
		*The copy machine made **copious** copies of the lecture notes.*
	엄청난 (양의), 방대한	

40	**oust** oust v.	remove, overthrow, depose
		to drive out or expel someone from a place or position
		*The people **ousted** the French king and had him executed.*
	몰아내다(쫓아내다/축출하다)	

SET 37

41 grave
grāv
adj.

important, profound, significant
serious
He was in **grave** danger.

심각한

42 radiance
ˈrādēəns
n.

elation, ecstasy, euphoria
great happiness
The bride was smiling with **radiance** as she walked down the aisle.

(행복감, 건강 등으로) 빛나는(환한)

43 regime
rəˈZHēm
n.

authorities, administration, government
a government
The old **regime** was toppled and a new system was set up.

정권

44 sanction
ˈsaNG(k)SH(ə)n
v.

authorize, warrant, consent
to officially permit or approve
China **sanctioned** its companies to do business with Taiwan.

허가, 승인, 인가하다

45 coherent
ˌkōˈhirənt
adj.

rational, reasonable, logical
logical and consistent
The lawyers were unable to give a **coherent** defense.

일관성 있는, 논리(조리) 정연한

46 immaculate
iˈmakyələt
adj.

unblemished, impeccable, unsullied
without any flaws or mistakes
The comic book was in an **immaculate** condition, still inside the plastic cover.

티 하나 없이 깔끔한(깨끗한)

47 discord
ˈdiskôrd
n.

strife, hostility, friction
disagreement between two sides
There was no **discord** in the cheerful family.

불화, 다툼

442 · LEAD VOCABULARY

48. deface
dəˈfās
v.

vandalize, tarnish, mar

to spoil the surface or appearance of something

*The Dada artist **defaced** the Mona Lisa painting.*

외관을 훼손하다

49. impart
imˈpärt
v.

convey, transmit, communicate

to pass on information

*Teachers have the responsibility to **impart** knowledge to their students.*

(정보, 지식 등을) 전하다

50. imbricate
ˈimbrəˌkāt
v.

overhang, overlay, flap

to overlap

*The roof tiles **imbricate** in a distinct pattern.*

겹쳐지다

SET 37 TEST

1. The teacher _____ the testing time when the computer malfunctioned.

2. The surprise gift _____ the child.

3. The reasons for buying the house was _____.

4. The number of lives the character had in the game slowly _____.

5. The chicks became _____ when the mother left the nest.

6. There was _____ cash inside the car.

7. The sun's energy concentrated by the magnifying glass _____ the ants.

8. Feeling blue is a _____ expression.

9. The Native Americans were _____ when the European family offered them food.

10. The children were allowed to eat _____ amounts of candy on Halloween.

---

1. protract 2. enliven 3. manifold 4. dwindle 5. vulnerable
6. petty 7. decimate 8. figurative 9. cynical 10. copious

11. The new business owner was smiling with _____ as the first customer walked in.

12. The president _____ American troops to be pulled out of the country.

13. The artwork was sold at a high price because of its _____ condition.

14. My grandfather _____ our family's secret before he passed away.

15. Feeling _____, the man sold all of his belongings and moved out of the country.

16. The ship was in _____ when the pirates aimed their canons toward them.

17. Allowing the child to eat candy all day _____ an evening of energetic mayhem.

18. The _____ of the rainforest had never seen people with clothes.

19. Work with no pay _____ upon the labor laws.

20. There was _____ in the senate on the issue of military intervention.

---

11. radiance   12. sanction   13. immaculate   14. impart   15. imprudent
16. peril   17. precipitate 18. aborigine   19. infringe 20. discord

SET 37

notes:

LEAD SET 38 VOCABULARY

SET 38

01 ancestor
ˈanˌsestər
n.

forefather, predecessor, antecedent

a person from whom one is descended

*Our **ancestors** came to this land on boats.*

조상, 선조

02 antagonism
anˈtagəˌnizəm
n.

enmity, opposition, feud

hostility or opposition

***Antagonism** still exists between China and Taiwan.*

적의, 적대감

03 prone
prōn
adj.

susceptible, inclined, predisposed

likely to suffer from

*Tom is **prone** to make the same mistakes unless he learns from Jerry.*

(좋지 않은 일을) 하기(당하기) 쉬운

04 multifold
ˈməltēˌfōld
adj.

assorted, diversified, varied

manifold

*The flowers in the garden are both **multifold** and luxurious.*

여러가지

05 deleterious
ˌdeləˈtirēəs
adj.

detrimental, inimical, harmful

causing harm or damage

*Gasoline cars have a **deleterious** effect on the environment.*

해로운, 유해한

06 hostile
ˈhästl
adj.

aggressive, belligerent, spiteful

unfriendly

***Hostile** actions were received when the enemy invaded our territory.*

적대적인

07 agriculture
ˈagrəˌkəlCHər
n.

farming, cultivation, husbandry

the practice of farming

***Agriculture** is important in South Korea's economy.*

농업

08 dissolve
dəˈzälv
v.

	melt, liquefy, disintegrate
	for a solid to become incorporated into a liquid
	*The sugar cubes **dissolved** in the hot coffee.*

녹다, 용해되다

v.

	disband, dismiss, terminate
	to end or dismiss a group or official body
	*The rebellion quickly **dissolved** when their requests were fulfilled.*

(사업상 합의, 의회를 공식적으로) 끝내다

09 broad
brôd
adj.

	spacious, extensive, vast
	large in area
	*The children ran around and played in the **broad** field.*

(폭이) 넓은

10 proximity
präkˈsimədē
n.

	nearness, closeness, vicinity
	close in space, time, or relationship
	*He was hiding in close **proximity** because I could hear him giggle.*

(거리, 시간상으로) 가까움(근접)

11 climate
ˈklīmit
n.

	weather
	the weather conditions of an area over a long period
	*The **climate** of Central America is humid and hot.*

기후

12 agent
ˈājənt
n.

	representative, emissary, envoy
	someone who represents another person or group
	*James Bond is a secret operative **agent** from England.*

대리인, 중개상

n.

	medium, instrument, vehicle
	someone or something that takes an active role or produces a desired effect
	*The revolutionists saw themselves as **agents** of freedom.*

매체(수단)

SET 38

13. dictate
ˈdikˌtāt
v.

- dominate, oppress, tyrannize
- to lay down with authority
- *Adolf Hitler **dictated** his own people without them even realizing.*

지시(명령)하다

v.
- recite, speak, utter
- to say or read out loud
- *Actors must **dictate** their script while matching the lips of the animation.*

큰 소리로 말하다

14. convex
ˌkänˈveks
adj.

- rounded, bulging, arched
- having an outline or surface that is curved like a circle
- *Contact lenses are in **convex** shapes to fit our eyes.*

볼록한

15. integral
inˈtegrəl
adj.

- essential, intrinsic, fundamental
- necessary to make something complete
- *Physical education is **integral** in a school curriculum.*

필수적인, 필요불가결한

16. catalyst
ˈkad(ə)ləst
n.

- impetus, stimulus, encouragement
- someone or something that stimulates an event
- *The monetary award became a **catalyst** for workers to try harder.*

자극(제)(추동력)

17. mislead
misˈlēd
v.

- deceive, delude, fool
- to cause someone to get the wrong idea about someone or something
- *In a fairy tale, the witch tends to **mislead** the princess into doing something bad.*

호도(오도)하다

18. commercial
kəˈmərSHəl
adj.

- trade, business, mercantile
- related to an interchange of good and commodities
- *The two countries decided to partake on a **commercial** venture.*

상업의

450 · LEAD VOCABULARY

19. diagnostic
ˌdīəgˈnästik
adj.

- analysis, examination, investigation
- concerned with the evaluation of problems
- Students take a **diagnostic** test before entering the university.

진단의

20. protrusion
prəˈtrooZHən
n.

- bump, projection, obtruding
- something that sticks out
- A **protrusion** of ice was sticking out of the glacier.

돌출, 돌출부

21. inspect
inˈspekt
v.

- examine, scrutinize, investigate
- to look at someone or something more closely, usually to find flaws or assess the condition
- The plumber came to **inspect** our overflowing sink.

(특히 모든 것이 제대로 되어 있는지 확인하기 위해) 점검(검사)하다

22. fuse
fyooz
v.

- amalgamate, merge, coalesce
- to join in order to form a whole
- Iron and carbon are **fused** to create steel.

융합(결합)되다(시키다)

23. subsistence
səbˈsistəns
n.

- survival, sustenance, existence
- a way of maintaining or supporting oneself
- The minimum amount of money required for **subsistence** determines minimum wage.

최저 생활, 호구

24. surplus
ˈsərpləs
adj.

- excess, superfluous, redundant
- more than what is required or used
- The bomb shelter had **surplus** food reserves.

과잉의, 잉여의

25. negligible
ˈneɡlədʒəb(ə)l
adj.

- trifling, minor, petty
- so small in amount or importance as to not worth considering
- Making a home movie is easy and efficient at a **negligible** cost.

무시해도 될 정도의

SET 38

26 indispensable
ˌindəˈspensəb(ə)l
adj.

crucial, vital, requisite

absolutely necessary

*Water is an **indispensable** requirement for an organism's habitat.*

없어서는 안 될, 필수적인

27 submissive
səbˈmisiv
adj.

obedient, compliant, passive

ready to change or adapt to the authority of others

*Long ago, servants had **submissive** attitudes toward their masters.*

순종적인, 고분고분한

28 devour
dəˈvou(ə)r
v.

swallow, consume

to eat hungrily or quickly

*The death row inmate **devoured** his last meal.*

(특히 몹시 배가 고파서) 걸신 들린 듯 먹다

29 seductive
səˈdəktiv
adj.

alluring, tempting, bewitching

tempting and attractive

*Her **seductive** voice led me to do her homework.*

마음을 끄는, 유혹적인

30 impair
imˈper
v.

weaken, damage, harm

to weaken or damage something, usually a human function

*Listening to music loudly will **impair** your ear drums.*

손상(악화)시키다

31 pervade
pərˈvād
v.

permeate, perfuse, saturate

to spread out to all parts

*The smell of freshly baked cookies **pervaded** the entire house.*

만연하다, (구석구석) 스며(배어)들다

32 competence
ˈkämpədəns
n.

capability, ability, proficiency

the ability to do something effectively

*The athletes showed varying degrees of **competence** on the field.*

능숙함, 능숙도

33. host
'hōst
n.

entertainer, manager, innkeeper
a person who welcomes or entertains guests
The **host** welcomed our family into his home.
(손님을 초대한) 주인

v.

hold, arrange, throw
to act as a host for an event
Our family decided to **host** this year's Christmas party.
(행사를) 주최하다

34. fathom
'faTHəm
v.

comprehend, understand, perceive
to understand a difficult problem after much thought
It is impossible to **fathom** the depth of love a mother has for her child.
(의미 등을) 헤아리다(가늠하다)

35. haste
hāst
n.

swiftness, hurry, rush
excessive speed or urgency in movement or action
Accuracy cannot be achieved with **haste**.
서두름, 급함

36. banish
'baniSH
v.

exile, deport, expatriate
to send someone away from a country or place as punishment
Thor was **banished** from Asgard for being reckless.
추방하다, 유형(유배)을 보내다

37. stingy
'stinjē
adj.

miserly, parsimonious, cheap
unwilling to give or spend
The **stingy** diner gave a very small tip to the waitress.
(특히 돈에 대해) 인색한(쩨쩨한)

38. multifaceted
ˌməltē'fasədəd
adj.

varied, adaptable, adroit
having many aspects
The swiss army knife is a **multifaceted** tool.
다면적인

SET 38

39 expend
ikˈspend
v.

spend, utilize, exhaust
to spend or use up
*The ship **expended** their energy on that last shot.*

쏟다(들이다)

40 refurbish
rēˈfərbiSH
v.

renovate, modernize, upgrade
to renovate and redecorate
*We decided to **refurbish** the house before we moved in.*

새로 꾸미다(재단장하다)

41 extricate
ˈekstrəˌkāt
v.

disentangle, liberate, extract
to free from a problem or difficulty
*The prisoner dug a hole to **extricate** himself from his cell.*

해방되다(해방시키다)

42 abolish
əˈbäliSH
v.

terminate, invalidate, annul
to officially put an end to something
*Slavery was **abolished** when the North won the civil war.*

폐지하다

43 caliber
ˈkaləbər
n.

merit, worth, competence
the quality of one's character or the level of their ability
*A man of his **caliber** should be leading the troops.*

도량, 재간

44 relinquish
rəˈliNGkwiSH
v.

renounce, yield, cede
to voluntarily give up
*The baby **relinquished** the toy when his mother offered him a cookie.*

포기하다(내주다)

45 extol
ikˈstōl
v.

eulogize, acclaim, laud
to praise enthusiastically
*The athlete was **extolled** for coming in first in the race.*

극찬(격찬)하다

46. tarnish
'tärniSH
v.

sully, stain, blemish

to lose or destroy the purity of

*The scandal **tarnished** the governor's reputation.*

더럽히다(손상시키다)

47. coup
ko͞o
n.

overthrow, takeover, deposition

a sudden, violent, and illegal obtaining of power from a government

*Caesar and his legion engaged in a **coup** which would make him the emperor.*

쿠데타

48. thwart
THwôrt
v.

foil, frustrate, prevent

to prevent from happening

*The terrorist attack was **thwarted** by the NSA.*

좌절시키다

49. abridge
ə'brij
v.

curtail, truncate, trim

to shorten or make it concise

*Scholars have **abridged** Shakespeare's works because they were too lengthy.*

줄이다, 요약하다

50. debase
də'bās
v.

degrade, devalue, demean

to reduce in quality or worth

*The original painting was **debased** when the artist accidently spilled paint on it.*

(가치,품위를) 저하시키다(떨어뜨리다)

SET 38 TEST

1. People suffering from the common cold are _____ to sneeze and cough.

2. Individuals who are sick will have a _____ effect on their coworkers.

3. The metal detector beeped louder in the _____ of the jewelery.

4. Yeast is _____ when baking bread.

5. Seats were removed from the airplanes to make room for boxes to be loaded for _____ purposes.

6. The _____ energy of the generator was stored inside a battery.

7. The new recruits were _____ to the drill sergeant.

8. Years of loud music _____ the musician's sense of hearing.

9. A news anchor's _____ is measured by how well they can react to sudden news feeds.

10. It was difficult for the scientists to _____ how the universe was created.

1. prone 2. deleterious 3. proximity 4. integral 5. commercial 6. surplus 7. submissive 8. impair 9. competence 10. fathom

11. Simba was _____ from the group because he was accused of killing his father, Mufasa.

12. The family _____ their backup money during the trip.

13. He was _____ from his debt when he won the lottery.

14. The man _____ his control of the company so that he could retire early.

15. The poor quality of the products _____ the clothing brand.

16. The programmer was able to _____ the virus from destroying the security system.

17. Oxygen is a _____ for rust.

18. The severance pay was a _____ for the unemployed man.

19. The _____ comment should not have bothered the woman.

20. Reporters write up their stories in _____ so that their articles can be on the next day's newspaper.

---

11. banish 12. expend 13. extricate 14. relinquish 15. tarnish 16. thwart 17. catalyst 18. subsistence 19. negligible 20. haste

SET 35

notes:

LEAD
SET
39
VOCABULARY

SET 39

01 opulent
ˈäpyələnt
adj.

lavish, grandiose, prolific
rich and luxurious
*Hollywood mansions provide **opulent** housing for celebrities.*
엄청나게 부유한

02 dogged
ˈdôgəd
adj.

tenacious, determined, resolute
having or showing persistence
*Starting a new business requires a **dogged** determination.*
완강한, 끈덕진

03 spacious
ˈspāSHəs
adj.

roomy, voluminous, sizeable
having lots of space
*The guest room is **spacious** even for a family of four.*
널찍한

04 flaunt
flônt
v.

parade, brandish, flash
to show off in order to incite envy or admiration
*My uncle **flaunted** his wealth by driving up in his new sports car.*
과시하다

05 sting
stiNG
v.

tingle, burn, hurt
to feel a sharp sensation or burning pain
*The scratch on his leg **stung** when he put on his pants.*
따끔거리다(따갑다, 쓰리다)

06 expulsion
ikˈspəlSHən
n.

removal, dismissal, discharge
depriving someone of belonging in a group
*An **expulsion** from school will have a detrimental effect in a person's career.*
퇴학, (조직에서의) 제명(축출)

07 fissure
ˈfiSHər
n.

crevice, slit, groove
a long narrow opening or crack in a rock or on the ground
*Years of no rain left the ground dry and covered with **fissures**.*
길게 갈라진 틈

08 inject
in'jekt
v.

administer, vaccinate, introduce

to put a liquid, such as medicine, into a person or animal's body using a needle

The nurse **injected** the vaccine in the man's arm.

(액체를) 주입하다

09 aerate
'erāt
v.

oxygenate, aerify, freshen

to mix with air

Wine enthusiasts know that wine should be **aerated** before being served.

공기가 통하게 하다

10 swell
swel
v.

expand, bulge, inflate

for a part of the body to become larger or rounder in size

His finger started to **swell** after being stung by a bee.

붓다, 부풀다, 부어오르다

v.

brim, overflow

to be greatly affected or filled with a specific emotion

I **swelled** with pride when my son received the award.

넘쳐흐르다

11 flair
fler
n.

aptitude, talent, knack

ability for doing something well

He had a **flair** for baking cakes.

(타고난) 재주(재능)

12 highlight
'hīˌlīt
n.

climax, zenith, summit

a significant part of an event or time

The **highlight** of our evening was watching the fireworks.

가장 좋은(흥미로운) 부분

v.

underscore, accentuate, stress

to emphasize

The professor **highlighted** that this would be on the final exam.

강조하다

13 phase
fāz
n.

stage, chapter, point

a period or stage in a series of events, process, or development

The Marvel universe is divided into several **phases**.

단계(시기/국면)

SET 39

14 essential
əˈsen(t)SHəl
adj.

crucial, indispensable, vital

absolutely necessary

It is **essential** to update the operating system on your computer for security reasons.

필수적인, 극히 중요한

15 optimal
ˈäptəməl
adj.

best, excellent, choice

best or most favorable

Engineers try hard to find the most **optimal** solution for problems.

최선의, 최상의, 최적의

16 consolidate
kənˈsäləˌdāt
v.

strengthen, secure, fortify

to make something more stronger or more solid

The soldiers **consolidated** the castle walls.

굳히다(강화하다)

v.

integrate, fuse, combine

to combine several parts into a single coherent whole

The different departments were **consolidated** into one large department.

통합하다(되다)

17 recall
rəˈkôl
v.

recollect, remember

to remember something

I **recall** getting an injection before falling asleep.

기억해 내다, 상기하다

v.

rescind, retract, cancel

to officially order someone or something to return

Several cars were **recalled** due to dysfunctional airbags.

회수(리콜)하다

18 don
dän
v.

dress, wear

to put on clothes

The princess **donned** a pink gown for the party.

(옷 등을) 입다(쓰다/신다 등)

19 frigid
ˈfrijid
adj.

freezing, frosty, icy

very cold in regards to temperature

The **frigid** arctic wind was cold even for the polar bear.

몹시 추운(찬)

20 intoxicate
in'täksəkāt
v.

befuddle, drunk, inebriate

to lose control of one's behavior by consumption of alcohol or use of drug

*The groom became **intoxicated** from too much alcohol at his bachelor party.*

(술, 마약 등에) 취하게 하다

v.

exhilarate, thrill, enthrall

to excite someone

*The bride became **intoxicated** when her favorite celebrity paid a visit.*

흥분시키다, 열중(도취)시키다

21 patron
'pātrən
n.

sponsor, financier, donor

someone who gives financial support to a person, organization, or activity

*Queen Elizabeth is a famous **patron** of arts.*

(화가, 작가 등에 대한) 후원자

n.

regular, frequenter, customer

a regular customer of a store or restaurant

*The **patrons** sat at their regular table in the restaurant.*

(특정 상점, 식당 등의) 고객

22 recite
rə'sīt
v.

deliver, speak, declaim

to repeat from memory in front of an audience

*The students **recited** Shakespearean poems in front of their parents.*

암송(낭송/낭독)하다

23 ode
ōd
n.

ballad, sonnet, song

a poem meant to be sung

***Ode** to Joy is a famous composition by Beethoven.*

(특정한 사람, 사물, 사건에 부치는) 시, 노래

24 illustrious
i'ləstrēəs
adj.

distinguished, acclaimed, notable

popular and respected for past achievement

*Her **illustrious** background gave her a teaching position in the university.*

저명한, 걸출한

SET 39

25 pseudo
ˈsoodō
adj.

- phony, imitation, sham
- not genuine
- The general public are not interested in **pseudo**-scientific theories.
- 허위의, 가짜의; 모조의

26 fledge
flej
v.

- to take care of a bird until it is able to fly
- The mother bird will **fledge** her chicks for a few weeks.
- 깃털이 다 날 때까지 (새 새끼를) 기르다, 독립시키다

27 refine
rəˈfīn
v.

- purify, cleanse, filter
- to remove unwanted parts from a substance
- The groundwater was **refined** until it was safe to drink.
- (어떤 물질을) 정제(제련)하다

v.
- hone, perfect, temper
- to improve something by making minor changes
- My mother **refined** her cooking skills by preparing the ingredients beforehand.
- (작은 변화를 주어) 개선(개량)하다

28 shear
Shir
v.

- shave, snip, trim
- to cut off hair
- Men **shear** off their hair before entering military service.
- (머리를) 깎다

29 stock
stäk
n.

- capital, funds, assets
- money raised by a business through the issue of shares
- The company's **stock** rose by 70% over the last year.
- 주식

n.
- merchandise, goods, commodities
- items inside a business or warehouse for sale or distribution
- Costco is famous for selling their **stock** in bulk.
- (상점의) 재고품(재고)

v.
- supply, equip, furnish
- to fill with goods
- I need to **stock** up my refrigerator before the sale ends.
- 채우다

30 sedulous
ˈsejələs
adj.

diligent, meticulous, assiduous

showing dedication and diligence

*A good secretary should be **sedulous**.*

(자기 일에) 공을 들이는, 정성을 다하는

31 oppress
əˈpres
v.

persecute, abuse, maltreat

to keep someone in hardship and servitude, especially through unjust authority

*The dictator **oppressed** the people by taking away their food.*

탄압(억압)하다

32 fortuity
fôrˈtooədē
n.

fortune, luck, accident

an occurrence that happened by chance

*It was **fortuity** that I was able to meet the guest speaker in the elevator.*

우연성, 우연

33 censor
ˈsensər
v.

delete, cut, redact

to delete a part from a whole which would be unacceptable

*The government **censored** parts of the movie before it was released to the public.*

검열하다, (검열하여) 삭제하다

34 taunt
tônt
v.

tease, provoke, ridicule

to make fun of or challenge someone with insulting comments

*The Joker **taunted** Batman until finally the dark knight started to chase him.*

놀리다, 비웃다, 조롱하다

35 exasperate
igˈzaspəˌrāt
v.

infuriate, enrage, inflame

to irritate and anger someone greatly

***Exasperated** by the Riddler's mysteries, Batman sought the help of the police.*

몹시 화나게(짜증나게) 하다

36 ludicrous
ˈloodəkrəs
adj.

absurd, ridiculous, foolish

so foolish and unreasonable

*His **ludicrous** suggestion was mocked by everyone in the office.*

터무니없는

SET 39

37 waver
ˈwāvər
v.

- hesitate, stall, dither
- to be indecisive
- *The child **wavered** choosing between a robot toy and a race car.*
- 결정(선택)을 못 하다, 망설이다

38 warrant
n.

- authorization, license, permit
- an official document that allows the police to arrest, search, or carry out a duty
- *Do you have an arrest **warrant** or are you just locking me up with no reason?*
- (체포수색 등을 허락하는) 영장

v.

- justify, sanction, validate
- to justify a course of action
- *The letter of recommendation **warranted** that he was a good worker.*
- 정당(타당)하게 만들다

39 verity
ˈverədē
n.

- truth, veracity, verisimilitude
- a true principle or belief
- *There was **verity** in Abraham Lincoln's speech.*
- 진리

40 mediocre
ˌmēdēˈōkər
adj.

- average, moderate, adequate
- of only moderate quality
- *His guitar playing skills were **mediocre** at best.*
- 보통 밖에 안 되는, 썩 좋지는 않은

41 astray
əˈstrā
adv.

- adrift, amiss, lost
- away from the correct path
- *The navigation device helped the driver not to go **astray**.*
- 길을 잃고

42 epiphany
əˈpifənē
n.

- revelation, insight, vision
- a moment of sudden insight or revelation
- *As I looked at the pictures again, I had an **epiphany**.*
- (뜻밖의) 새로운 발견, 직관적 인식

43 pivotal
ˈpivədl
adj.

- central, vital, focal
- of crucial importance
- *Helen was a **pivotal** character for the outbreak of the Trojan War.*
- 중심(축)이 되는

44 lush
ləSH
adj.

profuse, abundant, exuberant

growing luxuriantly

The Amazon Rainforest is a **lush** green rainforest.

무성한, 우거진

45 colossal
kəˈläsəl
adj.

gigantic, enormous, massive

very large

Cyclops is a **colossal** monster that appears in Greek mythology.

거대한, 엄청난

46 distraught
dəˈstrôt
adj.

distressed, devastated, frenzied

very upset and agitated

The parents were **distraught** when they found out that their son had died.

완전히 제정신이 아닌

47 altruism
ˈaltro͞oˌizəm
n.

selflessness, compassion, magnanimity

the principle of unselfish concern for or devotion to the welfare of others

Serving in hospice is a true act of **altruism**.

이타주의, 이타심

48 illicit
i(l)ˈlisit
adj.

illegal, banned, prohibited

forbidden by law

Teenagers were caught using **illicit** drugs.

불법의

49 premise
ˈpreməs
n.

assertion, basis, proposition

a basis on which logic stands

The **premise** for his argument did not make sense.

(주장의) 전제

50 leeway
ˈlēˌwā
n.

scope, latitude, slack

the amount of freedom to move or act

There is little **leeway** for any mistakes.

자유(재량)

SET 39 TEST

1. Rappers tend to wear _____ accessories, such as watches and necklaces.

2. _____ in the wrong neighborhood will end up in theft.

3. The boxing champion's strong punch _____ his eye.

4. The _____ solution to end the war without any casualties is to surrender.

5. The _____ resume quickly caught the attention of the employer.

6. The employee of the month was always _____, so he deserved the award.

7. Becoming the number one salesman was no _____; he worked really hard everyday.

8. His neverending questions _____ everyone in the group.

9. The manager _____ when he had to decide who to fire.

10. The man walked _____ after drinking too much.

---

1. opulent 2. Haunt 3. swell 4. optimal 5. Illustrious 6. sedulous 7. fortuity 8. exasperate 9. waver 10. astray

468 · LEAD VOCABULARY

11. Signing the Declaration of Independence was a _____ moment in the history of the United States.

12. The _____ statue was erected to honor the dictator.

13. _____ activities are quickly prevented by the police.

14. The company gave some _____ to its new employees so they could adjust to the new environment.

15. The _____ of the previous alpha male is a common sight to see in lion prides.

16. The hair designer had _____ when it came to cutting long hair.

17. The police officer _____ that this was the third strike, and the next one would result in going to jail.

18. The man _____ making a promise, but he was vague in the details.

19. _____ religions are common these days, especially in major cities.

20. Slaves in the south were _____ by their masters.

---

11. pivotal   12. colossal   13. illicit   14. leeway   15. expulsion
16. flair   17. highlight   18. recall   19. pseudo   20. oppress

SET 39

notes:

LEAD
SET 40
VOCABULARY

SET 40

01 wit
wit
n.
- intelligence, cleverness, shrewdness
- mental sharpness and innovative
- *It took a tremendous amount of **wit** for the general to win the war.*
- 기지, 재치

02 stance
stans
n.
- viewpoint, opinion, attitude
- the attitude of a person or group towards something
- *My **stance** in animal testing is neutral.*
- (어떤 일에 대한 공개적인) 입장(태도)

03 ferment
fərˈment
v.
- to undergo fermentation
- *Grapes are **fermented** to be made into wine.*
- 발효되다, 발효시키다

04 prohibit
prəˈhibit
v.
- forbid, ban, bar
- to not allow by law, rule, or authority
- *Individuals under the age of 20 are **prohibited** from drinking alcohol.*
- (특히 법으로) 금하다(금지하다)

05 painstaking
ˈpānzˌtākiNG
adj.
- meticulous, thorough, attentive
- done with great care and attention
- *Making this sculpture required **painstaking** attention to detail.*
- 공들인

06 byproduct
ˈbīˌprädəkt
n.
- consequence, ramification, aftermath
- an unintended result produced while doing something else
- *Poverty is a **byproduct** of economic prosperity.*
- 부산물

07 indefinite
ˌinˈdef(ə)nət
adj.
- unknown, unlimited, unspecified
- lasting for an unknown length of time
- *The convicts were sentenced to an **indefinite** time in prison.*
- 무기한의

08	**safeguard** ˈsāfˌɡärd v.	shield, screen, defend
		to protect from harm with an appropriate method
		*Iron Man wanted to **safeguard** planet Earth by shielding it with an armor.*
		(분실·손상 등에 대비하여) 보호하다

09	**conjunction** kənˈjəNG(k)SH(ə)n n.	concurrence, coexistence, combination
		the action of two or more things or events happening at the same time
		*Medicine was used in **conjunction** with physical therapy.*
		결합

10	**pathogen** ˈpaTHəjən n.	ailment, infection, germ
		a bacteria or virus that can cause a disease
		*The **pathogen** was traced back to bats from China.*
		병원균, 병원체

11	**permeable** ˈpərmēəb(ə)l adj.	porous, pervious, penetrable
		allowing gases or liquids to go through
		*The **permeable** rocks allowed rain water to go through.*
		(액체, 기체가) 침투할(스며들) 수 있는

12	**penetrate** ˈpenəˌtrāt v.	pierce, puncture, stab
		to force a way into or through a thing
		*The arrow had **penetrated** through his leg.*
		뚫고 들어가다, 관통하다

13	**aromatic** ˌerəˈmadik adj.	fragrant, scented, perfumed
		having a distinctive, yet pleasant smell
		*The **aromatic** candle helped her to relax.*
		향이 좋은

14	**gauge** gāj v.	measure, calculate, compute
		to estimate the size or amount of something
		*Scientists can **gauge** the energy released by different stars.*
		측정하다

SET 40

15. retrieve
rəˈtrēv
v.

- recover, reclaim, repossess
- to regain possession of
- My dog **retrieved** the ball from the bush.

되찾아오다(회수하다)

16. vacate
ˈvāˌkāt
v.

- evacuate, abandon, desert
- to leave a place
- The children **vacated** the school after the earthquake ended.

(건물, 좌석 등을, 특히 다른 사람이 이용할 수 있도록) 비우다

17. prospect
ˈpräˌspekt
n.

- expectation, anticipation, probability
- the possibility of a future event from happening
- There was no **prospect** for both sides to come to peace.

(어떤 일이 있을) 가망(가능성)

18. outlook
ˈoutˌlook
n.

- viewpoint, angle, perspective
- a person's point of view or attitude towards life
- She has a positive **outlook** on life.

관점, 세계관, 인생관

19. solitary
ˈsäləˌterē
adj.

- withdrawn, reclusive, isolated
- existing alone
- That man lives a **solitary** life on the island.

혼자 하는

20. vigil
ˈvijəl
n.

- patrol, observance, lookout
- staying awake to keep watch or pray
- The security guard's **vigil** is most important during midnight.

경계, (밤샘) 간호, (철야) 기도

21. trance
trans
n.

- daze, stupor, dream
- a state of half-consciousness
- The psychic put the volunteer in a **trance**.

(최면 상태와 같은) 가수 상태

22. supernatural
ˌso͞opərˈnaCH(ə)rəl
adj.

paranormal, mystical, unnatural

characterized by a force beyond science or natural laws

*Superman is considered a **supernatural** being from another planet.*

초자연적인

23. temporal
ˈtemp(ə)rəl
adj.

secular, worldly, material

related to worldly affairs, not spiritual

*The Church teaches the congregation to let go of **temporal** greed.*

현세적인, 속세의

24. serene
səˈrēn
adj.

composed, placid, tranquil

calm and peaceful

*Yoga is a **serene** exercise.*

고요한, 평화로운, 조용한

25. shabby
ˈSHabē
adj.

neglected, worn, ragged

in poor condition due to extended use or lack of care

*The house was in a **shabby** state since no one cared for the grounds.*

다 낡은(해진), 허름한

26. sensuous
ˈsen(t)SHo͞oəs
adj.

aesthetic, pleasurable, sensory

affecting or relating to the senses and not the intellect

*The painting appealed to the **sensuous** rather than shapes.*

오감(감각)을 만족시키는, (심미적으로) 감각적인

27. strain
strān
n.

pressure, demands, burden

a severe demand on the abilities, resources, or strength of a person or thing

*There is a lot of **strain** working in the emergency room.*

부담, 중압(압박)(감)

28. transact
tranˈsakt
v.

conduct, execute, perform

to carry out a business

*Company executives **transact** businesses on a daily basis.*

거래하다

SET 40

29 educe
ēˈd(y)o͞os
v.

develop, evoke, extract

to draw out or develop a potential talent

*After years of training, the apprentice was able to **educe** his inner powers.*

(잠재하여 있는 성능 등을) 끌어내다

30 upbraid
ˌəpˈbrād
v.

reprimand, rebuke, admonish

to find something wrong with someone

*The child was **upbraided** for pestering at the toy store.*

질책하다, 호되게 나무라다

31 amenity
əˈmenədē
n.

service, convenience, appliance

a desirable or useful feature of a place

*The five-star hotel offered **amenities** such as fitness center, pool, and game room.*

생활 편의 시설

32 archaic
ärˈkāik
adj.

obsolete, antique, primitive

very old

*The **archaic** media player had a slot for cassette tapes.*

낡은, 폐물이 된

33 forestall
fôrˈstôl
v.

preempt, avert, obstruct

to prevent by taking action ahead of time

*Taking vitamin pills will **forestall** unwanted diseases.*

미연에 방지하다

34 ominous
ˈämənəs
adj.

menacing, sinister, threatening

giving the impression that something bad is about to happen

*The **ominous** rain clouds approached the city.*

불길한

35 valor
ˈvalər
n.

bravery, courage, fearlessness

great courage in the midst of danger

*The soldier was awarded the medal of **valor** for saving his comrades.*

용기, 용맹, 무용

36 lucid
'lōosəd
adj.

- comprehensible, cogent, clear
- expressed clearly
- People have **lucid** dreams when they are undisturbed in their sleep.

명쾌한, 명료한

37 nostalgic
nä'staljik
adj.

- sentimental, wistful, yearning
- a sentimental or wishful yearning of bygone days
- When the song came on the radio, she suddenly felt **nostalgic** for her high school years.

향수를 불러 일으키는

38 surmise
sər'mīz
v.

- conjecture, deduce, infer
- to guess without strong evidence
- Judging by the look on his face, she **surmised** that something was wrong.

추측(추정)하다

39 oblige
ə'blīj
v.

- require, compel, obligate
- to make someone bound to an action
- Doctors are **obliged** by law to keep their patients alive.

의무적으로(부득이) …하게 하다

40 reprimand
'reprə,mand
v.

- rebuke, chastise, reproach
- to scold someone
- The workers were **reprimanded** for the poor quality in their project.

질책하다

41 memento
mə'men,tō
n.

- souvenir, keepsake, memorial
- an object kept as a reminder of a person or event
- This watch is a **memento** of my grandfather.

기념품

42 humble
'həmbəl
adj.

- meek, submissive, deferential
- not proud or arrogant
- The billionaire was a **humble** person, despite his net worth.

겸손한

SET 40

43 magnitude
'magnə,t(y)ood
n.

vastness, enormity, expanse

the size or extent of something

The sheer **magnitude** of the asteroid will destroy our planet if it collides.

규모

n.

significance, weight, consequence

great importance

Events of tragic **magnitude** will create trauma for individuals.

중요성

44 arouse
ə'rouz
v.

rouse, excite, stimulate

to excite or provoke someone to strong emotions

The president's speech **aroused** the people.

자극하다

45 ambiguous
am'bigyooəs
adj.

ambivalent, equivocal, enigmatic

open to more than one interpretation

Her **ambiguous** facial expressions stalled me from asking her out on a date.

애매모호한, 여러 가지로 해석할 수 있는

46 zenith
'zēnəTH
n.

climax, prime, crest

the point at which something is most powerful or successful

The French were at the **zenith** of their civilization under Napoleon's dictatorship.

정점, 절정

47 tumult
't(y)oo,məlt
n.

turmoil, disarray, chaos

confusion or disorder

The country was in a state of **tumult** when the neighboring country fired its missiles.

소란, 소동

48 transient
'tranSHənt
adj.

fleeting, transitory, brief

lasting only for a short time

Taking off a bandage produces a **transient** pain, which some might find excruciating.

일시적인, 순간적인

49 frail
'frā(ə)l
adj.

infirm, feeble, debilitated

weak and delicate

*The patient was **frail** and weak after the surgery.*

(허)약한, 부서지기 쉬운

50 vacant
'vākənt
adj.

empty, unoccupied, free

not filled

*The hotel had **vacant** rooms since it was a weekday.*

비어 있는, 사람이 없는

SET 40 CROSSWORD PUZZLE

Across

4. not proud or arrogant
6. to not allow by law, rule, or authority
7. to guess without strong evidence
8. to leave a place
13. to scold someone
14. to estimate the size or amount of something
15. lasting for an unknown length of time

Down

1. great courage in the midst of danger
2. existing alone
3. expressed clearly
5. to carry out a business
9. very old
10. a desirable or useful feature of a place
11. calm and peaceful
12. mental sharpness and innovative

1. valor 2. solitary 3. lucid 4. humble 5. transact 6. prohibit 7. surmise 8. vacate 9. archaic 10. amenity 11. serene 12. wit 13. reprimand 14. gauge 15. indefinite